VALENTINO ROSSI

The Definitive Biography

STUART BARKER

JOHN BLAKE

First published in the UK by John Blake Publishing
An imprint of Bonnier Books UK
80–81 Wimpole Street, London, W1G 9RE
Owned by Bonnier Books
Sveavägen 56, Stockholm, Sweden

www.facebook.com/johnblakebooks
twitter.com/jblakebooks

First published in hardback in 2020
Paperback edition first published in 2021

Paperback ISBN: 978-1-78946-418-4
Hardback ISBN: 978-1-78946-295-1
Ebook ISBN: 978-1-78946-296-8
Audio Digital Download ISBN: 978-1-78946-326-2

British Library Cataloguing-in-Publication Data:

A catalogue record for this book is available from the British Library.

Design by www.envydesign.co.uk

Printed and bound in Great Britain by Clays Ltd, Elcograf S.p.A.

1 3 5 7 9 10 8 6 4 2

© Text copyright Stuart Barker 2020, 2021

John Blake Publishing is an imprint of Bonnier Books UK
www.bonnierbooks.co.uk

CONTENTS

FOREWORD

BY KEVIN SCHWANTZ
500CC WORLD CHAMPION, 1993

*I*t's an honor to be asked to write the foreword for this book about Valentino Rossi. He's someone I've known of since 1989, although I don't think I got to actually meet him until 1990 or 1991 when we were all invited to a big, fun week in Livigno, Italy, where we went skiing and snowmobiling. There was a bunch of Italian riders and Graziano Rossi was there, as was a very young Valentino. I had already seen him racing a minimoto bike on a go-kart track near Misano. It was an endurance race and his team-mate was so much faster than anyone else out there, but when Valentino got on the bike it was noticeable just how much faster he was than even his team-mate. So, I felt like he was somebody we should keep an eye on because to have such a highly honed skill at such a young age was impressive. There was no doubt in my mind, there and then, that if he chose to go Grand Prix racing and really pursued it, he could be great at it.

VALENTINO ROSSI

Valentino burst onto the scene in the 125cc world championship just after I had quit racing. I didn't keep up with racing a lot at that time; when I walked away from the sport at the end of 1995 I just did my best to forget about it because I didn't want to be tempted back. So I didn't pay a lot of attention until Rossi started racing in the 500cc world championship in 2000. By that point I was excited about racing again and I predicted that, if he didn't dig himself a huge hole in his first few races on the 500, he would win the championship at the first attempt. But he did dig himself a hole by crashing too many times in the early rounds and Kenny Roberts Jr did exactly what he needed to do to win the championship. But the next year, Valentino absolutely dominated the class.

His impact on Grand Prix racing has been massive – and it was immediate too. He really did shake it up, but I guess none of us knew just how much until now when we can stand back and look at all he has achieved. To continue to compete at the level he's been competing at for so long is truly astonishing and he's been competitive in pretty much every championship he's raced in since 1996. I don't know that any other rider has had a career that's been quite so lengthy. It's easy for me to say he's the greatest of all time. I mean, I know Giacomo Agostini and I know Phil Read and I knew the late John Surtees, but to have raced for as long as Rossi has on 125cc, 250cc and 500cc two-strokes, and on such a variety of four-stroke MotoGP bikes from 800cc to 1000cc, definitely makes him the greatest of all time for me. Maybe he hasn't matched Agostini yet in terms of overall Grand Prix wins and championships, but he's won on a much greater variety of motorcycles, that's for sure. Maybe Surtees was a little more remarkable because he then got in an F1 car and won that championship too.

I've raced against Vale on supermoto bikes, in rally cars, and on motocross bikes and I've ridden with him at his ranch, and I can tell you that, when he puts his mind to it, whatever he rides or drives, and whatever surface it's on, from dirt to asphalt, he's always one of the fastest guys out there. He also proved, in a test at Barcelona in 2006, that he can get into a Formula One car and be just as fast as the top drivers. If he had lived in an era, like Surtees, when it was easier to get a seat in F1, who knows what he might have achieved on four wheels too?

The first time I went to Valentino's ranch I rode around for about twenty minutes or so before he showed up and came out on track to join me. He actually crashed as he was chasing me – not that I was setting such a great pace, he just made a mistake. Anyway, all the bikes have lap-timers and he looked at mine and said, 'What? Nobody comes here for the first time and does lap times like that!' He is just so competitive about these things; everything to him is a race or a challenge – his whole life is about lap times – and I thought, 'How does he get motivated, at the age he's at, to continue to go and train and practise and get ready for yet another 18-race MotoGP season?' And I realised that it has to be that inner drive he has to just beat everybody at absolutely everything he does.

I always struggled to motivate myself again after a couple of weeks off at Christmas. Not to ride the motorcycle, because that's absolutely the most fun you can have, but it was all the other stuff – the travelling and the media and the pressure and the PR events – that was difficult to deal with. So for him to stay motivated for as long as he has shows what a true competitor he really is. And it's got to be the kids at his academy that are keeping him so young and so fit and so focused. It will be great to see him when he does stop riding because, I promise you, he will be there to push those kids even harder than he pushed himself!

I see Valentino at races and he'll have a thousand people chasing him on his scooter all the time. When he sees me, he'll pull over and stop to chat and he'll have to fend off all those people constantly. But it doesn't seem to me that fame has changed him at all; he's got time for absolutely everybody and he always stops and signs autographs every chance he gets. Neither wealth nor fame has gone to his head.

Valentino has been so important for the sport – he's what the fans want to see. Marc Márquez has a pretty big following now, so you see a lot of red in the crowd, but five, ten years ago there was only yellow everywhere you looked. He's had the biggest following by far, to the extent that he's almost bigger than the sport itself.

When Vale retires, it will be interesting to see how well attended the races are and how popular MotoGP on television will continue to be. Maybe the Moto2 and Moto3 riders from his academy will have picked up enough of Valentino's mystique, and some of the air about him, and hopefully the support will continue. But will he be missed? Absolutely. I think it will take a few years for everybody to get used to not seeing the number 46 out there, that's for sure.

His racing achievements aside, the memory that sticks in my mind the most about how good Valentino is and how fame has changed him so little was when myself, Valentino, his father Graziano, Aldo Drudi and a few of Vale's other friends were having dinner at a restaurant in the seaside resort of Cattolica. In the middle of a really nice dinner, this kid walks up and taps him on the shoulder and says, 'Valentino, could I please have your autograph?' If it had been me and I had been having a quiet dinner with my friends and family,

I would have said 'Absolutely – I'm happy to sign that but not right now, I'm enjoying dinner with my friends. If you stick around, I'll sign something and do a picture afterwards.' Instead, Vale got up from his chair, signed an autograph, had his picture taken with the kid, then sat back down, like it was just part of his daily life. That's when I understood that he gets that kind of attention all the time, everywhere he goes. But he handled it like a true champ and it showed just how down-to-earth he really is as a person.

KEVIN SCHWANTZ
AUSTIN, TEXAS
MAY 2020

FOR WHOM THE BELL TOLLS

Sunday is a day of worship in the small town of Tavullia in central northern Italy, as it is in the rest of the devoutly Catholic country. It is a day to give thanks, a day to rejoice in the wonders of life, a day to gather together with family, friends and loved ones. A day when the bells of the church of San Lorenzo Martire in the centre of Tavullia ring out in celebration.

After fifty-five years of service, and at the grand old age of ninety-five, Don Cesare Stefano, the local parish priest, has pressed the button to ring the automated bells more times than he can remember. He has also rung them more times than is strictly necessary: 115 times more, to be precise.

For Don Cesare does not only ring the bells to announce mass, to celebrate weddings, or to mark religious festivals; he also rings them every time a certain member of his own flock wins a Grand Prix. Because there is another kind of worship that takes place in Tavullia: the worship of a local sporting hero who has made the pretty, but otherwise unremarkable, little hillside town globally famous. It is the worship of Valentino Rossi, the most famous, most popular and most loved MotoGP rider of all time.

It is 25 June 2017, and Don Cesare shuffles his way through the church he has served for over half a century to ring the bells once more. Valentino has won the Dutch TT at Assen and Don Cesare announces the latest victory to the local population, his bells peeling out over the rolling countryside that surrounds the rustic, medieval town.

In the main street of Tavullia there is barely even standing room to be had. Every inch is taken up with thousands of locals and visiting fans (more than two thousand partied in the streets until dawn when Rossi won the 500cc world title in 2001) craning their necks to watch the celebrations live from the Netherlands on a giant television screen. At the age of thirty-eight Rossi is back on top of the world, having beaten off yet another new generation of younger riders to take his 115th Grand Prix win.

The town centre is awash with yellow flags, banners, T-shirts, jackets, posters, scarves and hats, all emblazoned with Rossi's famous number 46 and his lucky colour yellow. Smoke from yellow flares chokes the air as fans sit on every wall, hang out of every window, crush together on the medieval streets and try, somewhat optimistically, to get served in the Bar Pizzeria da Rossi, which sits just metres away from the giant screen. The honking of innumerable car, scooter and air horns adds to the cacophony, bottles of Nastro Azzurro are clinked together, and the singing, chanting and celebrating can he heard for miles across the bleached-out fields that fall away to the Adriatic coast.

It's been over two years since Rossi has won a race, so the

townsfolk have gone into overdrive, as has Don Cesare. So excited is the old priest, he forgets to switch the bells off and they continue to ring, over and over and over. Nobody cares. It's a joyous sound and it has been absent for too long. Don Cesare, resplendent in his priest's robes and dog collar, ambles up from his church to join his exultant flock in the main street to share their joy. The bells keep ringing. They will do so for several hours.

This is Don Cesare's other congregation: the one that meets on eighteen Sundays during the summer months to worship another kind of god – a god of speed, a master unparalleled in the long history of motorcycle racing. And his latest win will ensure the celebrations in Tavullia carry on long into the night.

Don Cesare has known Valentino Rossi since his infancy and has followed every step of his illustrious career: the ups and downs, the thrills and spills, the injuries, the victories and defeats, the controversy, the growing fame, and the fabulous wealth that would see Rossi provide full-time employment for so many local townsfolk, not only in his pizzeria but in the nearby fan-club headquarters, the VR|46 store, and at his VR|46 ranch, just a few miles distant, which he set up to nurture a whole new generation of Italian motorcycling talent.

Sadly, this will be the last time that Don Cesare will get to enjoy such a glorious celebration of his home-grown hero. Just over one year later, on 6 July 2018, the venerable old priest passed away at the grand age of ninety-six, without seeing his boy take another win.

Huge crowds gathered to pay their final respects to Don Cesare but Valentino Rossi was not among them, as much as he would have wished to be. He couldn't because he was in Germany, preparing to race; preparing to go head-to-head with the greatest motorcycle racers on earth; preparing to risk his life yet again in the pursuit of glory, both for himself and for his home town; preparing to add to his legend and to give the people of Tavullia another reason to ring the bells of the church of San Lorenzo Martire. And there was no doubt in anyone's mind that Don Cesare would have given him his full blessing to do so, perhaps with a wink, a smile, a prayer and some final words of encouragement. 'Go on, my son. Show them. Show them all. I will be with you. Forza Rossi!'

CHAPTER 1

RAISING VALENTINO

'Valentino's first memories are of the paddock
and when he was at home he played with motorbikes
instead of other toys.'
GRAZIANO ROSSI

For centuries the small municipality of Tavullia in the province of Pesaro and Urbino nestled quietly among the rolling hillsides of central northern Italy, largely unnoticed by the wider world and of little significance to anyone except those who chose to call it home.

There were times, throughout history, when the municipality found itself caught up in the affairs of the wider world, most notably during the pre-unification struggles in Italy in the nineteenth century and again in World War II when the area became a hotbed for the Italian Resistance movement. But for the most part, Tavullia has been a sleepy little town and, until the late 1990s, its population of just over 7,000 could go about their business assured of tranquillity and anonymity. It wasn't even a tourist destination: the tourists flocked to the nearby Adriatic Coast, to Rimini and Cattolica for the beaches, or to Urbino and San Leo for the culture and architecture, leaving the people of Tavullia to live their lives in peace and quiet.

But on 14 March 1954, the birth of a baby boy in nearby Pesaro marked the beginning of a chain of events that would lead to Tavullia becoming famous throughout the world. The boy was born to a cabinet-maker and a housewife and he was christened Graziano Rossi. The surname was a common one in Italy, yet it would, in time, be elevated to iconic status.

Three years later, in the same town, another unremarkable couple – a truck driver and a nurse – welcomed a baby daughter into the world and named her Stefania Palma. The Palma family were close neighbours of the Rossis, and Graziano and Stefania would grow up together, become childhood sweethearts and, ultimately, marry in October of 1978. Their lives would most likely have remained localised and tranquil had Graziano not discovered a passion for motorcycles and found himself travelling around the world to race them.

It's easy to forget or to underplay the racing achievements of Graziano Rossi, given what was to come, but this is to do Rossi Sr a major disservice: no rider gains a place in the world's premier motorcycle racing championship without being astonishingly good, even in the 1970s when riders could still fight for podiums and wins on privately owned machinery. Graziano Rossi spent the prime years of his career battling with all-time greats like Barry Sheene and Kenny Roberts Sr. He was good, of that there is no doubt.

A somewhat romantic and gentle soul when not on a motorcycle (he was a primary school teacher before his racing career began), Graziano started racing motocross on a 250cc

Maico in 1971, when he was seventeen years old, and soon discovered he had a much wilder side when he donned a crash helmet. If he was a laid-back, humorous man in everyday life, he was an aggressive, wild-riding daredevil when he raced a motorcycle, and the balance seemed to work well for him, providing suitable outlets for both sides of his personality.

In 1975, when he was twenty-one, Graziano made his road race debut on a 250cc air-cooled Benelli at the Vallelunga circuit near Rome, and from that moment on his progress through the road-racing ranks was as swift as it was impressive. By 1978, he was racing in the 250cc Grand Prix world championship, traditionally seen as the second most prestigious Grand Prix category after the premier 500cc class (now MotoGP). In only his second year at world level, Rossi would take three race victories on his Morbidelli to finish the 1979 season in third place overall, behind Kork Ballington and Gregg Hansford, both on factory Kawasakis. His performances were impressive enough to attract the attention of team bosses in the 500cc class – the two-wheeled equivalent of Formula One.

During that same 1979 season, Rossi had made his debut in 500s with selected wild-card outings and had a best finish of ninth place at the Nations Grand Prix of Italy at Imola, which, to Rossi, was a local circuit. When Suzuki gave him an end-of-season outing, again at Imola, on one of its factory RG500s, Rossi beat both Barry Sheene and Kenny Roberts Sr (both world champions) and earned a full-time place in the world's premier motorcycle racing championship. For the 1980 season, he would be armed with a Nava Olio Fiat Suzuki RG500 and would contest a full season in the 500cc Grand Prix world championship. Graziano Rossi had reached the premier league.

Steve Parrish raced against Graziano on many occasions and spent a lot of time with him in the paddock, but it was the Italian's effect on women that he remembers most from that period. 'All the girls swooned over him, including my girlfriend at the time!' he says. 'Even Barry Sheene's wife, Stephanie, fancied Graziano – all the girls absolutely swooned over him. He had long hair down to his shoulders, his leathers always fitted nicely, and he had that lovely, genial attitude – he was just so Italian and a real smoothie. He was the pretty boy of the paddock.'

Always fast and loose on a motorcycle, Rossi was no stranger to crashing on four wheels either and went into the 1980 season carrying a head injury from a pre-season rally car crash in which he suffered serious concussion. 'It was a dickhead's crash,' he said of the incident. 'My fault totally.' However lightly he treated the crash in later years, it would have massive implications for his career and he would ultimately attribute this crash as marking the end of his upwards trajectory as a racer, believing that he never quite managed to capture his pre-crash form. 'I finished fifth in the world championship but didn't have the same form as previous years,' he admitted.

Rossi still managed to take two podiums that year, with his best-ever 500cc finish of second place coming at the fast and swooping Assen circuit in the Netherlands. He would end the season behind Roberts, Randy Mamola, his close friend Marco Lucchinelli and another Italian rider, Franco Uncini. Lucchinelli would clinch the world title the following year and Uncini the year after (Roberts had already become a three-time world champion in 1980), so it's clear that Rossi was racing in very good company and holding up well, despite feeling he had lost his best form after the rally car crash. It begs the question of how good Rossi might have been had he not suffered that head injury.

Don Morley is one of the most celebrated sports photographers in the world and worked closely with Rossi in the 1970s. He believes he could have gone all the way to the top. 'Graziano was an absolutely brilliant rider,' he says. 'He was one of those riders that, if you look at the statistics it doesn't look too good but in fact he was bloody good – in my mind he was one of the top four riders in the world at that time. I was the first person to spot and write about Mike Hailwood, I was the first to spot and write about Phil Read, and I was the first to predict the American domination of Grands Prix that took place in the 1970s and 1980s, and I felt the same way about Graziano Rossi – I felt he was definitely good enough to be world champion in the 250cc, 350cc or even 500cc class.'

Rossi, though, had a habit of crashing when he really didn't need to, like at the British Grand Prix in 1979 when he had a 2.5-second lead but crashed out with just three corners to go. Or, at least, that's how it appeared to outsiders. Morley insists that particular crash was more down to bad luck and Rossi having to over-ride his inferior Morbidelli. 'He was terribly unlucky over the years and that British Grand Prix was just one example. Kork Ballington and Gregg Hansford had the works, 250cc Kawasakis that were almost unbeatable, and yet Rossi very nearly beat them on his Morbidelli that was run out of a one-man-band kind of team; no back-up or anything like that. If he hadn't had that silly crash when he was trying to overtake a backmarker on the last lap then he would have beaten Ballington and Hansford and I think he could have been world champion that year. As it was, he finished third in the championship.'

With too many crashes, the injuries began to take their toll.

'Until then, injuries and pain were for other riders,' Graziano said. 'I never related racing to pain. After my accidents, my motivation suffered and I found I couldn't commit like before.'[1] He also found he couldn't quite remember things as well as before; to this day, Rossi Sr needs to be 'reminded of things', as his son delicately puts it.

He would race in 500cc Grands Prix for another two years but would never finish higher than eleventh place in the championship. Then, in late 1982, while riding a Marlboro Yamaha YZR500 at Imola, Rossi crashed at Villeneuve Corner at over 150mph and he finally knew his time was up. 'I was in a coma for half a day but Doctor Costa created one of his first miracles and saved my life. It was time to stop.'[2]

Costa is the Italian doctor who founded the Clinica Mobile, which, to this day, travels to every Grand Prix and attends to injured riders. Seen as nothing short of a miracle worker by Grand Prix racers, Costa has been responsible for saving the lives and careers of countless riders over the years. In any one season, the Clinica Mobile makes around 3,000 medical interventions across the three Grand Prix classes, and as well as saving Graziano's life, Costa would later attend Rossi's son in his hour of greatest need.

Speaking of Graziano's accident, Costa said, 'He was dead. Graziano Rossi died in that corner. Because that corner was very dangerous I had stationed a very good doctor there and he reached him within seconds and resuscitated him.'[3]

He may not have died but it certainly spelt the end for Rossi's riding career, as Don Morley explains: 'He had that terrible crash in the rally car and very nearly died. He suffered massive head injuries. When he later crashed the bike at Imola and banged his head again he was told if he did it one more time he was a dead man, so he had no choice but to stop racing. Without that injury I think Graziano almost certainly would have been a world champion.'

So Graziano Rossi had been given a second chance at life. But what to do with it? By the time he retired from racing, he was only twenty-eight years old and still had a full life ahead of him. He continued to race rally cars for fun, never professionally, but for the most part he simply focused on family life and raising his young child, who he was clearly very proud of.

'After taking time out to recover from the head injury in the rally car crash Graziano came back to the paddock to see us all and to show us his baby,' Morley says. 'He was immensely proud of him. Of course, none of us knew then the significance of what that baby would achieve. I remember Graziano greeting me like a long-lost friend and I took some pictures of him proudly holding his little baby boy. And that baby boy was Valentino Rossi.'

*

The medieval walled town of Urbino lies in the Marche region of central northern Italy, some twenty miles south-west of Tavullia. It is one of the most beautiful cities in the country, with a relaxed, elegant and cultured feel. A world heritage site, the university town was also the birthplace of the great Renaissance artist Raphael. On 16 February 1979, Urbino became the birthplace of another individual destined for fame and greatness, albeit in a very different field.

Valentino Rossi was delivered in Urbino just four months before his father had won his first 250cc Grand Prix. Many would later assume that Graziano and Stefania had decided on their first child's name because he was born two days after Valentine's Day, but this wasn't the case. Graziano's first motocross bike had been built by his best friend, who happened to be called Valentino. The pair had been inseparable in their youth as they worked a variety of odd jobs to fund their motocross racing ambitions. Graziano was devastated when Valentino was drowned in the Adriatic at just eighteen years old but he ensured that his friend's name would live on into a new generation. There was never any doubt in Graziano's mind that, if he was blessed with a baby boy, he would name him after his greatest friend: he would name him Valentino.

Graziano Rossi is one of life's good guys. Personable, grounded, laid-back, intelligent and fun-loving, whether by accident or design he hit upon a winning selection of character traits and, more than anything he might ever have taught his son about the art of racing a motorcycle, it is this that is his greatest contribution to the success of Valentino Rossi. Inheriting his father's easy-going manner and personable charm, as well as his happy-go-lucky outlook on life, has been a huge blessing for Valentino, not only when it comes to dealing with the inevitable disappointments of racing, but in dealing with the relentless pressures of global fame.

There's a slightly eccentric, hippy side to Graziano too, though even this is endearing. He may be the father of the greatest motorcycle racer of all time but he prefers to drive to race meetings all over Europe – largely because he hates flying – and to sleep in the back of his car in the paddock. There are no five-star hotels for Graziano and he even refuses his son's offer to stay in his multi-million pound motorhome because Valentino rarely retires before 1am and Graziano prefers an early night. 'I go in my car and sleep in it when I get there,' he has said by way of explanation for his seemingly eccentric behaviour. 'I like to stay in the paddock because I like to see

Valentino when he is relaxed at the end of the day. I don't want to say it is about money, but it does seem crazy to pay to sleep... I have a BMW estate and everything I need for a good night's sleep. It's as comfortable as any bed for me.'[4]

In 1982, after his head was shaved in hospital following his big Imola crash, Graziano decided not to cut his hair when it grew back. He had always worn it longer, even when he was racing, but would now take things to a new level. By the time Valentino started racing, Papa's hair was so long it was permanently tied back in a waist-length ponytail: he would only cut it off in 2000 after his son won the 500cc world championship. That had been the deal, that had been the promise, and Graziano saw it through. 'It wasn't for a bet,' he said at the time. 'It was just a display of appreciation and affection.'

This was the character of the father who would guide the young Valentino Rossi through his childhood years and, with hindsight, the boy could not have been in better hands – especially since mum Stefania provided the yin to Graziano's yang. While Dad was the eccentric hippy, Mum was far more rational and 'normal' and generally viewed as the more respectable and sensible of the two. A surveyor for Tavullia council, she hoped her son would grow up to become either an engineer or an architect, both highly respected professions in Italy, as elsewhere.

The contrast between Mum and Dad gave young Valentino a very balanced personality and he would later celebrate these two sides of himself with his famous sun/moon helmet design. For Graziano and Stefania, however, that contrast was perhaps too great and the couple would ultimately divorce in 1990 when Valentino was just eleven years old.

While he went to live with his mother in the village of Montecchio (ostensibly because she didn't give him as hard a time as Graziano when he came home late), Valentino spent just as much time with his father who lived only four miles away, and half a mile outside of Tavullia. There were no arguments, no traumas and, crucially for the eleven-year-old Valentino, there was no feeling of being torn two ways or being caught in the middle of a warring couple; his parents remained great friends and Vale was free to come and go as he pleased between the two households. 'We were all happy,' Valentino said, 'because they still had a good relationship and lived near each other.'

Of the divorce, Stefania told Rossi biographer Mat Oxley, 'I think he only married me because he was confused. We met at such a young age. I think that's why it didn't work.'[5]

Although Valentino lived with his mother, it was Graziano's house that had all the toys, and for a boy born into the Grand Prix motorcycle-racing paddock it was only a matter of time before he began to show an interest in them. 'Valentino's first memories are of the paddock, and when he was at home he played with motorbikes instead of other toys,' Graziano told Michael Scott when *Motocourse* first started taking a real interest in Rossi in 1997. (First published in 1976, *Motocourse* has become the definitive record of every Grand Prix season since. Valentino made his debut in the 1980–81 edition, pictured as a babe in his father's arms.) 'He was three years old when I finished bike racing. He had already begun to know some riders, to look at books and photos, and to speak about motorcycles.'[6]

Steve Parrish remembers a very young Rossi making a nuisance of himself at race meetings. 'I remember him messing about in the paddock when he was a kid, on a scooter or a bicycle, just getting in everyone's way. He was the same as everyone's else's kids at the time – like Kenny Roberts' [Sr] kids and all the others – just another little kid bumming around and growing up in the paddock.'

It wasn't long before the young paddock kid wanted to ride bikes himself and, according to Graziano, Valentino rode his first motorcycle before he could even ride a pushbike. In 1982, when Vale was two and a half years old, his father bought him a small minicross bike and the young Rossi immediately set about turning his father's house and paved back yard into a series of impromptu racetracks. The bike was styled like a mini chopper, and while neither father nor son can remember what make it was, they do both recall that it originally came with stabilisers, which only lasted three days before being removed. Valentino always was a quick learner.

It may seem ludicrously young to be riding motorcycles, but almost every world champion in the modern era started out riding by the age of three or four. There is no later substitute for growing up on a motorcycle and mastering the arts of balancing, sliding, throttle control and feel until they are second nature and it seems the younger this is achieved the better. Yet this trend is a relatively modern phenomenon. Just one generation before, it was quite possible to start riding at sixteen and go on to enjoy racing success. Nowadays, sixteen-year-old riders are winning world championship races: late starters have no chance.

The young Rossi was 'a bright and lovely kid' according to Graziano. Curious, inquisitive, good-natured and affable, though not prone to studying (his mother would read his schoolbooks to him when he showed no inclination to do his homework). More interested in playing guitar and football, Rossi found it easy to make friends in Tavullia and most remain part of his tight-knit inner circle to this day. Chief amongst them is Alessio 'Uccio' Salucci, who has acted as

Valentino's right-hand man at practically every Grand Prix since 1996; reassuring, helping and providing a constant in an ever-changing world, he's one of a small group of people who can treat Valentino as an equal because he knew him long before he became famous, powerful and wealthy. This fact alone is important: his presence and ability to speak openly and honestly to Rossi has a grounding effect that is beyond value. 'Vale's been there since my earliest memories; our parents were friends and we practically grew up together,' Uccio said in 2011. 'We're from a little village and went to the same nursery, schools... we've always been very close. I remember that in nursery our friends often played football, but we would go to a downhill slope we knew and ride a tricycle down it! It's a memory that is well fixed in my mind – even at that age we were taking big risks!'[7]

When he wasn't playing daredevils on a tricycle, Rossi was also given a good grounding on four wheels after his father built him a go-kart when he was five years old. The home-made kart had a 100cc engine bolted into a chassis designed to house a 60cc engine and it was, for such a young child, a brutal machine. When Vale started tagging along with Graziano and his friends on their trips to a local quarry to mess around with battered old rally cars, he would soon prove to be faster than all of them. And there were some seriously fast friends in the 'gravel gang', including three-times 125 and 250cc world champion Luca Cadalora (who would later act as a spotter for Valentino at Grands Prix, offering trackside observations on how Rossi's bike, and those of his rivals, were behaving on different parts of the track) and 125 and 250cc Grand Prix winner Loris Reggiani.

Valentino appeared to be a complete natural on four wheels, effortlessly learning the art of sliding on the loose gravel surface of the quarry, a skill that would serve him well in later years. It was almost inevitable that he would eventually wish to start racing go-karts and, at nine years old, he finally expressed this intention. The problem was that, in Italy, you had to be ten years old before you were eligible for a junior kart-racing licence. Graziano attempted to forge documents that would have allowed his son to race underage, but when this plan was foiled Valentino had no option than to wait until he was ten. At least he could get another year's practice in at the gravel pit.

Schoolboy motocross is usually the earliest form of motorsport that bike-mad kids take part in, as it doesn't have the same age restrictions as racing on tarmac. But Rossi never showed any desire to take up off-road sport, claiming he was attracted 'to the asphalt of the track'.

And so, the racing career of Valentino Rossi began on go-karts in 1989 – and he was immediately competitive. By April of the following year he had won his first race and by the end of 1990 he had won the regional championship, taking a total of nine wins along the way. The boy was clearly a natural on four wheels, but just as he was beginning to prove it, his interest was piqued by the newest craze to hit Italy: he discovered minimoto racing.

Minimoto racing took bike-mad Italy by storm. The bikes were scaled-down versions of proper Grand Prix race bikes and while they could be ridden by adults for fun, they could be ridden by kids in anger. When Rossi persuaded his father to buy him one, it marked the turning point in his life. It was, he said, 'the moment where my education as a future MotoGP rider really began'.

In 1991, he moved up to the Italian national junior go-kart championship, eventually finishing the season in fifth place overall, but he also won his first minimoto race and found that two wheels were even more fun than four.

Rossi's first proper race on two wheels took place at nearby Miramere in Rimini that year, under floodlights against a field of nineteen other riders. And not just kids – minimotos were so popular that a rent-a-racer culture quickly sprang up so anyone could rent a bike and enter a race for a few thousand lire. But none of them could touch Rossi that night. He led easily, took his first-ever victory on two wheels, and backed it up with another fifteen race wins that year on the multitude of mini racetracks that had sprung up along the Adriatic coast.

His time spent racing minimotos was both a happy and crucial one because the large number of riders involved meant he really had to learn how to race, not just ride fast. Sheer speed was not enough to get to the front of the pack – tactics were needed, as were elbows, aggression and fearlessness. When he eventually started racing in world championship Grands Prix on 125cc machines, Rossi applied the same wild-riding tactics as he had on minimotos, much to the chagrin of some of the older, more conservative riders. If racing go-karts against drivers with much better equipment had taught him how to lose with grace and look forward to the next race (a trait he would always maintain), then racing minimotos taught him how to fight for wins, and he proved to be very good at it, right from the outset.

'They are good training,' Rossi would later say of the pocket bikes. 'To have that much power in such a short wheelbase means that you do very long wheelies, and also that you slide them in the corners.'[8]

It was around this time that Graziano realised his son preferred to make his own mistakes rather than being told how to race. While he was always on hand to offer advice to Valentino, Graziano knew that his boy was not always receptive to the advice on offer. 'The last time I gave him advice as the father of a rider, he was ten years old,' he told journalist Maria Guidotti in 2015. 'We were at the pocket bike circuit of Cattolica, close to Misano. Vale was leaving from the pole position and he chose to take the start from the right side of the track because the first corner was on the right. I joined him on the starting grid and I suggested that he start from the left side so that he could pass on the outside. Vale looked at me from under the visor and told me: "Dad, let's leave it to me!"'[9]

Valentino preferred to learn his own way and if that meant learning the hard way by making mistakes, then so be it. As he said: 'If I make a mistake, it's necessary that I make my own mistake.' But that didn't mean he didn't at least take on board what his father was saying. 'I speak a lot with him because he is clever and always gives me clever advice,' Rossi explained, much later in his career. 'When I first started riding, when he said something I didn't listen – because I was young – but now I listen more. I think that is normal.'[10]

It was also around this time that the Rossi image that would later become globally famous began to take form. His traditional 46 race number is now even more famous than Barry Sheene's lucky 7. Sheene was the first world champion to decline the number-1 plate and stick with his number 7 when he had won the title in 1976. Rossi would be only the second rider to do this, twenty-five years later in 2001, and he started running it in his minimoto days. 'I discovered that it was the same number my dad, Graziano, used when he won his first GP, racing on the Morbidelli 250 in 1979 – the very year I was born,' Rossi explained. That is why I have decided to have 46 as my number for the world championship.'[11]

And then there was the Teenage Mutant Ninja Turtle soft toy, attached to the top of his helmet with suckers; a reminder that Valentino Rossi was still only a child, albeit a very fast one. Even today, the same old Ninja Turtle (Michelangelo, to be precise), now faded and frayed, travels in Rossi's suitcase to every race. It has been around the world some twenty-five times. 'It's my lucky charm,' Rossi explained. 'I bought it at the Co-op with my mum when I was ten and it's always been with me.' The turtle is no longer suckered on to his famous AGV helmet though; instead Vale has a turtle tattoo on his stomach for good luck. Motorcycle racers are a superstitious lot and Rossi is no exception: when you skate on the edge of disaster for a living, every little helps.

His helmet of choice was a Kevin Schwantz replica, as the wild-riding American and 1993 500cc world champion was Rossi's racing hero. His own gangly riding style would later be likened to that of Schwantz, a comparison that no doubt pleased Valentino.

It would no doubt also have pleased him to know that Kevin Schwantz himself witnessed one of these races and was astonished at how good Rossi was, even at this early stage. 'The first time I saw him race I was with Aldo Drudi [who would later become the painter of Rossi's famous helmets] and I went to watch him race a pocket bike at a go-kart track near Rimini – maybe Riccione. Aldo was telling me that this was Graziano's son and how fast he was on pocket bikes.'

The event in question was a two-hour endurance race with two riders in each team, each taking turns to do stints. Rossi's team-mate went out first and Schwantz was seriously impressed by his speed, but he got an even bigger shock when the young Valentino took his turn. 'Valentino's team-mate was noticeably faster than everybody else on the racetrack but when they made the rider change and Valentino got on the bike you noticed even more – maybe twice as much again – how much faster *he* was. He was so much faster than his team-mate and his team-mate was way faster than anybody else who rode in the first stint.'

Even at this early stage in Valentino's career, Schwantz knew he was witnessing something special. 'I thought, even then, here was someone who had found a way to work on, practise, and hone his racing skills on pavement at such a young age. And having a dad like Graziano who had raced as well? I thought it was just a matter of time till he got big enough and old enough to get into Grand Prix racing. So long as nothing else side-tracked him; so long as he didn't find something else he liked more than motorcycles – I mean, it was hard for me to find anything and it seemed like it was for Valentino too – but yeah, I realised he was special the very first time I saw him race.'

Now enjoying success on both four wheels and two, Rossi was going to have to make a decision as to which discipline to pursue, having spent two years dabbling in both. Although money has often been cited as the key factor in making this decision, Rossi insists his choice was more down to his greater passion for motorcycles, although he does admit that money played its part. While he always took his kart racing seriously, partly because the karting world is more professional even at the lower levels, minimoto felt more like playing to Valentino ('the way I saw it, I raced karts and played with minibikes'), and that sheer enjoyment of riding motorcycles never dissipated and was a key part in his success. While many other riders struggle to cope with the huge pressures of racing in multi-million-pound teams in MotoGP, Rossi has never forgotten the original reason he started racing in the first place – because it was fun. It's a well-known saying in the Grand Prix paddock that a happy racer is a fast racer and Rossi seems to be the living embodiment of this. When he snaps his visor shut and pulls out the of pit lane at any given MotoGP race, he is still that little kid with the Ninja Turtle suckered to his helmet, and it was this attitude that enabled him to remain at the top of the sport for far longer than any other rider.

Rossi has always had a natural passion for speed and, when combined with an equally natural curiosity about how to make things go ever faster, it proved to be a devastating combination. 'He was immensely curious, but kids are like that,' Graziano would later say. 'He really enjoyed accomplishing very difficult tasks, but kids also do that. Every kid has a talent, but sometimes they don't know they have it, or maybe they don't know for what they have a gift. Valentino had a big talent. Fathers make their kids play, first of all with the toys they like themselves. Valentino developed a great passion for speed. I think it's difficult not to become passionate about the game of speed. Valentino had talent, he enjoyed racing and this became his life.'[12]

But finance *was* also important in Rossi's decision to switch four wheels for two. Because of his age, he would have to move up to the 100cc category in the national go-kart championship in 1992 (he had been competing in the 60cc class up to that point) and that was going to cost 100,000 lire (around £40,000) for a full season. Knowing that this was going to be a huge stretch for his mother and father, it played a big part in Rossi's decision to ditch karts and focus on the much cheaper sport of minimoto racing. 'To me it wasn't hard to decide,' Valentino wrote in his 2005 autobiography, *What If I Had Never Tried It* 'My ideas were clear. I could feel the passion for motorbikes growing.' But he did also admit that money was an issue: 'Motorbikes were not my second choice. The doubts over money only contributed to my choice, but they were not the decisive factor.'[13]

While Graziano and Stefania both lived comfortably enough, partly due to Graziano's thriftiness with money, neither was fabulously wealthy and so, in the winter of 1992, after he had won the regional minimoto championship, Rossi made his decision, suddenly asking his father as they drove between Cattolica and Tavullia, 'Why don't we race motorbikes?' By this, Rossi meant full-sized motorbikes, not minimotos, because in 1993 he would turn fourteen and finally be old enough to race them. That would still be much cheaper than racing on four wheels and the path might even be smoothed over thanks to Graziano's extensive contacts in the motorcycling world. To the teenage Rossi it made perfect sense but it's not difficult to imagine Graziano's reaction – as a former top-level bike racer himself, he must have been proud that his son had chosen to follow in his footsteps, but the flipside is that every bike racer is all too well aware of the dangers the sport involves. Valentino's decision might prove to be a poisoned chalice. Should he be encouraged? It was difficult for Mum too. She had accompanied her husband to motorcycle races in an era when fatalities were all too commonplace before the advent of modern-day safety measures: she knew what could happen. But she also knew her son was careful and not nearly as devil-may-care as Graziano had been, so she supported Valentino in his decision.

Niall Mackenzie is a former 500cc Grand Prix rider and triple British Superbike champion whose sons, Taylor and Tarran, have both won British titles. As a parent, he remembers the moral dilemma he faced when encouraging his children to ride. 'When kids start riding minimoto bikes they can ride round all day and fall off as often as they like and never get hurt. Great fun. But then they get a taste for it and want a bit more and then, before you know it, you're standing at pit wall by the side of a proper, big racetrack and your kids are going past really fast on proper race bikes.' That's when Niall and his wife wondered what the hell they had done. 'But by that point,' he continues, 'it's too late. You can't tell them they're not allowed to do it any more. We wondered if we'd done the right thing. That's when I realised that, as parents, we're actually hardwired to look after our kids – not to give them dangerous things to do! That's when we had the really serious conversation with the boys about the dangers of the sport and I'm sure Graziano did the same thing with Valentino. As long as they're fully aware of the dangers and fully accept them, then all you can do is try to make sure they're as safe as they can be. All of us racers know parents who have lost their kids to racing, so we know it's not a game.'

The litmus test for Rossi's proposed career in bike racing would come at Misano, the international circuit that lies just a few miles from Tavullia and which still features on the MotoGP calendar today. Valentino's plan was to borrow a 125cc Aprilia Futura road bike from a friend and see if he had any natural talent for riding proper-sized motorcycles. Graziano agreed this was a wise course of action and the pair arranged to attend a public track day in November of 1992. It turned out to be a day that would change the face of motorcycle racing for ever and would lead to the greatest career the sport has ever witnessed.

CHAPTER 2
BOY RACER

'I thought, "Oh my God, get this kid away from me!"
because he was so noisy.'
NEIL HODGSON

Valentino Rossi's first time on a proper racetrack involved a modicum of deception and skulduggery. At thirteen years of age he was too young to be allowed out onto the hallowed tarmac of the Misano circuit, just nine miles north of Tavullia, for a track day. Undeterred, he waited for his older friend, Maurizio Pagano, to sign on in the race office, then borrowed Pagano's Aprilia Futura 125 and headed out on track pretending to be him. It was November of 1992 and it was the first time Valentino Rossi had ridden a full-sized motorcycle.

Although he struggled slightly with the size and weight of the Aprilia – at 140kg it was much heavier and physically much bigger than anything he'd ridden before – and also had to get accustomed to using clutch and gears for the first time in his life, he completed some safe and steady laps, finding his feet slowly rather than going all-out to impress and risking a crash.

While the 29bhp he had to play with was a far cry from the 290bhp MotoGP monsters he later learned to master, it was still a huge jump up from the 4 or 5bhp he had been accustomed to on minimoto bikes – and it was enough to seduce Rossi completely. After that first gentle foray into riding a proper-sized motorcycle on a proper-sized racetrack with billiard-table smooth tarmac, he was smitten and would never look back. And now that he had decided motorcycle racing was the way forward, he could really put Graziano's extensive contacts to good use.

Much has been made of the role played by genetics in the success of racing motorcyclists whose fathers also raced: it's the age-old nature-versus-nurture debate. As with so many things in life, the real answer lies somewhere between the two. If it were purely down to genetics, then every son of a racing father would be fast and that's clearly not the case. While it's quite common for paddock babies to later carve out successful careers for themselves (Kenny Roberts Sr and Jr, Ron and Leon Haslam, George and Carl Fogarty, to name just a few) it's more common for racers' sons to pursue other paths in life. 'I think it's fifty-fifty really,' Niall Mackenzie says of the nature-nurture issue. 'I've got a lot of friends who are ex-riders and their sons have shown no interest in bikes at all. They had grown up with bikes and I'm sure their dads didn't discourage them, but they just weren't interested. So, I think there has to be that initial spark from the son – they have to *want* to get on a little bike and tear round the garden. The higher up the ladder they get, the more they need to really want it because they *are* going to get hurt and they *are* going to have a lot of bad days and that's when you find out how much they want it.'

Not all traits are passed on from father to son, however. Steve Parrish feels Valentino has a natural racer's killer instinct that was absent in his father. 'I mean, there's clearly a great deal of Graziano in Valentino, but Graziano was the kind of chilled-out smoothie who just ambled around the paddock whereas Valentino is less laid-back and a bit more edgy and fidgety, so maybe he gets that from his mum. Valentino is more intense – but then, maybe Graziano taught him that he needed to be like that. Graziano wanted to win races, just like the rest of us, but I don't think he was as hell-bent on it as his son is. I think he maybe just lacked that drive, that fire in his belly, that Valentino has as a racer.'

Mackenzie agrees. 'Graziano comes from a different era, so he's a bit of a hippy type – he always reminds me of George Harrison and that whole era! He's just so laid-back and Italian. Valentino is a lot more like the whole racer package – totally focused, highly intelligent, really aware of everything that's going on around him. Graziano was just a cool dude who loved racing his motorbikes and going fast and living the life.'

So genes are only part of the story. What's more important is nurture, or rather, the guidance that racing fathers can offer and, perhaps even more importantly, the doors they can open for their children. They're far more likely to have pit bikes lying around and be willing to show their kids how to ride them and they're in a far better position to guide their children through riding schools and track days to see if there's any talent there. And, should there be any sign of talent, they have the contacts to be able to arrange rides with teams and to gain sponsorship by calling up old friends and calling in old favours. This, it would seem, is the real advantage of having a racing father and Valentino Rossi has openly acknowledged this. 'Graziano gave me a passion for motorcycles. Maybe if Graziano had a different job or chose another sport I wouldn't have had this passion. Also, when I started racing, he knew a lot of people in the sport and it was easier for me to get a ride at the start of my career.'[1]

Among Graziano's old racing friends were 1981 500cc world champion Marco Lucchinelli, 250cc Grand Prix winner Loris Reggiani, and 500cc GP race winner Virginio Ferrari. It was to them that Graziano turned when his son wanted to move up to racing full-sized motorcycles in 1993, just a few months after that initial try-out at Misano.

Few teenagers would have been able to call upon such racing luminaries to help them kick-start their careers. After receiving a call from Graziano, Virginio Ferrari called Claudio Castiglioni, the owner of Cagiva motorcycles, who agreed to help and placed Rossi in a team run by Claudio Lusuardi, a former 50cc Grand Prix rider (who raced at the same time as Graziano) turned race team manager. Rossi would ride a Lusuardi-prepared Cagiva Mito 125 in the hugely popular and competitive Italian Sport Production championship. Graziano would pay the mechanics' wages and travel expenses while Cagiva would supply the bikes and all the spares. It was a fabulous deal for an unproven rider and it simply could not have happened without Graziano's contacts and standing in the motorcycle racing world.

Rossi's debut on the bike was at a practice session at the Autodromo dell'Umbria at Magione near Perugia and it was not the brightest of starts; in fact, he fell off the bike immediately after leaving pit lane, on the first corner of his first lap. New tyres on a cold track were blamed, a common enough mistake but an excruciatingly embarrassing one on your very first ride with a team and on your official debut as a motorcycle racer. He did, at least, get his first crash out of the way without injury and managed to ride the bike back to the pits to be fixed up before heading back out on track.

Six laps later, it happened again. And the cause of the crash was the same again – pushing shiny new tyres too hard on a cold track. Tyres need heat to work correctly and Rossi lacked the experience required to be patient enough to work some heat into them before twisting the throttle open.

Team boss Lusuardi had to effectively teach Rossi how to ride a full-sized motorcycle from scratch, but he was immediately impressed by Rossi's willingness to learn. 'He came from minibikes and we had to explain to him the ABCs of driving a motorcycle with big wheels. The boy listened, listened, and continued to listen – always. He was very attentive to everything that happened to the bike. He was always bothering me with questions and always wanted to improve.'[2]

Immediately displaying a talent for improvising and inventing techniques to improve his riding, Rossi covered his rev counter with a sticker so the only part still visible was the crucial powerband between 10,500 and 13,500rpm. The Cagiva Mito operated best within these parameters, so Rossi only wanted to see the needle when it was in this zone. Below 10,500rpm the bike made very little power so the game was to keep the needle within the small segment of the powerband where the bike worked best. It was an early, but telling, sign of the way Valentino's mind worked. He was a thinker.

But Rossi was mortified with his performance at that first test. Two crashes in six laps were enough to not only give his team some cause for concern (although Lusuardi himself did not seem too upset), but Rossi too. As Graziano drove him home Valentino was almost in tears and seriously thought about quitting before he made a further fool of himself. 'You could see the disappointment in Valentino's eyes,' Graziano said of his son's perceived failure. 'He was almost crying. But these are the most important moments in a racer's career, when you find the strength to react and to show whether you're strong or weak.'[3]

Rossi discovered that day he wasn't weak. Nor was he prepared to let down all those who had helped him get this far. He made the decision to carry on, as much for their sakes as his own. It would prove to be a decision, made by a fourteen-year-old schoolboy, that would change the history of motorcycle racing.

It would also prove to be a decision that he would learn from and he would put that learning – if at first you don't succeed, try and try again – to good use over the next quarter of a century. Whether it was recovering and making a comeback after injury or simply finding the motivation to carry on pushing at 100 per cent on an uncompetitive Ducati (as he did in 2011 and 2012), Rossi always fell back on this same basic principle and refused to quit when the going got tough. Those embarrassing and confidence-sapping early crashes on his first proper outing on a full-sized motorcycle taught him that knocks will happen but it was how he chose to react to them that would determine who he was. No world champion in any discipline has ever had an easy ride to the top and Valentino Rossi was no exception. In fact, he would eventually become as famous for his mental toughness as he would for his riding skills, and that toughness was born out of moments like those Magione crashes.

He would also learn that perseverance and courage could

help turn things around very quickly. In the first round of the 1993 Italian Sport Production championship, held at the same Magione circuit that same weekend, Rossi would finish in ninth place. It was his first-ever race on a proper motorcycle and he finished inside the top ten. The signs were good, and Rossi was elated.

Lusuardi was elated too and could see that his young charge took to the Cagiva like a natural. 'Valentino immediately found himself at ease with the Cagiva Mito – the feeling with his bike was immediate.' He also believed the 125 Sport Production championship was the perfect place for young riders to learn their trade. 'The technical regulations were very restrictive, so the driver counted a lot. It was a preparatory class that allowed you to make the boy grow in every way – the management of a race, the management of the vehicle, learning to describe to the mechanics the feeling with the bike... it was the right way.'[4]

While Graziano was always on hand to help his son at races, he was more in the background than the foreground and never interfered by laying down the law on how his son should ride. Valentino, then as now, preferred to learn his own way, and if that meant learning the hard way by making mistakes, then so be it.

Rossi spent most of the 1993 season hovering in or around the top ten in the Sport Production championship, seemingly unable to make progress and finish any higher up the results sheets. But this all changed at the final round in Misano, as Graziano explained: 'It has never been necessary to push Valentino as he has always been totally motivated. He is generally a happy person but deadly serious when his visor goes down. Only once I felt he needed help. At the beginning of 1993 in the Italian Sport Production championship he was out of the top ten... and I could see he couldn't understand why. We worked hard at improving his confidence but it took until the last race where he qualified pole and finished third before he was back on form.[5]

Misano was Rossi's home track and he had already completed more laps on it than any other circuit. It was, after all, the track where he had first ridden a full-sized motorcycle the previous year. The other key factor was that Cagiva decided to give him one of their official factory bikes for that final round. Rossi's usual bike was more standard than the official bikes being ridden by his team-mate, Andrea Ballerini, who was fighting Roberto Locatelli for the championship. When the Cagiva factory prepared a special bike for Ballerini to help him win the title, Claudio Lusuardi offered Rossi Ballerini's spare machine. It was enough to make the difference and Rossi found himself sitting on pole position for the very first time – ahead of the two championship contenders, Ballerini and Locatelli.

So excited was Rossi by this new-found form, he completely fluffed the start and found himself languishing in twentieth place. Undeterred, he rode magnificently and fought his way through to take third. 'I was ecstatic,' he said of his first-ever podium finish on a real motorcycle. 'It always took me a bit of time to figure out how to be fast. But once I learned, I knew how to be fast – very fast. It was like that throughout the early stages of my career.'[6]

The result was enough to secure third place in the championship, and with Ballerini and Locatelli (who won the series) moving up to the 125cc Grand Prix world championship in 1994, Rossi became Cagiva's official rider in the Sport Production championship. But Graziano had other plans too. Realising that another year spent on production-based machinery would not teach Rossi about the intricacies of setting up a thoroughbred racing motorcycle, he arranged for his son to also ride in the Italian GP 125 championship in 1994 on a Sandroni. It was effectively a home-built bike, put together by local enthusiasts including Peppino Sandroni and chassis-designer Guido Mancini (Graziano's former race mechanic) and with an engine supplied by Aprilia.

For all its home-brew credentials, the Sandroni was fast and, more importantly, it gave Valentino experience on a real racing motorcycle. If he were to move up to world championship racing in the future, then this would be crucial. Racing motorcycles are infinitely adjustable beasts – almost every parameter on them can be changed and modified to allow the rider to get the 'feel' he needs to ride at the limit. Production-based bikes are far less adjustable, slower, and much heavier too, so the sooner Rossi could get onto a thoroughbred the better. Racing in the Italian national 125cc GP class would also introduce Rossi to racing on slick tyres for the first time – another skill he would need to master if he was planning to race at world championship level. He would also get to race against world championship riders from Italy, as it was common practice back then to take in the odd domestic round just to stay sharp and perhaps earn a bit of extra cash and gain more exposure for sponsors.

Of course, after finishing third in 1993, Rossi was aiming to win the Italian Sport Production championship in 1994 as well as learning the ropes in the pukka 125 racing class. Lusuardi was not best pleased with Graziano's master plan, feeling that it was too much for the young Rossi to take on so early in his career. The Cagiva team boss would have preferred his young charge to focus solely on winning the Sport Production championship before moving up to the national 125cc GP class the following year.

Fortunately for Rossi, the two championships did not clash. The 125 GP series was run during the first half of the season and the Sport Production championship mostly during the second, so he could at least concentrate on one at a time rather than having to jump between two very different motorcycles.

While he didn't set the world alight in his first races in the GP class (fourteenth in Monza and a crash at Vallelunga), his pace did improve as the season progressed and this prompted Aprilia to furnish him with a stronger engine for the last few races. At Misano he was hanging onto the leading group and holding a strong fourth place until his engine failed, but he fared better in the final round at Mugello where he faced 125cc Grand Prix world championship riders for the first time. He was clearly thrilled to finally be able to measure himself against some of the best 125cc riders on the planet. 'For me, at the time, the prospect of racing with a world championship rider was a dream,' he said. He didn't disgrace himself either and was delighted to finish fifth, just behind world championship rider Gabriele Debbia, whom he'd held onto for the whole race.

With many valuable lessons learned in the GP class, Rossi could then focus on the Sport Production series to round out his second season of racing. And it would prove to be an altogether more dramatic affair.

When asked about his son's fiercest racing rivalries over the years, Graziano Rossi has named Paolo Tessari, much to the puzzlement of less well-informed fans who expect to hear names like Max Biaggi, Casey Stoner or Jorge Lorenzo. Tessari is not a name familiar to most MotoGP fans, but he was the man Rossi had to beat in 1994 and he provided the first opportunity for Rossi to hone his race craft on a weekly basis. But despite the fierce rivalry that built up between them, the two became – and remain to this day – great friends. They even had a unique pact, according to Tessari. 'We slept in the same camper and we said that whoever won had to dedicate the victory to the other. He was like a brother. We had a unique relationship, we had fun.'[7]

So much fun that Rossi says the opening race of the 1994 Sport Production championship still stands out as one of the best of his life. 'Tessari and I duelled in a way I will always remember as one of the most fun races of my career,' he said. 'Even though I lost!'[8]

Tessari, on the Aprilia, and Rossi, still on his 1993 Cagiva while awaiting the new model, were well ahead of the rest of the pack in the opening race and constantly changing positions over the last two laps. Rossi took the lead in the very final corner but then immediately crashed out, handing the win to his rival and friend.

By the second round at Misano, Rossi's new bike had arrived and he put it to good use, taking his first-ever win on a real motorcycle. It was a historic moment and crucial for Rossi's confidence: it's one thing thinking you can win races, another thing entirely to *know* that you can. It has often been said that around 80 per cent of motorcycle racing happens north of the eyebrows; in other words, it's all about confidence, and nothing raises confidence like winning.

Tessari won the next two regional races and the pair headed to the four national finals agonisingly close on points. At the first final at Vallelunga Rossi's bike seized, handing the win to Tessari. In the next, at Mugello, he finished second before taking another win at Monza. And then came the very last round at Misano where Rossi would have 'home turf' advantage again. It was all to play for. His first title was in sight. And then the real drama began.

Aside from Tessari, Rossi also had strong competition from other championship hopefuls including Gino Borsoi and Stefano Cruciani, and it was the latter who would provide the first major drama of Rossi's career. On the last lap of the race Rossi was in second place – just enough to secure the title – until Cruciani made an over-ambitious, do-or-die attempt to overtake, nudged into Rossi's bike, and ran both himself and Rossi off the track. Cruciani rejoined the circuit ahead of Valentino and finished second with Rossi third. It was enough to steal the title from Rossi but the matter didn't end there. Rossi was furious. 'Cruciani arrive much too fast and knock me wide because he's fucking crazy!' he raged.

There was pandemonium in pit lane as the rival riders and team members pushed, shoved and fought over the highly dubious move. There were appeals and counter-appeals, and eventually Cruciani was disqualified from second place and Rossi was awarded his first-ever title – he was the 1994 125 Italian Sport Production champion.

Paolo Tessari was magnanimous in defeat and later acknowledged that Rossi's talent was, ultimately, far greater than his own. 'Even if I had won I would never have reached his level because Vale has always had an extra gear, as a pilot and as a person. I already knew he was special – he was very strong mentally.'[9]

This would be the last time Rossi would race in the Sport Production class. It had served its purpose as a basic training institution and it was time to move onwards and upwards, but he would always have the fondest memories of his time in the class. If there's one period in his career that Valentino tends to get nostalgic about, it's this one. In between races the riders would cause mayhem, organising massive water-bomb fights and midnight scooter races (with headlights switched off) on the very tracks where they would turn wheels in anger the following day. In his 2005 autobiography *What If I Had Never Tried It,* Rossi writes: 'Even today I remember with so much affection and nostalgia many of those races and the adventures I shared with kids who were my rivals on the track and my friends off it.'

He couldn't have known it at the time but now, at the end of his second season of racing, Rossi had started a pattern that would repeat itself right up until he was in the elite class of motorcycle racing – MotoGP. That pattern was deceptively simple: a year to learn, a year to win. He had taken a year to learn the 125 Sport Production championship before winning it and he would do the same in 125cc Grands Prix, 250cc Grands Prix and 500cc Grands Prix, before the premier class was rebranded as MotoGP in 2002 and Rossi finally settled into the very top level of the sport. He even followed this pattern in 1995: having learned the ropes in the Italian 125 GP championship the previous year, he would take the title in his second attempt. The only exception to the rule that governed the first nine years of his career came in 1995 when he also took part in the now defunct European championship – a once crucial stepping stone between national championships and world championships. He would finish third in that series but never returned to win the title in 1996 because there was simply no need: by then he had graduated to world championship level and there was no going back.

Guiding Rossi all the way through these early stages of his career was his engineer Mauro Noccioli, another trusted ally in Vale's formative years and a man who had a very keen perception of what made Rossi tick and how to get the best out of him. 'He was very difficult to work with at the beginning – he was just a child who wanted to play. On a Friday and

Saturday he would just mess about but he was so intelligent that he could change completely on a Sunday for the race, even from an early age. His freedom was so important to him and we knew that. He needed to have fun and needed to feel confident. If you stuck Valentino in the box all the time, then for sure he wouldn't go so fast. You can't make a child work for a whole weekend and put that sort of pressure on him. He was better off playing on his PlayStation.'[10]

A race engineer or crew chief's job is not only to tune his rider's motorcycle, it's also about tuning the rider's mind and making sure he's happy, comfortable and confident. They need to know their rider's personality, what they like and what they don't like, what kind of things affect their performances, what makes them settled, what makes them relaxed. Noccioli, even at that early stage, could clearly see what made Rossi tick and did all he could to accommodate him – and to let him be the young teenager that he was.

When he wasn't glued to his PlayStation, Rossi had showed enough promise during the 1994 season to capture the attentions of the Aprilia factory and was furnished with a standard RS 125R for both the Italian and European championships the following year. Rossi completely dominated the Italian series, winning the title with rounds to spare, but the European series proved a much greater challenge. In 1995, it was staged at world championship Grand Prix meetings, allowing Rossi to become acquainted with some of the tracks that would be used throughout his career, as well as being able to get a feel for the pressure of racing in front of massive crowds, meeting team bosses, getting his face known – it was all part of the grand plan. But most importantly, Rossi got to measure himself against the pace of the best 125cc racers in the world. He may not have been racing against them, but he could compare lap times from the world championship qualifying sessions and races with those that he and his European championship rivals were posting. And it proved to be quite a shock. 'It was quite depressing,' Rossi later admitted. 'I'd look at their times and then I'd consider my own and see just how far behind I was. There were times when I was as much as four seconds a lap slower. But at least now I had a reference point, something to aim for.'[11]

In order to try to bridge that gap, Rossi studied the world championship riders intensely, absorbing their race craft, their lines, their riding styles, their overtakes – no detail was too small. This was a masterclass from the best in the world and none of it was wasted on the young Valentino. He might never have applied himself in school, but this was an education that he was ferociously interested in and he became a model pupil.

Another huge bonus was befriending Japanese 125 world championship rider (and world champion in 1995 and '96) Haruchika Aoki, who happily showed Rossi round every new track they went to and explained the intricacies of each. Rossi loved the style and attitude of the Japanese 125 riders: they rode every lap like it was their last, had spectacular riding styles, were not afraid to crash, and knew how to have fun in and around the paddock, too.

In the 1995 125cc European championship, one of Rossi's greatest rivals was fellow Italian rider Lucio Cecchinello. Now owner of the LCR Honda team in MotoGP, in '95 Cecchinello was mounted on an HRC (Honda Racing Corporation) kitted Honda RS125 which, according to Rossi, was 'impossible to beat'. That didn't stop him trying though: 'I wanted to beat him, so I'd go, go, go and after, crash, crash, crash!'

The two had met when competing in the Italian 125 GP

championship the previous year but hadn't become close friends. 'We started to meet each other more often on track in 1995 and we were competitors in that period,' Cecchinello explains. 'He was riding for Aprilia and I was riding for Honda, so we were fighting each other for the European championship. I remember that he was already a really fast rider, even in his first year.'

There's an old adage in motorcycle racing which states that's it's far easier to teach a fast rider to stop crashing than it is to teach a slow rider to go fast. In these early years of his career Rossi was no stranger to crashing but that was nothing to be ashamed of: crashing is the only way to find out where the true limit is. A smart rider will, once he has found this limit, learn to ride just within it, skating on the edge of disaster but trying not to go over that edge too often. Rossi would eventually master this art, but he had a lot of learning to do first and would regularly crash in pursuit of Cecchinello. 'For sure he had a few crashes, but I don't think he had more than the other riders would average in a season,' Cecchinello says. 'He was definitely very fast and very aggressive on the brakes and on corner entry.'

He might not have admitted it at the time but Cecchinello does now concede that he had a faster bike than Rossi during that 1995 season. 'Yes, it's true that I had a very fast bike because I raced with Team Pileri and the team had a very good relationship with Honda and HRC, so I had a Honda 125cc GP bike with an HRC race kit and it was fast. Valentino's Aprilia was slower, but the chassis and handling was probably a bit better than my bike. But I still believe that he did incredible things with that Aprilia.'

Cecchinello remembers the German round at the Nürburgring as being a particularly fierce encounter and one that clearly demonstrated Rossi's never-say-die attitude. 'I won the race in the end but before I managed to create a gap between us he overtook me so many times and I had to keep fighting back to pass him again. He was a tough rider to race against out on track, especially because he was always giving you surprises! You would expect him to overtake you on the inside of a certain corner but instead he would pass you around the outside, which was amazing to see.'

Rossi's presence in the Grand Prix paddock was immediately noticed, though not always for the right reasons. Future World Superbike champion Neil Hodgson was racing in the premier 500cc class that year and remembers the teenage Rossi as a very noisy and slightly annoying presence. 'It was like he had ADHD!' he says. 'He was so loud and he had the loudest scooter in the paddock, too. And he had really weird hair. This was 1995 when he was racing in the European 125 championship, which had some rounds alongside Grand Prix meetings. He was battling at the front but didn't particularly stand out to me as a rider, I just always thought, "Oh my God, get this kid away from me!" because he was so noisy. He was certainly memorable though.'

But behind the tomfoolery, the young Rossi was a polite and well-mannered kid, as Niall Mackenzie recalls. 'I knew Graziano so he came up to speak to me at a party hosted by Diadora boots near Misano in 1994 and said, "I want you to meet my son," so he brought over a very young Valentino, who was really polite and always looked you in the eyes when talking to you. Graziano said, "This is Valentino and he's been doing really well with his racing." Now, I've met dozens – probably *hundreds* – of dads that have brought their kids over to me and said their sons were going to be great racers one day so I remember thinking, "Yip, another youngster that might, or might not, go somewhere," but I really shouldn't have doubted this one, knowing what we know now!'

During the 1995 season, Rossi also took in some rounds of the Ducados Open series, which was mostly based in Spain. It was, according to Mauro Noccioli, a highly beneficial experience. 'The Open Ducados in Spain was an extremely important series for Vale. He learnt how to race at circuits he wasn't familiar with and compete against people he didn't know. His family stayed in Italy and he spent a long time away from home but he learnt to deal with that. On the other hand, the European championship was too hard for him and it wasn't a great experience. He was still riding on impulse and needed to learn how to work with things like carburation and tyres. He was still very young but he was also a quick learner, so those things came with time.'[12]

The highlight of the Ducados series came at Jarama, where Rossi finished third behind vastly experienced world championship riders (and world champions) Jorge Martínez and Emilio Alzamora. But, racing aside, the venture also took Rossi away from home for long periods, making him more independent and giving him a taste of what it's actually like to be an international motorcycle racer. 'We would leave restaurants without paying and trash rental cars,' he said, clearly easing his way into the international bike-racer lifestyle without difficulty. He wasn't quite jet-setting yet, but it was a taste of things to come. Not everyone has the inclination to travel round the world every year, so if travel was going to be a problem it was best to find out sooner rather than later.

Despite some of Noccioli's more negative memories of the European championship, it wasn't a complete disaster for Rossi. After taking six podiums he eventually finished in third place overall behind winner Frédéric Petit and runner-up

Lucio Cecchinello. That was enough to guarantee his future – for one season at least – in the world championship, as the top three finishers qualified for a slot on the world stage the following year. Yet Valentino still felt he could have achieved more. 'In the Europeans I made too many errors this year,' he said shortly after the championship wrapped up. 'If I hadn't been stupid I would have had a chance but I made lots of mistakes and ended up third.'

But third place was enough: it was his passport to Grands Prix and a springboard to levels of success, wealth and fame beyond his wildest dreams.

CHAPTER 3

ROSSIFUMI

'Who is this Rossi?'
Ivano Beggio

While gifted with a natural intelligence, Valentino Rossi didn't like school, and his teachers didn't like him racing motorcycles, so something clearly had to give and, in 1996, it did. At the age of sixteen he finally decided to end his formal education and left the Liceo Mamiani high school in Pesaro before he had gained his high school diploma. It had been on the cards for some time. During the 1995 season, when he had been competing in the European championships, Rossi had regular, and at times prolonged, absences from school and would often reappear in class nursing injuries from crashes. 'I wasn't the best student,' Rossi himself has admitted. 'And I certainly wasn't the best in terms of paying attention in class... I really wasn't interested.'[1]

A particular pet hate was the history of art class: it was a subject Rossi despised, despite having been born in Urbino, home of the Renaissance master Raphael. It was, perhaps tellingly, Rossi's art history teacher who told him he would never make a living riding 'silly motorcycles'. It was a criticism which stung at the time but must now be a source of amusement and even a cause for smugness in one of the world's highest-earning sportsmen. Rossi now refers to his teacher's comment as 'one of the least accurate predictions in history'.

Although his teachers saw little promise in the restless young Rossi, he did have non-academic talents that were starting to be noticed by the movers and shakers of Italian motorcycle racing. Carlo Pernat is a guru of the MotoGP paddock and often referred to as the 'kingmaker' of the sport, having managed such brilliant riders as Max Biaggi, Marco Simoncelli, Roberto Locatelli and Alessandro Gramigni. In 1995, Pernat started receiving a lot of phone calls from his old friend Graziano Rossi. 'Graziano approached me many times that year,' he says. 'At that period, I was responsible for the Aprilia factory's racing programme – I was responsible for signing riders. Graziano called me a minimum of twenty-five times, always pressing me to come and see his son racing. Eventually I agreed and went to Misano to see Valentino racing. Honestly, he impressed me a lot. I immediately thought, "He's either a crazy man or a champion," because he was taking so many strange lines, all over the track. And the way he was slipstreaming and the moves he was making, he reminded me very much of Kevin Schwantz. When I was at Cagiva in 1987 we tested Schwantz on the bike, so I knew exactly how he rode. Vale was so similar to Kevin – they both made it look like they were just riding bicycles, just throwing the bikes around and having fun.'

Schwantz himself would later notice the similarities in

style. 'When Valentino first started riding in Grands Prix his style was fairly similar to mine,' he says. 'He was a fairly tall kid, compared to a lot of the guys on 125cc bikes, so he had kind of a more upright riding style, but I didn't notice a whole lot of similarities between his style and mine at that time. But then, once he got onto a 500, I saw it maybe a little bit more. And when he got onto a MotoGP bike his style had to change as electronics started coming into play, so then he was hung off the bike a whole lot more – much farther than I ever was.'

He continues: 'He's been able to adapt his riding style to whatever it was he rode, so that's a big tip of the hat to him. He's never actually told me that he shaped his style around the way I raced, but hearing him say that I was his hero when he was growing up and that he liked my style... I'm sure he tried to implement a little bit of it. He's always been pretty good on the brakes, which, if I had a strongest point, that was probably it. But I think it all just comes naturally to him.'

Although Grand Prix success was still some way off for Rossi at this point, Pernat had seen enough to convince himself. 'I was so impressed I said to myself, "Okay Carlo, you have to speak to Ivano Beggio [President of Aprilia Motorcycles] about signing this kid." But he told me I was crazy because I was proposing to sign Valentino for three years, not one, which is more usual. He was saying, "Who is this Rossi?"'

Undeterred, Pernat drew up a contract for his teenage protégé that would secure his services for the next three years, beginning in 1996. It was the first contract Rossi ever signed. 'In this first year we paid him 60 million lire, then 90 million the next year, and 180 million for the third year [around £28,000, £41,000 and £83,000 respectively]. For me this was good money but not a huge amount of money. The family of

Valentino was not so rich at this moment so I tried to give them the best deal I could. Beggio said to me, "Carlo, why you spend all this money?" I think he only stood by me because I had discovered Max Biaggi and Alessandro Gramigni and we had won a lot of races. After half an hour of discussion he said, "Okay, Carlo, you take this rider." I was very happy about this. I made two separate contracts because Valentino was still a minor, so I needed the signatures of both his father and his mother.'

As ever, it was Graziano who was key: 'I think Valentino should pay a lot of money to his father for helping him so much in the beginning,' Pernat explains. 'Because in those early years Graziano was very important for Valentino! He was always speaking with me, speaking with Vale's mechanic – he was like a shield for his son. When I made the contract, I speak with Graziano, when I get a sponsor, I speak with Graziano. For me, Graziano was a big part of the beginning of Valentino's career.'

Ivano Beggio was not alone in his scepticism about Rossi. After all, he hadn't yet proven himself to any great extent at that stage of his career. 'Not everyone believed in Valentino,' Pernat says. 'Jan Vitteven – the technical director at Aprilia – spoke to me and said, "Carlo, in my opinion Valentino will never be a champion." And Fabrizio Guidotti [another Aprilia employee and noted talent scout] felt the same. He was a fantastic talent-spotter of Italian riders – it was him who suggested Max Biaggi to me, who suggested Alessandro Gramigni, Roberto Locatelli and Stefano Perugini – but when I signed Valentino, Guidotti told me, "You made a mistake." Unbelievable. Two important people, two experts, thought I had made a mistake. I don't know why, probably because Valentino was always joking and having fun and didn't seem to be serious enough.'

But this lack of belief from certain parties wasn't Pernat's main concern at the time: the real obstacle was that he had nowhere to put Rossi. The contract was for Rossi to race in the 125cc world championship but Aprilia only fielded an official team in the 250cc class and Valentino wasn't ready for that. 'The problem at the beginning was that I didn't have a team to put Valentino in. Aprilia was mainly concentrating on the 250cc class and we already had Max Biaggi as our rider in this. We had no official team in the 125cc world championship for 1996, so I telephoned my friend Giampiero Sacchi [famed rider manager and team boss] and explained that I had a very strong rider and I said I would give him Valentino for free, I would give him the bike for free, and I explained that he could have all the space on the bike for sponsors if he would set up a team for Vale and this is what we did.'

Mauro Noccioli, already established as Rossi's engineer, would also join the team and Rossi would be given Stefano Perugini's factory Aprilia RS125 from the previous year's championship. 'Because he crashed a lot in the early days we did not give him an official factory bike for the 1996 season,' Pernat explains. 'We gave him a semi-official bike and, for me, this was important. Mauro was the perfect man for Rossi at that time because he was so strong. For the second season we gave Vale the official factory Aprilia bike. This is a good way to help a rider to progress; you give him the semi-official bike first to let him learn and to make mistakes and then you give him the faster, official bike. We did the same when he moved to the 250cc class; he had the semi-official bike in 1998 and the official bike in 1999. One year to learn, one year to win – this was our system of work, and it was a good system.'

So this was it. The team was in place and the contract was signed: Valentino Rossi was going to race in the world championship. He had even come up with a nickname for himself, intended as a tribute to one of his heroes in the 500cc class, Japanese rider Norifumi Abe. 'In 1994, I watched Norifumi Abe and I liked his racing style very much,' Rossi would later explain of his new moniker. 'Now I also like the Japanese 125 riders. They are very funny and I enjoy racing with them very much.'

So for his debut season in the 125cc world championship, Valentino Rossi would become Rossifumi, and a legend would be born.

*

It was a rude awakening. Italian national championship riders are one thing, European championship riders are another; but the quantum leap up to the level of world championship riders seemed completely insurmountable to Valentino Rossi at first. He got his first taste of the pace he would need to learn to ride at in pre-season tests at Jerez in Spain and simply couldn't believe what he was seeing. 'Fuck, it was incredible – they were so fast! It was like another sport, maybe four seconds a lap faster. I thought I would never be able to ride like that.'[2]

Rossi's childhood friend and right-hand man, Uccio Salucci, later remembered that initial despair. 'Valentino said, "Uccio, these riders are very, very fast – maybe too fast for me." I said, "No, Vale, why? This is the first test and we are very young!" And he said, "No... it's very difficult."'[3]

But while he hadn't been prepared to apply himself and learn about the history of art, this was a schooling that Rossi was only too eager to participate in and he set about doing everything he possibly could to learn how to go faster. Again, just as he had done in the European championship, Rossi stood trackside at every opportunity and studied the other riders' techniques: their lines, their braking points, the position of their bodies on the bikes. He watched everything, analysed everything, and absorbed it all with an obsessive fervour.

While he realised he had a lot to learn, Rossi refused to be intimidated by the world championship riders and once the racing began he very quickly started ruffling feathers. 'That was me at my craziest. I really was an absolute pest... I wanted to overtake everyone, come what may... In other words, I made people uncomfortable.'[4]

One of those he made uncomfortable was Jorge Martínez, a four-time world champion in the 80cc and 125cc categories and something of a veteran by 1996. Martínez had come from a more orderly and gentlemanly tradition of racing and was unaccustomed to the banzai tactics of the new generation who had grown up squabbling around minimoto tracks, where elbows were viewed as part of a riders' arsenal and desperate do-or-die moves were considered the norm. Rossi's first world championship race was at Shah Alam in the steaming heat of Malaysia on 31 March and he immediately incurred the wrath of Martínez. 'I was fighting for the podium with a group of five riders, then, in the middle of a slow corner Valentino braked, I touched him and crashed. I was very angry.'[5]

So angry, in fact, that as soon as Rossi had finished his race (in a very creditable sixth position) Martínez stormed into the young Italian's pit garage. 'He came to see me in my box with a lot of anger,' Rossi said. 'He wanted to kill me.'

Martínez knew Graziano Rossi and remembered the Italian introducing him to his son in the paddock when he was just a toddler. After a year of fighting Rossi on track, Martínez would say, only half-jokingly, 'I should have taken my chance then and run him over!'

Rossi claimed the incident had occurred because Dirk Raudies' bike seized in front of him, forcing him to brake hard, but however justifiable his defence the damage had been done and Rossi was forced to hide behind one of his mechanics, using him as a shield against the furious Martínez. He was, after all, just seventeen.

After taking eleventh places in both Indonesia and Japan, Rossi showed real promise with two fourths in Spain and Italy, just missing the podium by a tenth of a second in Jerez and by less than a second in Mugello. But there were too many crashes along the way; fifteen in total that season, though mostly during practice and qualifying sessions. He failed to finish in France due to yet another crash but did at least manage to set his first fastest lap in a world championship race before doing so.

And then matters came to a head at a damp Assen. After starting in a lowly twentieth position, after just three laps Rossi had fought his way through practically the entire field to put himself in second place. It was a breath-taking performance, ruined only by the fact that he then crashed out. Again. Team boss Giampiero Sacchi felt it was time to intervene and sat his rider down for a serious talk. All the crashes were straining the tight budget of Sacchi's small team but, even more importantly, he felt that Rossi was wasting his talent by riding too hard too soon. Sacchi also happened to be the personal manager of a certain Max Biaggi who was dominating the 250cc world championship on an Aprilia at the time. Biaggi was a Roman and, as a two-time world champion already, he was the darling of the Italian press. Rossi was not a fan, so Sacchi probably chose the wrong example when he explained to Rossi that if he kept on going about his racing in the way he was, he could only ever hope to be a Kevin Schwantz at best

(Schwantz won twenty-five Grands Prix but only one world title), but if he calmed down and learned discipline then he could be a multiple world champion like Max Biaggi. Rossi has since confessed that his immediate thought was 'Like Biaggi? Forget that! I'd much rather be like Schwantz,' but he kept his mouth shut and took on board what his team boss was telling him.

Next time out in Germany Rossi took a more sensible fifth place but would suffer yet another non-finish at the British Grand Prix, although this time it was due to a mechanical problem and no fault of his own. Despite his crash-happy attitude, Rossi had done enough to convince Aprilia that he was worthy of a little more support and the factory supplied him with an upgraded cylinder and carbon front disc brake ahead of the Austrian round. The upgrades had an immediate effect and at Zeltweg Rossi took the first podium of his world championship career with third place but had to watch his compatriot, Ivan Goi, become the youngest-ever winner of a Grand Prix at just sixteen years and a hundred and fifty-seven days old.

'I was very young, so I only realised in later years the value of that victory,' Goi says. 'But I was not surprised we were both so competitive because we came from a very difficult Italian championship that taught a great deal about competition. When Valentino moved to the world championship he had a great ability to quickly learn the new tracks so he was able to attack even the most experienced riders. I knew Rossi had talent, so I'm not surprised by what he went on to achieve. Everyone's dream is to become champions, both him and me. In that first year, however, we were the same.'

Many had expected Rossi to claim the accolade of being the youngest-ever winner of a Grand Prix and were disappointed when he didn't, but he didn't disappoint for long: the next round was at Brno in the Czech Republic and that would change everything.

The Czech Grand Prix was only Rossi's eleventh world championship race and he had taken his first podium just two weeks before. Momentum was building, a win was coming and everybody knew it – it was only a matter of when. The first sign that it might come at Brno was when Rossi took his first pole position in qualifying. The fast, flowing and undulating Brno circuit clearly suited both his riding style and his Aprilia, so the big question was whether Rossi had listened to Sacchi and would calm his aggression just enough to avoid another crash. He *had* to stop crashing or, as Carlo Pernat had elsewhere observed so bluntly, he would 'either be a champion or dead'.

The race proved to be a classic battle of youth versus experience as a seventeen-year-old Rossi again fought hard with thirty-four-year-old veteran Jorge Martínez. Both had problems early in the race: Rossi got a terrible start and was seventh after the first lap while Martínez dropped to ninth after accidentally selecting neutral. Both men fought their way back through the field, with Rossi initially taking the lead before his Spanish rival hustled through on lap ten. From there it was all about the two of them as they continued to trade places and pulled farther away from eventual third-place finisher Tomomi Manako. Martínez took the lead on the last lap, but Rossi refused to be denied and slipped back through and held his slender advantage to the flag to claim his first Grand Prix win.

So ecstatic was he at taking a maiden victory, Rossi punched the air with both hands as he crossed the finish line and almost crashed into the pit wall when his bike veered violently to the right. But he had the skill, coolness, and lightning reflexes to correct the situation and went on to enjoy his first world championship victory lap. In time he would become as famous for his elaborate post-race celebrations as he would for his riding but for now he just exuded sheer delight as he waved to the fans, punched the air in delight, and accepted countless pats on the back from his rivals.

But the real joy was in finally knowing that he *could* win at world championship level. That first win is a huge moment in any rider's career and it was no different for Rossi. 'I thought that all riders are divided into two big groups – those who win Grand Prix races and those who don't,' he said. 'And if you haven't won, then you never know.'

Now he knew. He was a Grand Prix winner. He could beat the best 125cc riders on the planet. He had arrived. Even Martínez was impressed by the youngster's skill, as Rossi later revealed: 'After my win he gave me his hand and said, "Fuck, you were strong!"'

He may have been a Grand Prix winner but Rossi was still just a teenager so the celebrations weren't exactly debauched that night, according to Uccio Salucci. 'On the Sunday evening we stayed in our very small camper and we drank some beer with our parents.' Rock stars they were not.

Rossi's win meant he and Graziano became only the third father and son pairing to both win Grand Prix races, the others being fellow Italians Nello and Alberto Pagani and British riders Leslie and Stuart Graham.

The Czech Grand Prix was a seminal moment for Rossi. 'It was a turning point because from then on my riding became somewhat more controlled,' he would say. He would still crash, as every rider pushing the absolute limits of physics and adhesion occasionally does, but he would learn to control his excitement just that little bit more, would accept second place when a win wasn't possible and would think more calmly about his race craft rather than throwing caution to the wind. Martínez noticed the change. 'In MotoGP we have seen many riders arrive who are very fast but crash a lot, so we ask the questions: "Will this new guy continue to be very fast but still crash too often or will he change this mentality?" Around this time Valentino made this change.'[6]

Giampiero Sacchi also saw the change as Rossi's confidence began to grow and his riding became more controlled. 'His mind changed. He became another person... He was now sure of himself inside; he had the conviction, something that normal riders don't have.'[7]

Rossi was also helped enormously by his natural curiosity and attention to detail. 'Valentino is one of the most curious people I have ever met,' says Carlo Pernat. 'I remember in that first season in 1996 he asked me about *everything*! "Who is this man?" "Why is this green?" "Why is it made like that?" He was as curious as a monkey about everything! But that is probably one of the best characteristics of Valentino. Curiosity is a form of intelligence.'

Despite his new-found conviction in his abilities, the last four races of the season were largely disappointing for Rossi. After leading the Italian Grand Prix at Imola, he could only manage fifth place at the flag due to a faulty spark plug robbing him of revs. In Spain, he was wiped out by a crashing Masaki Tokudome, and in Brazil he crashed both in practice and in the race before the spark-plug issue returned at the final race in Australia, leaving him languishing in fourteenth place. It had been a year of learning and of over-riding a bike that didn't quite have the speed of the full factory machines he was up against. 'It was necessary for me to ride crazy because my bike was so slow,' Rossi said in summation of his debut Grand Prix season. 'And when you ride like this all the time it's possible you crash.'[8]

A lowly fourteenth place was not how Rossi wanted to finish his first season of Grand Prix racing, but there were a lot more positives than negatives to reflect on at year's end. He had won a race, taken two further podiums, and set one pole position as well as a fastest lap. He was beginning to tick all the boxes and managed to finish in ninth place overall in the world championship (which was won by Haruchika Aoki) despite having to learn new circuits, a new team and a new bike, as well as becoming accustomed to all the travel involved. He had also made a name for himself, not only among fellow riders, teams and all the movers and shakers in the Grand Prix paddock, but also with the fans who instantly took to the infectiously cheerful Italian with the floppy long hair and flamboyant riding style. He was a hit from the off but even he could never have imagined just how outrageously popular he would eventually become.

Rossi had certainly done enough to impress his bosses at Aprilia, who decided to supply him with an official, full-factory RS125 for the 1997 season. Rossi's old sparring partner from the European championships, Lucio Cecchinello, who finished six places behind Rossi in the 1996 world championship, says he saw the potential of a more experienced Rossi and a full factory effort even then. 'After his performance in the world championship in 1996 we all knew that he could win the world title in '97 – also because Aprilia was fully committed and behind him.'

As well as supplying him with the latest factory bike, Aprilia's Carlo Pernat also allocated more staff to Rossi's AGV-sponsored team, which was still led by Giampiero Sacchi with Mauro Noccioli remaining as Rossi's race engineer. In fact, Pernat had been so impressed with Rossi's performance in 1996 that he offered to fast-track him up to the 250cc world championship in 1997, but Rossi declined the offer – against his father's advice. Rossi's whole career, as short as it was at that point, had been spent on 125cc machines and he wanted to close the circle by winning the world championship before moving up to the intermediate 250cc class. He was still relatively inexperienced in world championship racing, so another year in the same class to allow him to perfect his race craft and fine-tune his circuit knowledge was not such a bad idea. He would still only be eighteen in 1997: there was time enough. He was only prepared to switch to the 250 class as 125cc world champion. 'I would only move to the next level once I had conquered the level I was in,' Rossi said.

★

If he had shown promise in 1996, Rossi was utterly dominant in the 125cc class in 1997. From the 15 races held that year he took 11 wins, 13 podium finishes, 4 pole positions and 7 fastest laps to end the season with an 83-point advantage over Japan's Noboru Ueda. It was a stunning display of riding and, when coupled with Rossi's increasingly flamboyant post-race victory celebrations, was a recipe for instant stardom. In Italy at first and, soon afterwards, globally, Rossi became a phenomenon, the new darling of motorcycle racing and a clear threat to the most popular Italian rider of the time, Massimiliano Biaggi.

Known to all and sundry as Max, the 'Roman Emperor' was a very different character to Rossi. Sombre faced, immaculately dressed, proud, aloof, arrogant, even, Biaggi was everything Rossi was not. He preferred to eat alone (a very un-Italian trait), he cultivated his image extremely carefully, he dated famous Italian models, he was feted by the mainstream Italian press and he had no interest in making friends in the paddock. 'I don't come to the GPs to make friends,' he stated. 'I come for business and I go home from the track as soon as I can.'

There was a troubled history behind Biaggi. He had been abandoned by his mother as an infant, hence the loner stance and the obsessional drive he displayed in everything he did, a drive fed by his need to feel worthy. There was no doubting that Biaggi was a complex character but he was also sublime on a motorcycle. By the start of the 1997 season he had already won three consecutive 250cc world titles and would add a fourth that year before moving up to the premier 500cc class.

And yet here was a long-haired, happy-go-lucky teenager from Tavullia starting to steal Biaggi's thunder – and his press coverage. Motorcycle racing is hugely popular in Italy, almost as big as football. It's a mainstream sport, which means its stars – and particularly the home-grown ones – are prime fodder for the mainstream press. Biaggi dating a glamorous model was front-page news, so it must have bruised his ego when the eighteen-year-old Valentino Rossi suddenly became the darling of the press and began to attract all the headlines.

Few people are better qualified to assess the troubled relationship between Rossi and Biaggi than Carlo Pernat who, as well as discovering Rossi, had also been Biaggi's manager. 'They were two completely different people,' he says. 'Valentino is a very likeable man. He is always smiling. He's the same on television interviews as he is in a bar or in the paddock – he is full of fun. You are born with this kind of nature, you don't learn it. Biaggi is Roman and that is another mentality. He was the first Roman rider who arrived at the top level and he was so strong, and not friendly. He was the complete opposite of Rossi, one hundred per cent different, so it was impossible that these two people could be friends.'

Biaggi was the first Italian rider of the modern era to become mainstream famous. Giacomo Agostini had set the precedent in the 1960s but gossip magazines and celebrity-obsessed websites and television shows had not yet emerged, so his impact was arguably not as great. 'Biaggi became extremely famous outside of the sport and was constantly featured on television shows and in magazines and newspapers,' Pernat says. 'When Rossi arrived he made a similar impact; not because he wanted to but because the television stations and newspapers followed him wherever he went. And so this caused a big clash about the mentality of Biaggi and the mentality of Valentino. Biaggi suffered a lot because all the media started going to Valentino as he was more fun and more likeable. Biaggi is a real champion on a motorcycle but Valentino is so strong with people. So Biaggi was destroyed in the mind by the sheer normality of Valentino. For sure, it was a complete psychological victory.'

Rossi may not have had many personal dealings with Biaggi by the start of the 1997 season but he had already formed a dislike of him from what he had read in the press, seen on television, and heard from others. Even before he started racing Rossi had reason to dislike Biaggi: Rossi was a fan of Loris Capirossi and since Biaggi was a racing rival of Capirossi, this placed him in the enemy camp. Two other riders who shared a mutual hatred and intense racing rivalry were Kevin Schwantz and Wayne Rainey, the two Americans who won four 500cc titles between them from 1990 to 1993. Rossi had been a

Schwantz fan, Biaggi had been in the Rainey camp. It seemed that, in everything, the pair were polar opposites.

But the direct origins of Rossi and Biaggi's soon-to-be-famous rivalry began in 1997 at the opening round of the world championships at Shah Alam. Biaggi won the 250cc race first time out on his new Honda (he had left Aprilia after a messy falling-out and switched camps to the Japanese firm) while Rossi won the 125cc race, prompting one journalist to ask Rossi if he dreamed of being the Max Biaggi of the 125 class. 'I'm sorry,' Rossi retorted, 'but I think it's going to be him that dreams of being the Rossi of 250'!

He knew his barbed comment would provoke the proud Roman, but Rossi didn't care. To him, life was a game, racing was fun – who cared what Biaggi thought? And then, at the very next round in Japan, the pair found themselves together in a restaurant at Suzuka. Spotting Rossi sitting with a group of Italian journalists, Biaggi marched straight up to him 'as if he was trying to intimidate me' and said, 'Before talking about me, you should wash your mouth out.' Within earshot of the Italian press, Biaggi couldn't have created much more of a sensation had he pulled the pin on a live grenade. Rossi, eight years Biaggi's junior, returned the Roman's stare but kept his mouth shut. It would be the last time he did so when it came to Max Biaggi. The feud between them would continue for the next ten years in Grands Prix and would even extend beyond that: to this day, Rossi refuses to even have Biaggi's name published on his official website. When he needs to be referred to it's always as XXX XXXXXX. Childish? Perhaps, but their feud would get dangerous too – there's nothing childish about trying to elbow an opponent off a racetrack at 150mph. But that was in the future. For now, the seeds had been sewn, the lines had been drawn and the fans would have to choose which camp they were in. Most pitched their tents around Rossi's. Most, but not all.

The seeds of another long-standing Rossi tradition were also sewn in 1997: it was the year he began his colourful post-race celebrations. They were minimal at first – a jester's hat on the podium after winning the French Grand Prix, a Superman-style 'Superfumi' cape after a stunning win in Holland (where he had to slow to adjust his brake lever before scything his way through a ferociously fast and tight pack of riders to sneak a win by a tenth of a second), and a Robin Hood hat and bow-and-arrow set on the podium at Donington Park, which he clearly felt was close enough to Nottingham and Sherwood Forest for the gag to work.

The celebrations, usually dreamed up in late-night bars in Tavullia with his close friends, helped to inject a bit of fun and colour into Grands Prix and reminded people that motorcycle racing is a sport, a celebration of speed and daring, and should be enjoyed as such. 'When I started winning GPs we decided we should try to make some big fun because back then all the riders were very, very serious,' Rossi explained to his biographer Mat Oxley in 2001. 'We just wanted to do something new to show the big emotion of winning races.'

In his autobiography Rossi admitted he had studied other riders and what they did on celebration laps and found it all very droll. So his increasingly elaborate celebrations were calculated and deliberate – an antidote to the dullness that had gone before. 'How boring,' he wrote. 'They win and then all they do is wander around with their country's flag. We said, "Why don't we do something nobody has ever seen in motorcycling?"'[9]

It's fair to say that Rossi achieved this at Mugello in 1997 after taking yet another win. Nobody in motorcycling had ever seen a race winner taking a blow-up sex doll for a victory lap. Rossi had bought the doll a year earlier with the hope of displaying it had he won his home Grand Prix at Misano. He didn't, so the doll remained unseen. But around the time of Mugello in 1997 (Rossi's second home round) the press began speculating that Max Biaggi was dating supermodel Naomi Campbell and for Rossi the temptation was too great. The doll was dug out and fitted with a red T-shirt bearing the name 'Claudia Schiffer' – Campbell's great rival in the modelling world. To everyone except Max Biaggi and his entourage, it was hilarious, a breath of fresh air, as Rossi had intended when first studying other riders' victory laps. It harked back to the 1960s and '70s when the likes of Mike Hailwood and Barry Sheene had actually managed to enjoy their racing and have fun with it, as well as being devastatingly fierce competitors. It was displays like this that made Rossi stand out from all the other talent in the GP paddock and which, just as much as his results, made him famous and adored in equal measure. Perhaps most satisfyingly for Rossi, it was also a perfect way to have another dig at Biaggi.

The full head bandage he sported on the podium at the penultimate round in Indonesia – after taking his eleventh victory of the season – alluded to a rather more serious incident. Back home in Italy the previous weekend, Rossi had been in a Porsche 928 with his father at the wheel. A gifted rally driver, Graziano decided to drive into an industrial estate and see how far sideways he could step the car out. If there was ever any doubt as to how Valentino inherited his joy for life and carefree attitude, it's never necessary to look any further than Graziano. But on this occasion Dad lost control, the car rolled and then struck a lamppost. Fortunately, there were no serious injuries but Valentino suffered a concussion and this in turn led to his first real problems with the Italian press. The following day it was (wrongly) reported that Valentino had been at the wheel of the car and, worse still, had been driving while under the influence. Somewhat shocked that the press, who had doted on him thus far, could suddenly turn nasty if that helped to sell papers, Rossi would learn to be a little more cautious in his future dealings with them. 'I was very, very angry,' he said of the press. 'It was a big shock.'

Former Grand Prix commentator for the BBC Steve Parrish is another who remembers Rossi's colourful character and extravagant celebrations as being a breath of fresh air for the sport. 'Rossi was the first rider to do really good celebration laps after winning races,' he says. 'A lot of riders have copied that since but he was the first. And I think that smiley, bubbly personality just won people over. Rossi is also very good at hiding his nerves. Some riders might say they don't get nervous, but I don't believe them. But Rossi was very good at hiding it. And it's not just immediately before a race – you're nervous throughout the whole weekend and intensely focused on what you're doing.'

Rossi was very good at switching off, he explains, and being that charming, funny character for the cameras. 'When people approach riders for autographs and selfies before a race, I mean, imagine what that would be like if you were just about to go in for a really important job interview or a final exam – having to stop thinking about the job in hand and forcing a smile and a chat with someone who's asking you silly questions. Riders have got so much going on in their heads before a race, so to try and switch that part of your mind off and be nice to people – relations, guests, sponsors, TV crews – it's very, very difficult and it takes a certain kind of person to do that. And Rossi is one of them.'

For all his tomfoolery on victory laps, Rossi had seriously matured as a rider during the 1997 season and curbed his former crash-happy attitude. In 1995, he suffered more than twenty crashes in the Italian and European championships, in '96 he had fifteen in Grands Prix, but in 1997 he crashed just three times – and only one of those was in a race. Apart from the incident at Suzuka when he crashed out ('I thought I could win – now I just think I'm an idiot') and his sixth place in the final round in Australia, caused once again by a spark-plug problem just like the previous year, Rossi was on the podium at every other race and in the middle part of the season he took six consecutive wins between the French and British rounds.

Rossi put some of this new-found maturity down to having a faster motorcycle. 'The better bike helped my concentration,' he said. 'When you've got a slow bike you push too hard and sometimes lose concentration.'

Rossi's race engineer, Mauro Noccioli, also saw his rider's style change out on track. 'Suddenly, in March 1997, everything changed,' he said. 'Vale had learned how the Aprilia worked and decided he wanted to take his own lines on the track. When you look at him you will see that his lines are different to all the other riders. His two years of experience helped him but that is something you can't teach a kid; it was just a natural development.'[10]

For Rossi, winning the world championship was the highlight of his young, but already very eventful, life. 'When you start to race you hope that one day you will become world champion,' he later told BT Sport in a television interview. 'It was an unforgettable moment in my career because the first time you become world champion is really like a dream come true.'

In winning the 125cc Grand Prix world championship, Rossi had brought the first chapter of his career to a neat close. Since moving up from minimotos to full-sized motorcycles, he had only ever ridden 125cc machines: in the Italian Sport Production championship, in the Italian GP125 series, in the European 125cc championship and in the world championship. Now that he had won the biggest prize in 125cc racing it was time to move onwards and upwards, but not before keeping a promise he had made to himself. By now, Rossi's hair had grown out of control, forcing him to wear an Alice band much of the time to keep it out of his eyes. He had promised himself that if he won the title he would finally cut it off. He held good on his promise but not with a standard short back and sides; instead, he had it shaved close and dyed electric blue with a number one bleached on the back of his head. It was the first of many crowd-pleasing hairdos that added to the pantomime that was Valentino Rossi. He would later dye it bright orange to race in Holland, red, white and green to race at home, then there were the red, orange, two-tone black-and-white hairdos and the Afro wig. It was all part of the show, all part of the colour and spectacle that the young Italian brought to the Grand Prix paddock, and his public loved him for it.

As already mentioned, Graziano Rossi had, for years, sported hair so long it was down to his waist and permanently tied in a ponytail. He too made a solemn vow to cut it off when his son won the world championship, but not this one. Only when Valentino had won the premier 500cc class would the sacred Graziano locks fall to the barber shop floor. For now, they remained, though Graziano was clearly proud of his son's achievement: 'I knew he was a good, fast rider – I didn't know if he was good enough to be champion. This year he raced very well because he showed he could control the situation in a race.'

In 1998, Rossi would take a step closer to achieving his goal of being 500cc world champion. He would move up to the 250cc class with Aprilia – the class that had been dominated by Max Biaggi for four years. It would have been the stuff of dreams for the Italian press to report on the two arch enemies duelling it out in the same championship for the first time, but it would have to wait: at the same time that Rossi moved up to 250s, Biaggi upgraded to the 500cc class. He was one step ahead of Rossi, but their time would come.

CHAPTER 4

VALENTINIK

'It was not always easy working with Valentino.'
CARLO PERNAT

*F*ame does not sit easily with everyone. His antics during the 1997 season might have been calculated to encourage it, but when Rossimania really took off Valentino quickly realised he had created a monster. 'It is a big problem for me,' he explained in that first real year of his fame. 'I don't want to be famous, I just want to have fun with my friends. I'd prefer to go for a ride to the beach.'[1]

Rossi's reluctance to embrace his growing fame might explain his curious disappearing act at a major function held at the end of 1997 to celebrate both his world title and that of F1 driver Jacques Villeneuve. Carlo Pernat: 'It was not always easy working with Valentino. He was so young when he was riding for Aprilia. In 1997, when he won his first world championship, Jacques Villeneuve won the F1 world championship for Renault and Valentino wanted to meet him. I knew the chairman of Renault, so arranged for Valentino and Villeneuve to appear on stage in Bologna at a special event along with the championship-winning bike and car. The place was packed and there were so many media people there. Twenty minutes before he was due to go on stage, Valentino told me he had to go to the toilet and then he just completely disappeared.'

To this day, Pernat has no idea why. 'Even now when I ask him where he went he never gives me an answer! Maybe there was some girl involved, I don't know! But it was really embarrassing for everybody and it made me look very bad in front of my bosses. But this is Valentino! And he was very young at the time.'

However he truly felt about it, Rossi generally handled fame well. He was always courteous with fans and happy to spare the time to talk with them and pose for photographs. He was still, at this point, largely a darling of the Italian press (although he'd had his fingers burned over the car crash incident) and would hang out with Italian journalists in the press room at Grands Prix and always had plenty to say to television reporters, in Italian at first but as his command of the language improved, also in English.

World champion motorcycle racers cannot avoid being famous to a certain extent, but they're usually only revered in the closed world of racing; send them down the high street in any city outside of Italy and Spain and they will usually go relatively unnoticed. It's only at race meetings and motorcycle shows that they're swamped by fans and treated as demi-gods. There have been very few motorcycle racers who transcended their sport and became household names in their own lifetimes: Geoff Duke, Giacomo Agostini and Mike Hailwood were all known outside the confines of their sport, but it was Barry Sheene in the 1970s who took fame to a whole new level, at least in terms of motorcycle racing. Sheene was front-page news whenever he dated a new girl, appeared on numerous television shows (sometimes as a presenter), was the face of a Fabergé television ad campaign, featured in non-motorcycling magazines and ultimately became mainstream famous to the point that practically everyone in Britain knew who he was. Yet even Sheene's considerable fame would eventually be outstripped by Rossi, aided by the fact that the Italian lived in the digital era when his every move, opinion and statement could (and would) be recorded and broadcast.

Yet if Rossi had truly hated fame from the outset he could have done something about it. He could have knocked the crazy post-race celebrations on the head, could have abandoned the increasingly wacky hairstyles, refused to give as many interviews as he did, tempered down his flamboyant presence both in the paddock and on Italian TV. But with less fame comes less wealth, fewer sponsors, fewer endorsement deals and, more importantly for a racer, less power in the paddock and, therefore, lesser motorcycles. Rossi's fame would eventually reach such levels that he became the most powerful man in the Grand Prix paddock, able to influence the development of motorcycles that he rode and to have his views heard, and taken seriously, when it came to concerns about safety, about riders' wages, about anything that mattered. With fame came power, so, however inconvenient it may have been at times, it was something to be tolerated. The benefits far outweighed the disadvantages and he was very much aware of this. 'I have to do adverts, go to gala events and dinners,' he said. 'I don't like it but it's better than getting up each morning to go to work in a factory.'[2]

Besides, Rossi couldn't exactly change his own natural character and, no matter how contrived the post-race celebrations were, they were also a reflection of his own fun-loving personality and he couldn't temper that any more than he could stop winning races; he was just being himself and his character was such that it would always make him stand out from the crowd. The boy simply couldn't help it.

By the start of the 1998 season, Valentino was just short of six feet tall and far too big for a tiny 125cc machine. He was, arguably, even too big for a 250cc bike, but one of those would at least offer him a little more room to squeeze his gangly frame onto.

As strange as it sounds with the benefit of hindsight, not everyone was convinced that Rossi could be a success in Grand Prix racing's intermediate class. Winning on a 125cc machine making around 45bhp is a very different thing to mastering a bike of double the capacity and more than double the horsepower: the Aprilia RSW250 he would race in 1998 made over 96bhp yet weighed just 96kg. That's a serious power-to-weight ratio and would necessitate a lot of learning on Rossi's part. So much so that he said of his promotion to the class, 'On a 250 I feel I'll be starting again from zero.'

Graziano was hardly oozing confidence about the move either, despite suggesting his son should have made the transition the previous year. 'I am not sure if he will be fast enough to race in the 250 class' was his pessimistic assessment.

The plan was the same as his assault on the 125cc world championship had been – a year to learn and a year to win. Rossi was placed in Aprilia's official factory team (though not on the very latest full-factory bike) alongside his countryman and erstwhile hero, Loris Capirossi, and Japan's Tetsuya Harada. Right from his first test on the bike he was fast, although he did use a little bit of trickery to bolster his speed. Knowing the press would be watching him keenly on his debut, Rossi arranged for Dunlop tyre technicians to fit his Aprilia with super-soft and ultra-sticky qualifying tyres. As the moniker indicates, 'qualifiers' are usually only used during qualifying sessions to determine a rider's place on the starting grid. They're so soft they're only good for one or two very fast laps, then deteriorate rapidly. They would never normally be used in testing but Rossi wanted to make a point, wanted to prove to the media that he was going to be a force in the larger capacity class. He set a blistering pace with the qualifiers (the press was unaware he was using them) and stole all the headlines again.

Being fast over one showy lap for the press was one thing, but if he hoped to be fast over a complete season on these much more powerful bikes, Rossi was going to have to learn some other tricks too. Jeremy McWilliams was entering his second season in the 250cc Grand Prix world championship in 1998 and would witness Rossi's adaptation to the class at close quarters. 'It's actually not such a big difference, believe it or not,' the Ulsterman says of the step up from 125cc to 250cc bikes. 'It was a fair bit easier back then than changing from a Moto3 bike to a Moto2 bike nowadays. The 125 and 250 had quite similar characteristics. The 250 had a lot more grunt – maybe twice the power – but the power-to-weight ratio on a 250 is probably the most ideal of any Grand Prix bike ever produced, so I don't think the transition was that difficult. Rossi immediately took to it – he was immediately fast on it and was soon winning races. I think everyone expected him to and he made the transition look very easy.

'When Rossi jumped on the 250, I feel that was the real start of his story. He understood that he could not only be a

125cc world champion but could translate that ability onto a bigger, faster bike and become a 250cc world champion too. He was so quick and so competitive back then that I think everyone just expected him to do it. And he did.'

Carlo Pernat agrees that the progression from 125 to 250 was a natural one for Rossi. 'I was sure he would be okay on the 250. Back then it was not such a big step up from the 125cc class to the 250cc class and I felt that, in that period, riders who could win races on a 250 would be able to ride a 500cc bike. It was a very natural progression back then; now all the classes are very different.'

By the time he moved up to the 250cc class, Rossi had drifted apart from his race engineer, Mauro Noccioli, feeling that the older man was telling him how he should ride instead of allowing Rossi to work things out by himself. 'Nobody was going to tell me how to ride' was Rossi's blunt summation of the situation and so, setting a pattern that he would repeat in the future whenever he felt his team was not completely working for him, Rossi demanded some staff changes. 'At the end of 1997, Vale arrived in my office and told me he was moving up to the 250cc class,' explains Pernat. 'I said, "Okay" and then he told me which team members he wanted. He asked me for Rossano Brazzi as his chief engineer, I don't know why. The problem was that, four months before, I had signed Loris Capirossi and promised he could have Brazzi. So after speaking to Vale I suggested to Loris that he would be better to have Mauro Noccioli as his engineer instead and he accepted. I only told Capirossi and Noccioli the real reason for this last year! [2019]'

But while he managed to secure the services of Brazzi, Rossi didn't quite get all the staff he wanted and Pernat was left to wonder how different his own life might have turned out had Rossi got his way. 'It was at this same time that Valentino asked me if I would be his manager, but for me it was impossible because I was working at Aprilia. If I had my time again then I would have agreed to manage him and probably my life would have been very different.'

Pernat says it was at the end of the 1997 season in which Rossi had been so dominant on the 125 that both he, and the remaining doubters at Aprilia, started to fully realise what they had on their hands. 'He had won eleven Grands Prix that year, his post-race celebrations were becoming really famous and I understood I was standing in front of a phenomenon, not just a world champion. A phenomenon is more than a world champion; a phenomenon is Barry Sheene, it's Maradona, it's Björn Borg, it's Cassius Clay… Valentino is like this. They have something more than the other people. In fact, I think they need to have five things: as well as talent they need to have character, a sense of humour, a mental strength and a certain humanity. It's difficult to be a phenomenon!'

Rossano Brazzi was formerly chief engineer to both Loris Reggiani and triple world champion Luca Cadalora and was a highly respected two-stroke engine tuner. A serious man whom Rossi has described as 'a bit dour' on occasion, Brazzi nevertheless knew his business and was impressed by his new charge's talents and attitude right from the outset. 'When Valentino arrived to my team in 1998 he was very highly motivated as he was already 125cc world champion. He had a little trouble setting up the bike at the beginning because, of course, it is a lot different to a 125. However, he was never afraid to try things and even though he made a few mistakes and crashed out of the first couple of races he soon adapted his way of thinking to the bigger bike.'[3]

Rossi would later say that Brazzi was the first man to truly realise his potential as a rider. The engineer was convinced they should be challenging for the title in that very first year on a 250 whereas Valentino had slightly different ideas, saying, 'I just wanted to enjoy myself and learn about the tracks and bikes while having some fun.'

Of his first ten races in the 250cc class, Rossi failed to finish half of them. In the first round in Japan it was through no fault of his own as his factory Aprilia broke down. But he crashed out on the last lap in Malaysia while fighting Harada for the win; he crashed out of the lead at Jarama in Spain, crashed again in Britain and didn't even complete the opening lap before crashing out of the Czech GP at Brno. Four crashes and one breakdown in five of the first ten races doesn't sound like a great record, but it was what Rossi did in the other five races that impressed: a second place at Jerez, another at Mugello and yet another at Paul Ricard in France. And then, in only his seventh race on a 250cc machine, he won. The venue was Assen in the Netherlands, one of the truly great Grand Prix circuits and a happy hunting ground for Valentino over the years. The victory was as much down to Brazzi's shrewdness and technical expertise as it was to Rossi and his supreme riding skills. The Aprilia factory had supplied Rossi, Capirossi and Harada with new exhausts for the race, but Brazzi refused to fit one on the bike, believing that it retained too much air and so if the engine overheated, it would break. Both Capirossi and Harada ran with the new exhausts and both broke down. Brazzi had been Rossi's choice as race engineer: it had clearly been a good one.

After the non-finish in Britain, the third place in Germany, and the non-finish in the Czech Republic, Rossi was ten rounds into his first season on a 250cc bike when everything changed. Despite being pitched against far more experienced rivals, including his own team-mates, Rossi completely dominated the final four races of the season, winning every one of them.

It may not have been apparent to anyone at the time but, with the luxury of hindsight, Jeremy McWilliams now believes that Rossi's riding style on a 250 ultimately changed the way every Grand Prix rider rode. 'That big, gangly riding style of his just seemed to work. Looking back now, we can probably understand it a bit more because it's clear he had great levers [rider-speak for long limbs, which can help to flick a bike through corners] and he was all over the bike like a spider, his arms and legs hanging out everywhere. He probably didn't understand or realise it at the time but it seemed to really help – the fact that he could put a lot of his body parts outside of the bike helped him to lever the bike about on track and prevented the tyres from being on maximum lean angle all the time. Through the corners he didn't sit "in" the bike, he sat more outside of it.'

McWilliams goes on to explain that even though he's not that tall Rossi seemed to have very long arms and legs and really used them to his advantage. 'I think those were possibly the early signs of the riding styles we see today, with more bodyweight outside of the bike. It definitely helps with tyre management and keeping the motorcycle off maximum lean for long periods. He actually changed his riding style in later years in order to stay competitive with the likes of Marc Márquez and his other younger rivals, but it was Rossi who instigated the change in riding style that we saw in Grand Prix racing.'

Rossi could hardly have been any more popular in Italy as it was, but when he turned up at Imola with his motorcycle, his leathers, his helmet, and even his hair painted and dyed in the tricolours of the Italian flag, his legend was assured. The sell-out crowd went crazy at the sight and the Rossi replica helmet business went into overdrive. Since then there have been more than sixty different AGV Rossi replica helmets made available to the public.

After winning the Catalan Grand Prix in Barcelona, there was another famous celebration and one of Rossi's personal favourites – Osvaldo the chicken. The gag started during friendly football matches in Tavullia when Rossi's team kit featured an imaginary sponsor in the form of a local businessman called Osvaldo who was in the poultry business, his shop name plastered all over the team kit, much to the players' amusement. After Rossi had worn his football shirt as a bit of a joke at Imola he was contacted by a man who designed mascots for basketball teams. He had a spare chicken suit that had never been used. Was Rossi interested? Valentino didn't need to be asked twice and so at Catalunya fans were treated to the rather unusual sight of race winner Rossi taking a man-sized chicken for a lap of honour. When asked if Rossi would be penalised for his stunt a race official replied, 'It is forbidden to carry a passenger but the rules say nothing about chickens.' But Dorna (the company that owns MotoGP) officials *were* getting rather weary of Rossi's time-consuming post-race celebrations. Fearing his lengthy gags would interfere with the tightly controlled running of races and that they encouraged fans to storm the track, words were had. As usual, Rossi paid no heed: 'I'll do the same thing again because I like to amuse the fans.'

It was all goofy stuff but it brought a breath of fresh air to the Grand Prix world, which had become awfully serious in the premier class with the utter dominance of the rather more laconic and abrasive Mick Doohan. The Australian champ had brought a new kind of intensity to the paddock and, thinking that this was the key to success, other riders followed suit, making the paddock a largely fun-free zone. Rossi would change all that; no less focused, he just somehow seemed to be able to enjoy his riding at the same time and this would be a huge factor in his ongoing success.

Gags aside, Rossano Brazzi's belief in his rider had clearly been justified with Rossi's dominant form towards the end of the season. 'Vale's true potential came clear at the end of that first season when he incredibly went on to win the final four races, having won just once before that at Assen. We knew then that he was ready to win the world championship in the following season.'[4]

It was the final race of the 1998 season that was the most dramatic. Capirossi went into the race with a four-point advantage over his team-mate, Tetsuya Harada, meaning he had to win the race to win the title. With 25 points awarded for a win and 20 for second place, the points situation also meant that if neither rider completed the race then Capirossi would still win the title. Without a mathematical chance of taking the championship, Rossi sat back in a safe third place on the final lap as his two team-mates battled tooth and nail for the win. Harada held a seemingly unassailable lead going into the final corner, but Capirossi made an extremely ambitious do-or-die lunge and knocked his rival off his bike. Rossi went on to win the race while Capirossi finished second and took the title. Meanwhile, Harada's hopes lay alongside him in the dirt. 'He could have killed me,' the Japanese rider said in astonishment at the move. Capirossi was unrepentant: 'It was for the championship – I had to try something.'

The desperate move would have major ramifications. First, Capirossi's points were taken away (but later reinstated after he appealed), then Aprilia refused to give him a bike for the following season despite being contractually obliged to. Capirossi took the firm to court and was awarded a €2 million payout. He spent part of the money on a Ferrari and put 'Aprilia' on the registration plates, just to rub it in. It remains one of the most controversial last-corner moves in the history of racing.

The incident meant Rossi was promoted to second place in the championship, just twenty-three points behind Capirossi, and he must have regretted the four crashes he had early in the season – one less of those and he might just have been 250cc world champion at the first attempt. But it was still a spectacular performance and it set him up perfectly for a full assault on the title in 1999. 'I'm pretty happy with what I've done this year,' he said on reflection. 'I think I can ride a 250 at 90 per cent. Next year I don't need to be much faster in outright lap times, but I need to be consistently fast, lap after lap. I also need to make less mistakes and I need to be stronger.'

He would be.

*

After three years in the world championships Rossi decided it was time for a change of alter ego. It was out with Rossifumi and in with Valentinik, a name he had dreamt up while on holiday in Tunisia in 1998: 'The name Valentinik comes from a comic strip featuring Donald Duck [known as Paperino in Italian]. In the story, he turns into Super Donald [or Paperinik] sporting a mask and a cape. But he's not a superhero like Superman – actually, he doesn't have any luck and wreaks havoc everywhere but he is really funny and likeable. So that's how "Valentinik" came into being.'[5]

It is perhaps no coincidence that one of Rossi's great heroes, Barry Sheene, had also famously sported Donald Duck on his crash helmet, although in the Londoner's case that was down to 'Donald Duck' being Cockney-rhyming slang for a certain popular swear word.

'I needed something new after the difficulties of 1998,' Rossi explained. So Valentinik it was: a goofy superhero who was ready to wreak havoc in his assault on the 250cc world championship.

Rossano Brazzi knew his boy was ready. 'At the start of 1999, Vale was feeling very confident. He was very sure of himself but a couple of problems at the beginning of the season – like when his chain came off at Paul Ricard – knocked it out of him a little bit. However, he showed his character by winning nine races altogether that year and I think he proved to the world that he was the best talent around at that time.'[6]

The most marked difference in 1999 was that the crashing stopped. Rossi finished every single race apart from the French Grand Prix – which Brazzi alluded to – when his chain came off. Jeremy McWilliams had some close, hard races with Rossi during the year and shared the podium with him in Holland. He was impressed by the Italian's progress in his second year in the 250 class. 'He was so impressive in 1999 – there was Rossi and then there was everybody else. I had a pretty decent year and was happy to get on the podium a number of times, but Rossi was just absolutely gone and that season was really the start of his greatness. He was amassing a huge following at that stage with all the post-race antics that everyone then started to expect him to do after every race.'

But what impressed him more than anything about Rossi that season was that he didn't crash. 'The 250cc class was so competitive back then that you had to be riding absolutely on the ragged edge all of the time and, as a result, it was the norm to destroy bikes quite often and pick up injuries. It went with the territory. We all seemed to be crashing – and crashing quite often – but Rossi just seemed to be invincible and didn't make any mistakes. There were times in 1999 when Rossi didn't look like he needed to ride at one hundred per cent even though everybody else clearly was.

'I've always thought that Rossi was a very fair rider too. A lot of people wouldn't agree with me and I'm sure there have been a few incidents over the years, but he always gave me room and there were plenty of riders who didn't – and Max Biaggi would be the epitome of that. Loris Capirossi was a dirtier rider than Valentino, too. I always thought Rossi was pretty fair, to be honest.'

Fast and aggressive but fair with it, the only chink in Rossi's armour now was that he still hated riding in the wet, as his two lowest finishes of the year proved. Seventh in Japan and eighth in Valencia, both times under sodden skies. 'I remember that, in the beginning, he was afraid of racing on water,' Carlo Pernat explained of his signing. 'When it rained he didn't want to leave his camper. But then he learned to also ride when it was wet.'

For Rossi there was an added bonus to racing in the quarter-litre class – he could stay in bed longer. In the 125cc class he had to be awake at 7am in order to make the first practice session, but because the bigger machines went out after the 125s he could sleep until 9am. 'I keep strange hours,' he confessed. 'At home I never go to bed before one or two in the morning and I never get up before 11am if I can help it.' And that was on week nights; when he went out with friends on a Saturday night Rossi would never arrive home until six or seven in the morning. The odd hours he kept would eventually lead to him sleeping through a practice session and would necessitate a new system to make sure he was out of bed in time.

Rossi's work ethic away from the track was slack by today's standards. Most top racers now train for around six hours a day, often more, a fact which might surprise non-enthusiasts who tend to think that all a rider has to do is sit on a motorcycle and steer it. But forcing a racing motorcycle to change direction at high speed requires a lot of strength; braking forces are immense, racing in the heat and humidity of countries like Malaysia is utterly exhausting, and it's not unknown for riders to vomit inside their helmets (and carry on racing) in these conditions. Racers also get injured regularly and the fitter they are, the quicker they heal. Being in pristine physical condition also benefits mental fatigue during a race, so modern Grand Prix riders train like Olympian athletes, but in 1999 Rossi was still relying on his youth to get him through. 'When I get home after a GP I like to spend five days doing nothing – just relaxing and catching up with my friends,' he confessed. That would change with age but Rossi has never been the most die-hard enthusiast of physical training and much prefers to keep 'bike fit' by riding dirt bikes.

By now Valentino had learned how to turn each race into an event, a theatrical performance on par with a stage show. No one knew what livery his bike would be in (at Mugello in 1999, for example, it was covered in psychedelic swirls and twirls), what his helmet design or his leathers would look like, nor what crazy antics he would get up to on his victory lap, should he win the race. Even his hair would become a talking point amongst fans, many of who were even younger than Rossi. And that was all on top of the hugely entertaining on-track battles he always seemed to be involved in. By 1999, Rossi was already changing the demographics of a Grand Prix crowd. Once the domain of older men who were motorcycle enthusiasts and general petrol heads, the races were now attracting hordes of teenyboppers who would stake out Rossi's camper van in the paddock in the hope of meeting their pin-up boy. Rossi was a pop star every bit as much as a motorcycle racer.

For the 1999 season, Rossi was the sole rider with a full-factory Aprilia, meaning there would be no repeat of the tensions that had built up between himself and his two Aprilia team-mates, Capirossi and Harada – not to mention between their chief mechanics – the previous year. 'The atmosphere in Aprilia was terrible,' Rossi later said of the 1998 season. 'All the chief mechanics were fighting, you know, it was an Italian team. "Ah, you have the best cylinder" this and that and so on.'[7]

Capirossi had agreed an eleventh-hour deal to ride for Honda, so would still be a threat, but Harada had moved up to the 500cc class, leaving the likes of Tohru Ukawa (Honda) and Shinya Nakano (Yamaha) to challenge Rossi for the title.

He might have been well on the way to becoming a superstar, but Rossi was still just twenty years old and still very much a mama's boy. Just before Christmas he had bought his own house but his mother had insisted on moving in with him. 'I wanted to live alone but she said no,' Rossi quipped, though he didn't seem at all put out by this restriction on his liberties. Besides, having family and friends around would prove crucial in keeping him grounded and normal as his fame continued to grow. There would be no drug-fuelled rock star parties for Valentino and his friends – it was still all about scooters, pizza, ice cream and the odd beer or two. Harmless, innocent fun that kept him very closely in touch with reality and with the way he had always lived. He would get his adrenalin rushes and brushes with disaster, his buzz, his rush, out on track, and in 1999 there were plenty of opportunities.

Many believed Rossi would simply run away with the '99 title after his dominant end to the 1998 season, but things didn't quite work out that way and he had to fight hard for victories. A misfire on his Aprilia in the opening round in Malaysia meant he could finish no higher than fifth and a wet race in Japan (his first on a 250) saw him languishing down in seventh place at the chequered flag and protesting, 'I prefer to ride my bike on dry land.'

Then came Jerez in Spain and the first of nine victories that year. Rossi won by over five seconds despite slowing to cross the finish line, standing up on his footrests, hands clasped behind his back in majestic style. He then celebrated with one of his most beloved victory laps, parking his bike, vaulting the trackside hoardings and disappearing into a Portaloo in front of a packed grandstand. 'I saw the loo before the race and it looked strange – one toilet on its own by the side of the track,' Rossi explained. 'So I decided to go in it if I won. When I went inside all the 100,000 fans went quiet then when I came back out the noise was incredible.'[8]

While some of Rossi's post-race antics were elaborately contrived and designed to appeal to a specifically Italian sense of humour, this was a simple, universal gesture that had the crowd in stitches. Motorcycle racing had simply never seen anything like it before. The boy was a loon and the crowd loved him for it. The organisers, not so much: Rossi was officially reprimanded after his stunt.

The French Grand Prix saw Rossi's only non-finish of the year when his chain jumped the sprockets and came off completely. Then, at home in Mugello for the fifth round of the championship, the love for Rossi started to get out of control. Turning up with his bike, leathers and helmet painted in the aforementioned 'peace and love' livery, he drew the crowd wild with another dominant win and a monumental wheelie down the entire length of the kilometre-long start/finish straight. Whipped into a frenzy, the Italian fans stormed their way onto the circuit during Rossi's victory lap, making it very difficult for him to get round safely, even at cruising speed. When a TV cameraman jumped out onto the middle of the track Rossi was forced to brake so hard to miss him that he actually fell off his motorcycle. Rossi tried to shrug it off with good grace as always, noting merely, 'The people are crazy – they invaded the track. I was swamped before I could reach my fan club and fell off.' But it gave race organisers pause for thought: if this was going to be the new norm then additional crowd security measures were going to be required.

Another win followed in Catalunya after an epic battle with Tohru Ukawa and, more briefly, with a bumblebee when it flew through his visor aperture and got inside his helmet. Rossi's rapid and smooth progression through the Grand Prix classes and his lack of injuries received during that time had led many to believe he had a charmed life and the incident with the bee did little to disprove it. While most other riders would have been stung, Rossi simply lifted the visor on his helmet and the bee flew away without harming him. Charmed indeed.

The race of the year was undoubtedly at Assen, with the top five riders crossing the line within 0.74 seconds of each other. Rossi gave everything he had but just could not keep ahead of Loris Capirossi when it mattered and only just managed to hold off an equally determined Jeremy McWilliams for second place.

It was at the British Grand Prix in July that the rumours

first began to circulate that Rossi would be moving up to the premier 500cc class the following year on a factory V-Four Honda in a team run by Mick Doohan. As a five-time champion of the class, Doohan was one of the all-time greats but his career had been cut short following a horrific 135mph crash in Jerez just two months previously. He would be the perfect mentor for Valentino in the top class and Honda would need a rider good enough to take over from the formidable Doohan but, for now at least, it remained no more than rumour.

After winning in Britain Rossi chalked up another two victories in Germany and the Czech Republic, amassing enough to take the championship lead as he headed back to home turf at Imola for a second Italian Grand Prix. The gags continued. This time, Rossi turned up at the circuit with his head shaved into a monk-like tonsure – an exact replica of his mechanic Rossano Brazzi's hair. This time Rossi's livery was in the form of the Italian flag: his bike, leathers and helmet green on one side, red on the other, and white down the middle. He couldn't have been more adored by the partisan Italian crowd, although he did lose out to Loris Capirossi in the race and afterwards offered a most revealing explanation as to why: 'He had nothing to lose while I succumbed to nerves. I started thinking about the world title, about my mum. I lost my concentration, making it even harder not to mess up.'[9]

He may have seemed invincible from the outside but Rossi was only just out of his teens and clearly didn't yet possess the ironclad levels of self-belief that others suspected.

Proving he had still not conquered the art of riding in the wet, Rossi came home a sodden eighth in Valencia before returning to winning ways in Australia, South Africa and Brazil.

His convincing win in Brazil – the ninth of the season – put Rossi far enough ahead of Ukawa in the championship table that he could not be beaten, despite there being one more race to go in Argentina. It also meant that, at twenty years of age, he became the youngest 250cc world champion of all time, beating the late, great Mike Hailwood by a year.

Nine race wins, two pole positions (Rossi never was, and never would be, a pole position specialist, preferring to use qualifying time to work on a race set-up rather than on one fast lap), ten fastest laps and enough points to take the championship from Ukawa and Capirossi with a round still remaining. It had been an impressive performance. To celebrate his title, Rossi stopped on the victory lap to pick up his friend Flavio Fratesi who by now was heading up the Valentino Rossi fan club. Fratesi, sporting a long white beard, was dressed completely in white and wore a pair of angel's wings. This was Rossi's 'guardian angel', the spirit that had seen him through the season and assured his second world title. The gag was made more amusing by the need to comply with health and safety regulations – the guardian angel was forced to wear an open-faced helmet. It was, naturally, a replica of Rossi's own.

Valentino would bring the curtain down on his 250cc racing career with a third place in Argentina after suffering tyre problems and would then prepare for the biggest test of his abilities so far. He was moving up to the 500cc class to ride the fastest, fiercest, most brutal motorcycles in the world. Only the very best of the best could tame the 200bhp missiles and win races, let alone championships. Rossi was about to find out if he really had what it took.

CHAPTER 5

500

'For him to get on a 500 and just go? For me,
it was pretty impressive just watching it.'
KEVIN SCHWANTZ

'**A**t the beginning when you try first time the 500... ah
fuck! The 500 is another world – the bike come from
another world.'

Rossi's concise description of his first impression of the most
fearsome racing motorcycles on the planet spoke volumes.
Ever since the motorcycle Grand Prix world championship
began in 1949, the premier class had been for 500cc bikes.
This was the class for the world's most elite riders, the class
that sorted the men from the boys, the class that created
legends – from the inaugural 500cc world champion Les
Graham through to the likes of Geoff Duke, John Surtees,
Mike Hailwood, Giacomo Agostini, Kenny Roberts, Barry
Sheene, Freddie Spencer, Wayne Rainey, Kevin Schwantz,

Eddie Lawson and Mick Doohan. It is the two-wheeled equivalent of F1; there is simply no faster or tougher class to race in. It is the apex of motorcycle sport.

The bikes were ferociously powerful, extremely light and notoriously difficult to ride. They also bit back severely when riders got things wrong. Accelerating faster than an F1 car, a 500cc GP bike weighed just 130kg but made 200bhp, enough to give them a top speed of around 200mph on the faster tracks on the GP calendar. And in an age before electronic rider aids, all of that power had to be controlled by the rider's right wrist and it was laid down on the ground through a tyre contact patch no bigger than the palm of a human hand. The potential for catastrophe was ever present: in the six years prior to Rossi's debut, five-times world champion Mick Doohan had had his career cut short by injury, as did 1993 world champion Kevin Schwantz. And Wayne Rainey – the champion between 1991 and 1993 – had been left paralysed and in a wheelchair for life after being thrown from his Yamaha YZR500 at Misano. By the year 2000, when Rossi stepped up to the premier class, ninety-nine riders had lost their lives in Grand Prix racing across various classes. It was, and remains, a highly dangerous sport and the 500s the most vicious of all racing motorcycles. As Rossi said: 'Racing 125s was like a game, racing 250s was serious, but 500s are very serious. They're dangerous.'

Jeremy McWilliams, who raced against Rossi in both the 250cc and 500cc classes, explains: 'There was a significant difference between a 250cc Grand Prix bike and a 500cc Grand Prix bike – much more so than the difference between a 125 and a 250. A 500 wasn't very much heavier than a 250 but it had about twice the horsepower. Rossi's style on the 250 worked quite well on the 500 when he moved up – he looked very similar on both bikes. But being a good 250 rider does not automatically mean you're going to be a good 500 rider. Look at riders like Tetsuya Harada; he was a brilliant 250 rider but was never very successful on a bigger bike. I've seen an awful lot of very good 250 riders looking very mediocre on a 500 and that's down to just how much raw power the bigger bikes have. Riders have to adapt themselves to be able to work with that and not every rider can.'

In fact, in the history of Grand Prix racing only one man had managed to win the 125cc, 250cc and 500cc world titles – Britain's Phil Read, an eight-times world champion and a true legend of the sport. That's how difficult it is to adapt.

Former 500cc Grand Prix rider Niall Mackenzie also spotted something that Rossi was doing right – *understanding* how to get the best out of a 500. 'The trick, with riders who have been more successful than me, is that they figure everything out at the time. I mean, I understand everything now, looking in from the outside, but the trick is understanding it all when you're young and doing it. Erv Kanemoto [famed Honda crew chief] would tell me lots of things and I'd go, "Yeah, yeah, yeah," but I didn't really know what he was on about! Stuff like using the back brake in the corners and squaring the corners off and picking the bike up early for the exit of the turn... Kenny Roberts would tell me the same things but, again, I didn't really know what he meant – I didn't get the technicalities. I get it now but, at the time, I was just riding the bike as fast as I could and trying to stay on it! But people like Kevin Schwantz and Mick Doohan and Valentino Rossi all instinctively understood those things at the time, so they could act upon them and become better riders.'

Another big part of Rossi's success had always been down to good decision-making and careful thinking about which manufacturers to ride for, which teams to ride for, and which crew chiefs and mechanics to have around him. His move up to the 500cc class – the biggest move of all – was, as always, well thought out. Staying with Aprilia was not a realistic option; the RSW-2 500 that the Italian manufacturer ran in the class was uncompetitive and not worthy of his talents. Honda's NSR500, on the other hand, had won the world championship for the last six years and would eventually go down as the most successful 500cc race bike of all time, ultimately taking a total of 133 wins between its introduction in 1984 and the end of 500cc Grand Prix racing in 2001 (when the class was replaced by 990cc four-stroke motorcycles and renamed MotoGP). It was the only realistic choice. Honda was, after all, the largest motorcycle company in the world and that meant massive resources, but the deal they offered Rossi was only about half of what Aprilia had offered him to stay in the 250cc class (rumours put Aprilia's offer at £2.3 million, an unprecedented amount of money for a 250cc rider). But racers are not motivated by money – they're motivated by the need to win, and to win, you need a winning bike. For the 500cc class, Honda's NSR500 was that bike.

And yet, while Rossi had been in talks with Honda since midway through the 1999 season, he refused to sign a deal until he could have the crew chief he wanted. Jeremy Burgess is a laconic Australian and something of a legend in the Grand Prix paddock, having taken world titles with Freddie Spencer and Wayne Gardner in the 1980s as well as five consecutive titles with Mick Doohan between 1994 and 1998. With Doohan having been forced into early retirement due to injury in 1999, Burgess was now free and Rossi insisted on having him. The only problem was, after having been in the GP paddock since 1980, Burgess wanted to take some time out and asked for time to think about Rossi's proposal. Rossi had made it very clear to Honda that he would not sign for them unless he could have Burgess, even if that meant staying in the 250cc class for another year, something that he seriously considered. He was still only twenty years old. He could have cruised to a few more 250cc world titles (Max Biaggi had lingered in the class long enough to pick up four before moving to the 500s), commanded astronomical wages, and moved up a few years later when he was older and more experienced. But that had never been Rossi's style and when Burgess agreed to postpone his retirement and embark on a whole new adventure, Rossi put pen to paper and became an official Honda rider. He even got to choose his own crew – and that meant Burgess's crew, who had taken Doohan to those five world titles. Many of them would remain with Rossi for the rest of his career. Rossi was even allowed to put together his own team in Italy – funded by Honda Europe and Honda Italy and with title sponsorship from Italian beer firm Nastro Azzurro and Playstation. That meant he didn't have to join the official Repsol Honda team, which had a more formal feel that didn't sit so well with Rossi – as would be proven rather dramatically in 2003.

Although Honda insisted the Repsol team was the only official one, Rossi was essentially given the same equipment as Àlex Crivillé, Tady Okada and Sete Gibernau and had almost as much technical support from the factory. He would want for nothing, yet he would have more freedom to do his own thing. It was a perfect arrangement and far preferable to the pressure-cooker atmosphere in the Repsol camp. 'We ended up creating a fantastic little team,' Burgess later said. 'We were ostracised out there – we were doing it on our own.

They [Honda] knew they had to give him a good bike because of who he was and there was a group of five of us and one Japanese engineer and we just set ourselves up next door [to the official Repsol Honda team] and went about our business. It was chaos in the Repsol team. We just used to look over and go, "Oh, Jesus."'[1]

Rossi would also have one other strong ally in his camp aside from Burgess – Mick Doohan himself. Although talk of Doohan running his own team had faded after the withdrawal of proposed sponsor Shell, he did agree to work as a mentor for both the Repsol Honda team riders and to oversee Rossi's first year in the premier class. 'We were actually going to be team-mates if I could have made it back in 2000 but that never came to fruition so Valentino ended up with my entire race team,' Doohan explained. 'He then got the [Nastro] Azzurro sponsorship and it became a separate team. We were originally going to have different sponsorship for a two-rider team, which I had been speaking to him about, but it was then all taken over by Honda and I was contracted to become general manager of racing for them.'[2]

Rossi was still contracted to Aprilia until 31 December 1999, but the owner of the firm, Ivano Beggio, to his eternal credit, gave his rider permission to test with Honda before the year was out. A true lover of the sport, Beggio did not want to hold a rider back or deprive him of any chance to progress – unlike some manufacturers today who insist on sticking to the letter of their respective contracts. Due to this kindness, Rossi first rode a Honda NSR500 at Jerez in December while still under contract to Aprilia.

Given that it was a seminal moment in the history of Grand Prix motorcycle racing, Rossi's debut on a 500 was so low-key that the man himself was disgusted with his new employers.

Expecting to find massive race transporters, lavishly equipped garages, hordes of attentive Japanese staff and an immaculately turned-out bike, Rossi could barely believe his eyes when the reality turned out to be a rented van, a shoddy-looking bike with mismatched fairings and fuel tank, Jerry Burgess and just two other mechanics. It could have been practice for a club race, only with a much more expensive bike.

Rossi, as things turned out, was no better organised. His helmet had been stolen so he had to borrow one of his old ones that he'd given to Tetsuya Harada and, having brought the wrong leathers (he was unaware that Aprilia's condition for allowing him to ride the Honda was that he had to wear his Aprilia leathers during this initial test), he had to borrow an ill-fitting set from Aprilia rider Marcellino Lucchi and cover up Lucchi's name with tape. It was all a bit of a shambles and about as far removed from Rossi's fantasy 500cc debut as it could have been, but once he was actually on the bike none of that mattered. What mattered was that, when put to the ultimate test in motorcycling – the art of riding a 500cc Grand Prix bike – Rossi was immediately impressive. By the second day (when his own leathers turned up) he was already posting times that would have been fast enough to set pole position in that year's race, held six months previously.

Burgess was impressed. 'We quickly learned that he's very good at working on set-up. When he comes into the pits he's like a computer – he gives you a list of six or eight things he wants looking at, like a download. He's more analytical than the rest of them.'[3]

And while Burgess was impressed with his new boy's method of operating, Rossi himself was impressed with the bike. 'I loved its violent character,' he said. 'It was so intense that you got an adrenalin boost every time you shifted gears.'

It didn't take long before Rossi learned just how quickly a 500 could bite back if maltreated. During his second test on the bike at Phillip Island, he crashed. He had already been warned by future rival Sete Gibernau that he was still riding the bike like a 250 with high corner speeds, huge lean angles and wide, sweeping lines. A 500 needed to be ridden differently to play to its power advantage. Corners had to be 'squared off' by braking heavily then using the power to spin the rear tyre through the apex of the corner before lifting the bike as upright as possible, as early as possible, to get it onto the fat part of the rear tyre so more acceleration could be used to launch onto the straight, thereby gaining vital mph down the straight. Rossi ignored Gibernau's friendly advice and landed heavily, and at great speed too.

It would take Valentino much longer to truly master the art of riding a 500, and he would suffer many more crashes before he did, but he at least had pace on the bike right from the outset and, as the old racing saying goes, it's easier to teach a fast rider to stop crashing than it is to teach a slow rider how to be fast. The signs were good.

Race fans were understandably excited to see Rossi in action for the first time on a 500 at the opening round of the 2000 season at Phakisa in South Africa, but the event would be notable for another reason too – it would mark the very first time that Valentino Rossi and Max Biaggi would race against each other. After years of verbal jousting in the press, the two would finally meet on track, Biaggi with two years' experience on a 500, Rossi with just a handful of tests. It was not yet an even fight but that wouldn't stop Rossi from trying to beat his nemesis at the first attempt.

It had, as Max Biaggi himself pointed out, felt like the two had been racing rivals for years, thanks to the long-standing war of words in the press, but this was in fact the very first time that they would actually face each other on track: 'I was in 250 when Rossi rode 125 then in 500 when he rode 250' Biaggi said. 'Now we will race against each other – but it feels as though he has been racing against me for years.'

The implication was subtle, but it was there nonetheless. According to Biaggi it had been Rossi who had been trying to prove he was better than Biaggi for all these years, not the other way round. Now it was time to find out who was the better rider.

Things did not get off to a good start for Rossi: he crashed out of the opening two rounds in South Africa and Malaysia and, when he did finally finish a race in Japan, it was down in eleventh place. Those first few races on a 500 proved to be something of an eye-opener for Rossi, as Burgess later recalled. 'He didn't know how hard to go on the warm-up lap… He said in the 250 class it was like… it would all start, and then I would look around to make sure everyone had got going, and then we'd settle down and race. But on the 500s they're racing on the warm-up lap. They're trying to knock you off!'[4]

It was hard, and for the first time since he had made his debut in the 125cc GP class, Rossi started to doubt his own ability. Had he reached his peak in the 250 class? Was the 500 a step too far? Could he ever really hope to master the fastest race bike on the planet? Nobody knew, not even Valentino. But at round four in Jerez, he found out. After qualifying on the front row for the first time he followed it up with his first podium – third place behind Kenny Roberts Jr and Spain's Carlos Checa.

This massive turnaround in his fortunes was partly down to Rossi and Burgess working closely together and realising that both crashes had been attributable to a weak spot in the Honda's engine, mid-corner, that was unbalancing the bike. Their solution had been to retain the 2000 chassis but to slot an older 1999 engine into it. It cured the problem and the combination was retained for the rest of the year. The magic had begun: Valentino Rossi and Jeremy Burgess would form one of the most effective rider/crew chief partnerships in the history of motorcycle racing.

Another third-place finish and fastest lap of the race followed in Le Mans (Rossi had set the fastest lap on his debut in South Africa shortly before crashing out), before the Grand Prix circus headed for Mugello and Rossi's first home race in the premier class – and it would serve up the first of many epic battles between Rossi and Biaggi. The two had yet to truly battle close together on track but that was about to change. Biaggi had, incredibly, won on his 500cc debut in 1998, the first rookie in the class to do so since Kenny Roberts Sr twenty years before. With that feat, Biaggi had managed to outshine Rossi, so he still had the bragging rights, but that situation was not to last for too much longer.

In qualifying, Biaggi, Rossi and Loris Capirossi were split by just 0.13 seconds and it was every bit as close in the race, the three Italians trading blows repeatedly until, with less than two laps to go, Rossi made a break for it and promptly crashed his NSR. Biaggi also went down on the last lap after riding so close to Capirossi that his front brake lever touched his rival's rear tyre and caused him to crash out. The race win went to Capirossi and the fans were left wondering for a while longer whether Max or Vale was the better rider.

When rain started falling in Catalunya, Rossi should have been afraid: riding a 125 or 250 in the wet was bad enough for him but this would be his first wet race on a fire-breathing two-stroke 500 – another proposition altogether. But just like he had with every other negative aspect of his riding over the years, he managed to address it and correct it, this time by remaining calm as many of his rivals fell in the treacherous conditions. He tip-toed his way home to another third place and finally laid the wet ghosts to rest. He achieved something else at Catalunya too – he beat Max Biaggi for the first time. In the first race in which they had both finished, Rossi came out on top, two positions ahead of the Roman, in what was Rossi's first season in the class and Biaggi's third. True, the Honda was a better bike than the Yamaha, but it was a warning shot, nonetheless. This one would run and run.

Crew chief Jerry Burgess instigated a new practice following the Catalan Grand Prix: from now on he would act as Rossi's alarm clock. Never a keen morning person, Rossi had somehow managed to sleep through half of morning practice and arrived in his pit box in a state of shock. 'When I wake up I always have a big confusion for the first five minutes,' he said. 'Then I remember "Oh fuck! I'm at the world Grand Prix!"'[5] From now on, Burgess's first task of the day on any given Grand Prix weekend would be to knock on his rider's motorhome door and get him out of bed.

It was fortunate that Rossi had managed to conquer his fear of riding in the wet at Catalunya because the next two races would also be rain-affected. In Assen, he came home a steady sixth and then came the British Grand Prix, which was now effectively another home round.

Rossi claimed he had moved to London in 2000 because he had become too famous in Italy and could no longer live a normal life there. While he was a huge star amongst bike racing fans in the UK, the sport is nowhere near as popular as it is in Italy, so he was relatively unknown to the general public and could walk the streets largely unrecognised. Yet, for someone who loved their home town and their friends and family as much as Rossi did, it seemed an odd decision.

He took a sixth-floor apartment in St James's Square, just off Pall Mall (though he would later move to Mayfair, close to The Ritz) and told the UK media how much he loved living in the capital. 'You have all the world in one city,' he said. 'Lots of good restaurants with different types and styles. It is also a good place at night. I hope I will live here a lot longer. I always enjoy it. It is my place – I have no plans to go. I can do normal things like go for a walk, go shopping, go to the restaurant without any big problems.'[6]

He did have one slight problem in August of 2001, however – he was mugged on the streets of the capital. 'There was this guy who wanted my mobile,' he explained. 'Luckily, I had it clutched tightly in my hand. He hit me hard, thinking it would make the phone drop to the floor, but it didn't. We looked in each other's eyes and he ran.'[7]

Clearly as tough on the streets as he was on track, Rossi did like his nightclubs (a particular favourite was the original Chinawhite club in Piccadilly, now relocated to Fitzrovia) and also the underground London music scene, but without his close-knit group of Tavullian friends? Something didn't quite fit. He would fly them over to stay with him and would also spend as much time as he could back in Italy, but it's doubtful that London could ever truly feel like home for a boy from Tavullia. It was some years before the whole truth emerged and it became apparent that there were certain tax benefits to be had by living in the UK and, with Rossi now making serious money, the move made sense from a financial standpoint.

It would not end well. In 2007, Rossi would have cause

to regret his decision but, at the time, British race fans were delighted that the most popular man on two wheels had chosen to make the UK his home and it seemed fitting that Rossi's first-ever victory in the 500cc class came at the British Grand Prix at Donington Park on 9 July 2000, just one week after another icon of the sport, Joey Dunlop, had tragically lost his life in a road race in Estonia. The racing world was still in mourning and under dark clouds at Donington, both literally and metaphorically, as Rossi and his rivals lined up to attack a track that was treacherously damp and slippery.

The race turned into an epic three-way battle between Rossi, Kenny Roberts Jr and Joey Dunlop's fellow Ulsterman and friend, Jeremy McWilliams. 'I was on a twin-cylinder Aprilia while Rossi was on a four-cylinder Honda, so I didn't get to spend an awful lot of time in close-quarter battles with him that year because I just didn't have the performance from the V-Twin,' McWilliams remembers. 'But in certain scenarios – like in mixed weather conditions as we had at Donington or on short, tight circuits where the four-cylinders couldn't use their horsepower advantage – it was very competitive.

'I was a pretty decent wet-weather rider and I truly thought I had the race won at Donington when I started to break away mid-race. If I'd had any idea about tyre management back then I wouldn't have tried to win it by ten seconds! But Rossi was very smart that day and just waited for the right time to pounce. He's done that with so many riders – he just watches them, learns where he might be a little bit faster, then makes his move. He timed it perfectly at Donington, waiting until two or three laps before the end and then had a go at it. He executed it perfectly and I had no answer once he went through. That was his first win in the premier class and he racked them up pretty quick after that.'

For the last seven rounds of the season Rossi's consistency was superb. He was on the podium at every race except in Valencia where he crashed out while fighting with Roberts for second place. It appeared he had mastered the 500: the boy had become a man. The biggest drama occurred en route to the Czech Grand Prix in Brno. Rossi had forgotten his passport and might well have missed the round – and valuable points – but instead he simply hid away in the back of his motorhome and smuggled himself into the former Iron Curtain country, meaning he took part in the Grand Prix as an illegal alien.

Not content with mastering the subtle and dangerous arts of riding 125cc, 250cc and 500cc two-stroke Grand Prix bikes, Rossi also got to ride a Superbike for the first time in 2000 when he took part in the single most important stand-alone motorcycle race in the world – the Suzuka 8 Hours. Held annually in Japan since 1978, the endurance race was a chance for the dominant Japanese factories (Honda, Yamaha, Kawasaki and Suzuki) to go for glory and, better still from Honda's point of view, to humiliate their rivals on home turf: Honda owns Suzuka.

It's a race where no expense is spared and the bikes, although based on production models, are every bit as exotic as Grand Prix machines. In Rossi's case it was a four-stroke, 1000cc, V-Twin Honda SP-1 – about as different to his GP bike as it was possible to get. The conditions were different, too. The heat and humidity of a Japanese summer can be overwhelming and it's common practice for riders to be placed on intravenous drips after each session to replace vital fluids. They also have paddling pools filled with iced water to plunge straight into, even though they can't immediately feel the benefit, such is the elevation in their core body temperatures. Lasting eight hours, with two team-mates doing alternate one-hour stints, Suzuka is one tough race. Rossi's team-mate was Colin Edwards, an affable Texan who would go on to win the World Superbike championship that year and eventually become Rossi's team-mate in MotoGP.

Chris Herring was commercial manager for HRC in World Superbikes at the time and worked with Rossi at the 8 Hours. 'When Rossi decided to move up to the 500cc class from the 250cc class everybody wanted to sign him. During his negotiations with Honda he listed all his demands and one of them was that he'd like to do the Suzuka 8 Hours at some point in the future. The HRC guys couldn't believe their luck that they were not only getting potentially the best 500cc Grand Prix rider in the world, but he also wanted to do the 8 Hours! So it was a no-brainer for Honda to sign him. And Rossi was very genuine about wanting to do the 8 Hours – he really wanted to have a go at it; he wasn't just trying to keep Honda happy.'

Despite the intensity of the biggest single race on the motorcycling calendar, Herring says Rossi took everything in his stride. 'All the time when I was with him at the 8 Hours, whether it was in the garage or in the riders' room at the back of the garage, or in the Italian restaurant at Suzuka at night, he was just as chilled as you could ever imagine. I remember he almost fell asleep one night in the restaurant – that's how relaxed he was. Nothing bothered him. He went out, he did the lap times, he let the medical people put him on glucose drips and in ice baths and never complained. He just took everything in his stride.'

Rossi and Edwards made a formidable team and Rossi took to the 'softer' and easier-to-ride Superbike with ease; too much ease according to Edwards, who had to work hard to try and convince his team-mate not to go so fast. 'I spent the whole of the race in 2000 telling Valentino to slow down! He was just so, so fast and he didn't seem to understand the endurance pace needed. In the end he crashed.'[8]

Rossi managed to get the bike back to the pits and have it repaired but, ninety-four laps into the race, Edwards then crashed, set the SP-1 on fire, and ended the dream team's chances of a finish. But Rossi had loved the experience and, always a fan of all things Japanese, vowed to return the following year to make amends.

After crashing out of the Valencia Grand Prix, and with three rounds still remaining of the 2000 season, Rossi and Burgess got their heads together, studied footage of him on the bike, and realised he was still hanging onto a bit of his 250cc riding style. It had to go. He had to learn to turn the bigger bike with the rear wheel instead of pushing the front too hard and, as a consequence, overloading it and crashing. And by the time the pair got to the next round in Brazil they had it nailed. Rossi finally felt comfortable sliding the rear, squaring off the corner, and lifting the bike up immediately to squeeze the power out of it. The reward was his second 500 GP win and his first in dry conditions.

A second place in Japan and a third in Australia saw him round out the year in second place in the championship, 49 points behind Kenny Roberts Jr, who became the first (and still the only) son of a 500cc world champion to win the title himself. Kevin Schwantz was impressed with the speed at which Rossi adapted to a 500. 'I think that I said he would win the championship in his first year, as long as he didn't dig himself a huge hole in the first three or four rounds. But that's exactly what he did – I think he scored one point compared to however many points Kenny Roberts Jr scored [Rossi, in fact, scored 5 points from the first three rounds while Roberts took 55] and yet Rossi only lost by a handful of points at the end of the season. So, he made a few mistakes in those first races and crashed too many times. But he was amazing. Back then it seemed like it took everybody a couple of years to figure out how to ride a 500, so for him to get on a 500 and just go? For me, it was pretty impressive just watching it.'

It was Kenny Roberts Jr's first and last world title. Rossi's time had come and the American would never get another look-in. A further 39 points behind Rossi at the end of the season was one Max Biaggi. In their first year of racing together, Rossi had come out on top. He had won the first battle but the war would rage on. And in 2001, it would reach a crescendo: things were about to get dangerous.

CHAPTER 6

THE DOCTOR

'It was not very nice. He hit me when
my hands were held down.'
MAX BIAGGI

One year to learn, one year to win. If the pattern was
to be adhered to then the 2001 500cc Grand Prix world
championship was Rossi's for the taking. It would hold a very
special significance too, as 2001 would be the last year that
two-stroke 500cc machines would make up the entire grid of
the premier class championship.

When the world championship was introduced in 1949 the
bikes had all been four-strokes, but by the 1970s two-strokes
had gained the upper hand. Lighter and more powerful than
the four-stroke opposition, they became the bikes to beat and
remained so for over three decades, but 2001 would be their
swan song. The following year they would make way for a
new era of environmentally cleaner four-stroke racing and,

while some of the grid would continue to run 500s during that transitional year, they would be completely phased out by the midway point of the 2003 season.

Valentino Rossi had grown up idolising the 500cc racers, considering them the most skilled of all riders as they had to control the notoriously hard-to-ride two-strokes in an era before advanced electronics and rider aids. Mick Doohan perhaps best summed up the skills needed by 500cc riders, by holding up his right wrist when asked about the emerging traction control technology and saying, 'This is my traction control.' Rossi badly wanted to add his name to the list of 500cc champions – the men he considered to be the greatest riders of all time – and this was his last chance to do it. It was now or never.

Rossi had grown up a lot in 2000. Riding the most fearsome race bikes in history will tend to have that kind of effect on a person. As he was forced to concentrate more on mastering the 500 he became noticeably quieter in the press and the silly haircuts disappeared, as did, largely, the wacky post-race celebrations. The pressures of riding in the premier class and of dealing with the by-now suffocating attentions of the world's media were beginning to show on Rossi's increasingly gaunt and serious face. Speaking of the cessation of his famous post-race celebrations he said, 'I am young and like to enjoy myself, but I stopped everything after the race, not because it is the 500 class, but because of my situation. It's very heavy, especially in Italy.'[1] Speaking of the fickle nature of the Italian press he added, 'If you make some show after one race then the next race you don't win, then they say you are an idiot.'

Some traditions remained, however. Rossi had always enjoyed having an alter ego and a self-styled nickname and for the 2001 season he would introduce what would become his final and most famous moniker – The Doctor. There are differing stories as to how it came about. Rossi himself offered at least two different explanations, the first being that he heard a 'Doctor Rossi' being paged in an airport and simply found it amusing, so adopted it; the second had more thought behind it: 'With 500s you need to be quiet, calm and thoughtful, more like a doctor.' Others felt the name perfectly described the surgical precision with which Rossi now went about his racing; he had matured into the ultimate professional, a man who carefully dissected his opponents. Graziano Rossi offered perhaps the simplest explanation of all: 'In Italy, "the doctor" is a name you give to someone for respect; it's very important.'

*

The battle for the 2001 world championship was an all-Italian affair fought out between Rossi, Loris Capirossi and Max Biaggi but despite some very close races, the final outcome was never in any serious doubt.

After showing such promise in 2000, every team and sponsor wanted Rossi for the 2001 season including, it was reported, Marlboro, the company that was sponsoring Biaggi on the Yamaha at the time. But Rossi was such a fervent anti-smoker that he had it written into his contract while at Aprilia that he would not ride under tobacco sponsorship. This stand garnered him an even greater following amongst young, anti-smoking Italian fans, though his stance did promise to limit his future options if strictly adhered to and he would eventually be forced to give way. But for 2001, he remained with Honda in his one-man team, again sponsored by Italian beer giant Nastro Azzurro.

Jerry Burgess noticed a new-found maturity in his rider. 'There was a big change in him from 2000 to 2001, like he was coming out of being a teenager and becoming a man. In 2000 everything had been pretty spontaneous, in 2001 things were more methodical and thought out.'[2]

Rossi's pre-race ritual formed part of that methodology and, once established, would remain unchanged for the remainder of his career. Before each session and race he would walk to the front of his garage, squat down and take hold of his bike's right footrest, bow his head and take a few moments, just him and his machine. 'Usually before the start I crouch beside my bike, I talk to her, tell her that from then on it will be just me and her, that we will try to get on the podium and that she must give me a hand in the difficult points. She has never answered me yet but I believe in it so much, if she spoke to me I would not be surprised!'[3]

Like all top sportsmen Rossi simply needed a ritual to adhere to in order to become fully focused on the job ahead. It's a bridge between two worlds; a way to shut out the noise and activity in the paddock, to prepare himself to ride a motorcycle at 200mph and to dance on the very edge of catastrophe. Once on the bike the ritual continued – Rossi would stand up on the footpegs and pull his bunched-up leathers out of his backside before settling into the saddle. This act also served a very practical purpose in that it simply ensured his leathers were comfortable and not digging in anywhere they shouldn't. Only when everything is just right can a sportsman then concentrate fully on getting the best out of himself with absolutely no distractions. But when an act, even a practical one, is repeated often enough it becomes a necessary ritual and that in turn can become superstition. Rossi has admitted that his pre-race routine does have at least a small element of superstition to it. 'It also bring me good luck,' he said. 'But especially is for my concentration... When I make like this it is for concentrating, for getting myself alone with the bike.'

Perhaps it was because of his runaway success in 2001 that those rituals remained unchanged for the remainder of Rossi's career, as long-time mechanic Alex Briggs has explained. 'His process has always worked and if you watch any other great sportsman they will have the routine. You watch a golfer, they will have the same routine for teeing off, same routine for putting. All the good guys have a routine.'[4]

The season kicked off at Suzuka in Japan where Rossi's rivalry with Max Biaggi reached new heights. As the two were disputing second place behind Garry McCoy, Rossi attempted to overtake Biaggi on the outside as the pair came onto the start-finish straight. Biaggi veered over, forcing Rossi closer and closer to the edge of the track. Biaggi then thrust out his elbow and pushed Rossi away from him, off the track and onto the dirt at around 140mph. 'I touched with Biaggi when I tried to go round the outside of him,' Rossi said at the post-race press conference. 'He lifted up his elbow, forcing me on to the edge of the gravel and I was quite scared. I had to become a motocross rider at 220kmh and I can guarantee you that's not a nice experience on a 500.'

Biaggi tried to put a bit of spin on the situation and actually blamed Rossi for his actions: 'When Valentino tried to come past he could have caused an accident – I just put my arm up to stop us from crashing.'

But the last laugh went to Rossi. After forcing his way past Biaggi on the following lap he then slowed mid-corner, took his left hand off the handlebar, and flipped his middle finger up at his rival before going on to win the race and handing

Honda its 500th Grand Prix win – at a circuit owned by the firm itself.

Rossi always maintained Biaggi's actions had been deliberate and later offered a more detailed account of proceedings. 'We had a really good fight over the first few laps. We touched a few times on the brakes but I don't mind that because it's racing. But on the straight he saw me coming on the outside and tried to push me off the track. He saw me and thought to himself, "You're going off." This is very dangerous and I was pretty scared.'[5]

Pretty scared he may have been but Rossi certainly wasn't scared off, as he made quite clear. 'I hope it doesn't happen next time and we put it behind us, but I don't really mind if not.'

The rules were clear – there were none. Biaggi on his Yamaha and Rossi on his Honda, both now experienced in the premier class, would now have the head-to-head they'd been building towards for years. Loris Capirossi on another Honda would join the party on occasion as a spoiler, but the 2001 season was all about Rossi and Biaggi.

After taking first blood in Japan, Rossi won the next two races in South Africa and Spain while Biaggi could only finish eighth and eleventh, but the Roman struck back in France, taking his first victory of the year with Rossi in third place.

Rossi's outrageously loud Hawaiian colour scheme of blue and white swirls (which even extended to his mechanics' shirts) didn't prove lucky at home in Mugello; he crashed out of second place on the very last lap in freezing wet conditions while Biaggi salvaged a third place. Reluctantly superstitious, Rossi never again rode with a special livery for his home Grand Prix. 'I am superstitious, yes,' he has admitted. 'Eighty per cent of riders have some superstitions. I understand it may be stupid but it's like this.'

The feud between Rossi and Biaggi was everything the Italian press had hoped for. The two greatest Italian riders of the modern era, who made no secret of their hatred for each other, duelling it out round after round in pursuit of the greatest prize in motorcycle racing. The rivals were already generating endless headlines across the world, but the frenzy that followed the Catalan Grand Prix took things to a whole new level. Rossi won the race quite comfortably from Biaggi ('Passing him was like the best orgasm,' Rossi would later say) but it was the post-race clash that grabbed all the headlines.

The narrow stairwell that leads to the podium at the Circuit de Barcelona-Catalunya is hidden from public view, but on the day in question was crowded with officials, team members, cameramen and other interested parties. It was hot, it was noisy, the riders still had adrenalin coursing through their veins. Rossi's crew members were excited and pumped, Biaggi's were dismayed and Biaggi himself was deeply unhappy at having been beaten by Rossi yet again. The Roman wanted to make his way to the podium and get it done with as soon as possible; the ongoing celebrations of Rossi and his crew were only rubbing salt into his wounds. According to Rossi's version of events, in pushing his way through the throng of people, Biaggi elbowed Rossi's manager, Gibo Badioli, out of the way. When Badioli protested, Biaggi shoved him again, at which point Rossi interceded. 'I rushed up the stairs. Biaggi was waiting for me at the top. His eyes were red, he was furious. I'd never seen him like this. There were slaps and punches. People screaming.'[6]

In Biaggi's account, it was Rossi who pushed *him* before attacking him. 'It was not very nice. He hit me when my hands were held down.' A race steward, who wished to remain anonymous, agreed with Biaggi and told *The Telegraph* that 'Rossi landed a solid blow to Biaggi's face as tempers rose and they were being pulled apart.' But according to another witness, Biaggi headbutted Rossi's team boss Carlo Fiorani, before managing to get a blow in at Rossi as well.

Whatever happened, whoever instigated events, whoever struck the most blows, it was an ugly scene and thankfully an extremely rare one in motorcycle racing. The two rivals were swiftly separated by team members and security staff, the podium ceremony went ahead, and then came the traditional post-race press conference, although none of the assembled journalists were privy to what had just happened. One particularly observant scribe did, however, ask Biaggi what had caused the mark on his face. 'I must have been bitten by a mosquito,' was the Roman's laconic reply. It was a good put-down, comparing Rossi to an annoying insect – a pest to be swiped at – but it only served to arouse the curiosity of the press. Both men tried their best to appear calm and collected and no further reference was made to the incident during the conference but, in time, the truth would out – or rather, various versions of it would.

Rossi and Biaggi were summoned to the race stewards' office to give their versions of events. It is inconceivable that both men would escape penalties or even one-race bans in the current MotoGP paddock, but back in 2001 they were the main players, the two championship contenders, and their rivalry was galvanising a new-found interest in MotoGP worldwide. The stewards decided to let them off without any penalties being imposed. Had they penalised either rider, it would only have caused even more drama. Instead, Rossi and Biaggi were told to play it down, deflect questions from the press and, most importantly, *not* to do it again. A truce was agreed upon and the two were forced to shake hands in front of photographers and journalists at the next round in the Netherlands. But the charade fooled no one; not the stewards, not the press, not the fans, and not the two riders – the pair didn't even look at each other while limply shaking hands. They would remain the most bitter of enemies even if, from then on, as Rossi said, they would have to 'continue to detest each other privately'.

As global press officer for the factory Yamaha Racing Team, Alison Forth worked with both men during her career and recognised that the two were polar opposites. 'They were like chalk and cheese,' she says. 'I'm not surprised they physically came to blows at Catalunya because they were such different characters. Max wears his heart on his sleeve much more than Valentino, so you really know what he's thinking. I had quite a close relationship with Max – I think I was like a mother figure to him – and in some ways I actually found it easier to deal with him because I knew exactly where I stood with him and I knew what he was thinking. Max allowed me to be a bit more in charge of him, even though he had terrific mood swings. Vale was much more in control of himself and knew exactly what he wanted, but I was probably less close to him on a personal level. But I really liked them both – they were both really nice guys in their own ways.'

Back on the racetrack Biaggi was the first to take revenge, winning the Dutch Grand Prix from Rossi, while Valentino turned the tables in Britain. A poor-handling Honda hobbled Rossi's chances in Germany, meaning he could only finish seventh while Biaggi won again. The German Grand Prix marked the end of the first half of the season and as the riders went into their summer break Biaggi had closed Rossi's championship points lead to just ten. It was all still to play for. But before battle could recommence, Rossi had the small matter of the Suzuka 8 Hours endurance race to attend to once more.

Returning for a second successive year with the 2000 World Superbike champion Colin Edwards as his team-mate (the American would add a second title in 2002) on the Honda SP-1, there would be no mistakes this time around. Having led the race the previous year before crashing out, this time the all-star pairing secured victory at the world's most prestigious stand-alone motorcycle race ahead of fellow Honda riders Alex Barros and Tadayuki Okada.

Chris Herring was impressed with Rossi's work ethic at Suzuka. 'In the garage he was very calm and professional and determined and absolutely committed to what he was doing – exactly the way he approached every Grand Prix. The 8 Hours race is very full-on, workwise. Riders have to fly out to Japan at least twice for testing then on race week there's pit-stop practice every night, again and again and again. But Rossi is a grafter – he's prepared to put the work in. There was no holding back. If he had to do something he'd give it one hundred per cent per cent. And he watched and analysed everything and asked endless questions in order to learn more.'

Rossi's childhood hero Kevin Schwantz feels that Rossi's work ethic is his strongest point as a rider. 'I think his greatest strength is that he's able to work on the bike every last minute of every session. He gets out there and gets to work and even when it's not right during Sunday morning warm-up he's in and out of the pits, still working on things. That's a good rider, that's a great rider, but that's also having really good guys that you're confident to work on stuff with. My theory always was, as a rider, that I was always gonna figure something out that was gonna make the bike better; I was gonna figure out a way to get it round that 180-degree corner faster. It's that "work on it as long as you possibly can" attitude.'

As well as working relentlessly to make his bike faster and better at every race, Rossi also had the ability to get the most out of it even on days when it wasn't behaving perfectly – another key ingredient in the biological make-up of a champion. 'Even better than that hard-working attitude is the understanding of what you've got underneath you and how to just get the most out of it.' Schwantz continues. 'If that means a third-place result or a fifth-place result, whatever it might be, that's what you gotta do and that's how you win championships. I think that's Rossi's greatest strength – he just works and works and works on the bike. Like I said, even on Sunday-morning warm-ups he's still making changes to make the bike better if it's not the fastest thing out there. A lot of us would give up on Saturday afternoon if we didn't have anything and couldn't qualify well and just think, "Oh well, Sunday's gonna be a pretty long day." You'd make a few changes but you'd never try to reinvent the wheel 'cos, if you were making a little bit of progress, you wouldn't want to go backwards.'

That fierce work ethic translated into a race win at Suzuka. It was Rossi's first and last win on a Superbike and was yet another feather in his cap, especially given the importance of the race to the Japanese manufacturers and, in particular, to his Honda bosses. But he made it clear, to his team-mate at least, that he had no intention of returning to the gruelling event which, on top of a season of Grand Prix racing, was proving too much. Three jet lag-inducing trips to the sticky, humid heat of a Japanese summer for testing and racing, getting used to a very different motorcycle then having to adapt back to his Grand Prix bike, and all while most of his rivals were refreshing themselves on a summer break – it was far from ideal, which is why top Grand Prix riders no longer take part in the event. 'I could see Valentino was desperate to win so he never had to come back to Suzuka,' Edwards later said. 'We were leading going into the final hour and as we swapped riders in the pits Valentino looked at me with the look that said we have to win this because I never want to come back.'[7]

Perhaps more importantly, the trip to Suzuka in 2001 also gave Rossi his first chance to test the five-cylinder, four-stroke, 990cc Honda RC211V he would campaign in the new era of MotoGP that would begin in 2002. He only completed eight laps and the track was not completely dry but first impressions of the bike were not good. 'For sure the bike I ride was too small for me,' he said. 'You can see from the pictures. It's very beautiful but maybe the aerodynamics don't work for a rider my size. So, there is some necessary work.'[8]

Those negative first impressions would soon change and Rossi and the RCV would eventually make a devastatingly effective combination, but for now he had the last-ever 500cc world championship to think about.

The season recommenced at Brno in the Czech Republic and from here on in, with one exception, it was a Rossi rout. He won every race apart from the Valencian round, where a heavy downpour immediately before the start of the race meant it was a tyre lottery and Rossi could only struggle to eleventh place. Two rounds later, the Australian Grand Prix provided the most suitable farewell to the 500cc era that anyone could have hoped for. There were still another two rounds of the 2001 season (and thus the 500 era) remaining, but neither was as spectacular as the Australian round at Phillip Island.

The weekend didn't get off to a great start for Rossi. Sleeping in at his hotel room and running late as he so often did in the mornings, he was rushing to make the start of the first practice session when Australian police clocked his hire car at 96mph in a 40mph zone. Locals were astonished that he managed to escape a stint in jail; instead, he was only banned for six months and handed a £400 fine. Sometimes being Valentino Rossi makes life just a little bit easier.

The race itself was the closest in the history of the 500cc class, with just 2.9 seconds covering the top nine riders at the chequered flag. The first rider under that flag was Rossi, even though he didn't need to be. Before the race he stated: 'I need only finish eighth but I don't think that is a good way to win the title.' Such was his dominance of the class by this point in the season that Rossi was no longer focused on just winning the world championship, he had the luxury of deciding in which manner he would win it.

Even better, he won it by passing Max Biaggi on the very last lap and crossed the line just 0.01 seconds in front of him. It was the perfect way for Valentino Rossi to win his first 500cc world title and the very last 500cc world title at the same time. 'The stakes were huge,' Rossi said of the race against Biaggi. 'It wasn't just about the world title – at stake were the future paths of our racing careers. I desperately wanted to be the last-ever 500cc world champion.'[9]

And he forever will be. Rossi had comprehensively destroyed Max Biaggi in the duo's first proper head-to-head season in the premier class and he won his first 500cc championship with two rounds to spare. Biaggi did manage, through gritted teeth, to appear magnanimous in defeat, saying, 'Congratulations to Rossi, who has been good, smart and clever to use at the best what he has in his hands.'

Amidst the celebrations, there was also a sadness and sense of loss at the passing of an era in Grand Prix racing. The fabulously noisy, smelly, vicious and fearsome-to-ride 500cc two-strokes were to be consigned to the racing history books as a new age of four-stroke technology and electronics dawned. They would be sadly missed. Rossi had achieved his lifetime ambition in winning the same title that his own heroes had won, on the same brutal bikes. He had won 11 of the 16 races, set 5 pole positions and recorded 11 fastest laps. He had beaten his arch-rival Max Biaggi and become just the third rider in history to win more than ten races in a season and only the second rider in history (after Phil Read) to win titles in the 125cc, 250cc and 500cc classes. And to cap it all off he won the 580th and last-ever 500cc race – the Brazilian Grand Prix on 3 November 2001. He simply couldn't have done any more.

The winner of the premier class in Grand Prix racing is traditionally invited to pen the foreword for that year's *Motocourse* – the world's most comprehensive motorcycle racing annual that has been published since 1976. Rossi was clearly delighted that he was now being compared to the all-time greats of motorcycle sport. 'Winning the world championship means so much to me,' he wrote in his foreword. 'I dreamed about it as a boy. Now I am the only person to win 125, 250 and 500 titles after Phil Read. When people talk about him and Mike Hailwood and Giacomo Agostini, they talk about the greatest racers of all time.'[10]

The rampant success of his 2001 season had made Rossi the new benchmark in Grand Prix racing – the man every rider had to beat, the man rewriting the record books and the man now with the biggest target on his back. But could he master the new MotoGP machines? With a completely fresh start, manufacturers were now building all kinds of different motorcycles with three, four, and even five cylinders and no one knew which would prove to be the most effective design. In 2002, Valentino Rossi, and every other rider on the grid, would be starting from scratch.

While Rossi's mother Stefania had travelled all the way to Australia to watch her son fulfil his dream, dad Graziano – who hates flying – watched the race at home on television. He then wandered down into Tavullia to visit his barber and keep a promise he had made to himself several years earlier. The ponytail that he had been growing since he had his hair shaved off for surgery in 1982 fell to the barber shop's floor. His boy was champion of the world. His hair didn't matter. They had done it.

And with that, the curtain was brought down on the fastest and most hard-fought championship ever devised for motorcycles. The new era of MotoGP had a lot to live up to – but it would prove to be even faster.

CHAPTER 7

MOTOGP

'If Valentino did come to Yamaha,
he would not have a chance of winning.'
MARCO MELANDRI

Since 1975, when Giacomo Agostini became the first man to win the 500cc world championship on a two-stroke machine, the bikes had dominated the class. Almost three decades later, with environmental concerns coming more to the fore and with two-strokes having somewhat stagnated in terms of development, a major shake-up of the world's premier motorcycle racing class was instigated. The championship would change its name to MotoGP and would be contested by 990cc, four-stroke motorcycles. With so much more power (over 230bhp at that point) came more electronics to help control it, and the modern age of racing had begun. Not for the last time in his career, Valentino Rossi would have to learn to adapt and learn to ride yet another kind of motorcycle.

He got off to an inauspicious start. After stating that the old two-stroke Honda NSR500 was the most exciting bike he had ever ridden, Rossi was perhaps biased against the all-new, four-stroke Honda RC211V before he even rode it. It certainly wasn't love on first ride. Pulling into the pits during his first test of the bike at Suzuka in 2001, Rossi's first words were, 'That's it – you guys can race it!' He wasn't happy. 'These bikes are fast, but they don't give the same feeling of power as two-strokes. The new bike wears the tyres too much. I want the old one back.'[1]

Rossi genuinely wanted to contest the 2002 MotoGP season on his old two-stroke (which was still eligible for the class during this transitional season) but Honda would never have allowed it. This was a chance to lead the way in a whole new technology and a company like Honda was never going to go backwards and flee from the challenge. Besides, Honda had been among the loudest voices pushing for the change to a four-stroke championship as 500cc two-strokes no longer had any relevance to street bikes, which had been going down the four-stroke path for years.

Things slowly improved as the magical combination of Rossi and Burgess began to refine the package. Rossi created a wish list of changes he wanted made to the bike and was due to test a modified version in January 2002, but after contract negotiations with Honda stalled, he was refused permission to test. It was the first real indication that the harmony between Rossi and Honda wasn't quite what it should be, and that situation would only worsen over the next two years.

By the time the first-ever MotoGP race was staged (on 7 April 2002, at Suzuka in Japan), Rossi's bike had been transformed and he was finally singing the praises of both the RCV and Honda. 'The problem was that the Japanese testers who did the first riding would never say, "This is shit," they just say, "Yes, this is quite good," so when I arrive the bike has big problems. To make better you must say, "This is good," or "This is shit."[2]

With a new contract signed and some blunt observations about what was wrong with the RCV, Rossi and his employers had worked together to produce a motorcycle that he felt he could push to the limit and on which he could challenge for another world title. 'They did everything I asked of them,' he said. 'They made an incredible effort and now the bike is performing very well. I'm still excited when I think of the thrills I got from the 500cc bike but I must admit that these four-strokes have incredible performance.'[3]

That new contract saw Rossi become the highest-paid rider in the history of motorcycle racing. It was a two-year deal that was worth £10 million. To put that in context, Mick Doohan in his prime (a five-time 500cc world champion) was paid between £3 million and £4 million a year, and World Superbike legend Carl Fogarty around £1 million per year. And the more Rossi won, the higher that figure would rise.

★

The new era of Grand Prix racing began as the old one had ended, with Valentino Rossi winning. With the new technical regulations allowing for a great degree of innovation, the manufacturers unveiled bikes with three cylinders (Aprilia), four cylinders (Yamaha and Suzuki) and even five cylinders (Honda). Some riders, most notably Brazil's Alex Barros, fought bravely on their old 500cc two-strokes, but there would be no farewell wins for the old regime: if you wanted to win in MotoGP now, you needed a four-stroke.

Rossi felt the new generation of bikes were easier to ride

for a wider range of riders whereas only a very select few could ever claim to have mastered the old 500s. 'The 500's power was more wild so the bike was more difficult to ride,' he said. 'But if you took risks in the final laps you could make the difference against the others. It's not impossible to do that with the RCV, just more difficult.'[4]

The biggest difference the fans noticed was the sound. While the near-identical two-strokes had all chimed in together with their high-revving, trebly soundtrack, the four-stroke engines were of such differing configurations that the noise they generated when all out on track together was as varied as it was astonishing and went a long way to winning over opponents of the new formula.

The first race in Suzuka was wet and this handed an advantage to local 'wild card' riders who had superior track knowledge of the Suzuka circuit in those conditions. This knowledge was an even greater advantage given that most riders had not even ridden a MotoGP bike in wet conditions at this point. One of those local heroes, Akira Ryo on the Suzuki, proved to be Rossi's main challenger, surprising not only Rossi but also his own team and even himself. Ryo rode out of his skin to lead in the early stages, but once Rossi had settled in and got the feel for the RCV in the wet he stormed past and won the race relatively comfortably, though Ryo was equally thrilled with his well-earned second place, one ahead of Yamaha's Carlos Checa. Rossi had won the last race of the 500cc era and the first of the MotoGP era: he was starting to look like a very special rider indeed.

Despite taking such a historic race win, the rift between Rossi and his Honda bosses grew to new and, for the first time, very public dimensions. At the post-race press conference in Japan, Honda team manager Noriaki Nakata was asked if this first win was down to the skills of his rider. In answering, Nakata heaped praise on almost everyone in the Honda set-up but made no mention of Rossi. It had long been Honda's belief that it was their superior motorcycles and the skills of their engineers and designers that won world championships; riders were a very expendable part of the process and could be easily replaced. As Jerry Burgess would later note, riders were 'like lightbulbs' to Honda – when one was worn out they simply screwed in a new one. Nakata's implication was that the bike, and not the rider, had won the Japanese Grand Prix. Few implications could raise Rossi's temper more. 'They only want to highlight the bike and make sure it's not overshadowed by me,' he protested. 'They can't have taken kindly to the fact that last year we gave their official riders a kicking with a satellite team.'

For a Japanese company like Honda that expected unquestioning loyalty from its staff, this kind of comment was simply unacceptable. And in public too. The writing was already on the wall.

The results on track, however, were spectacular. Following his win in Japan, Rossi would finish second in South Africa due to clutch problems creating wheelspin (allowing his Japanese team-mate Tohru Ukawa to take his only MotoGP victory) but would win the next seven races and completely demoralise the rest of the field.

Following Rossi's first home win at Mugello in the sixth round of the season and his defeat of arch-rival Max Biaggi again, Rossimania reached new heights and started causing some serious concerns for the sport's governing body. As soon as the chequered flag fell, thousands of Rossi fans invaded the track while riders were still circulating – perhaps not at race pace but still fast enough to cause serious injuries should they strike anyone. Fortunately, no one was hurt, but the president of the Fédération Internationale de Motocyclisme (FIM), Francesco Zerbi, promptly issued an open letter to all riders warning of the dangers of 'inciting the public' by playing to the crowds. In what was a rather absurd attack, he wrote:

> Motorcycling races have been also the victims of fanaticism and imbecility. Thus, as stadiums are often invaded, provoking material damages, now the tracks where the world championships are held are also subject to the same evil. If… the invasion of a football stadium is serious, the invasion of a racetrack is even more serious. The invasions now take place while the riders are still racing on their bikes at very dangerous speeds. Perhaps it is nice to see Valentino or any other rider throw his racing clothes and his shoes to the public, but are we sure that this does not incite the public?

It hardly seems fair to blame the riders for being too popular; the onus of responsibility for crowd control should surely fall to the FIM, Dorna and the various race organisers. But racing had never experienced a rider as popular as Valentino Rossi and the FIM simply didn't know how to handle the situation. The letter was ostensibly written to all riders but was clearly aimed at Rossi. What was he supposed to do? Stop winning races? Try to make himself less popular? Ignore the crowd and all his fans on his victory laps? The FIM's attitude seemed to be remarkably out of touch with the sport, but, if nothing else, the letter stands as testimony to Rossi's incredible popularity and the passion that he aroused in race fans the world over, but particularly at home in Italy.

Rossi didn't care. While Zerbi was sweating he had reverted

to his elaborate post-victory celebrations, and this time he was stopped on his victory lap by members of his fan club dressed up as policemen who handed him a speeding ticket. It was a convincing enough ruse to fool Rossi's grandmother, who called to ask what had happened to her speed-happy grandson. It also showed that Rossi felt more comfortable riding the bigger bikes: his celebrations had become less frequent during his first two years in the class as the strain of racing the world's fastest bikes took its toll, but now, safe in the knowledge that he was the king of the class, he could afford to clown around on occasion and where better to do it than at Mugello?

As one of BT Sport's MotoGP presenters, Neil Hodgson has witnessed the Rossi effect at Mugello on many occasions and says every time feels special. 'To see Rossi race at home in Mugello is an astonishing experience. The track invasion with thousands of fans after the race, the yellow smoke going off everywhere, the noise – it's one of those moments where you instantly realise, "I'll remember this in years to come – this is pretty special." It's more like a massive music festival than a motorbike race and that's all down to the Rossi effect. I've been there when he's not even been on the podium and the crowd still chants his name so relentlessly that the organisers have to get him up there anyway or the crowd would never disperse.'

By the time the summer break came around after the German Grand Prix, Rossi had a 96-point lead in the championship over team-mate Tohru Ukawa, with seven rounds still to go. He had never been so dominant. Biaggi languished a further 15 points behind Ukawa in third place. Biaggi would make some amends by winning in the Czech Republic when the championship resumed (Rossi crashed out) and again in Malaysia, but those were to be the only two wins of the season for the Yamaha rider. Throughout the year he would repeatedly bemoan the fact that Rossi was only winning because he was on a Honda – and he wasn't alone in thinking this. Biaggi's argument was given some credence when Alex Barros – who had finally been given an RC211V for the Sepang round in October after having spent the year on the old 500cc two-stroke NSR – won first time out on the machine Rossi had been racing all season.

The Honda was clearly the superior bike among the new generation of MotoGP machines and Rossi was tiring of accusations that he was only winning because he was on one. But what to do about it? In the fifty-three-year history of the premier Grand Prix class, only one rider had won on two different makes of bike in two consecutive years – Eddie Lawson, who had accomplished the feat on a Yamaha in 1988 and a Honda in 1989. But what kind of rider would give up his seat on the best bike on the grid just to prove a point? That would take a special kind of madness. Or confidence.

So it seemed more than convenient for Rossi when the news broke in August 2002 that Biaggi would be joining him at Honda for the 2003 season, though not on the same full-factory bike and not in the official team. Instead, he would be in a satellite team riding a year-old version of the Honda RC211V. They might be set to become Honda team-mates of a sort, but the war of words between Rossi and Biaggi continued unabated. 'In appearance Valentino has a friendly, clean and beautiful personality but in reality he's not like that,' Biaggi said in 2002. 'It's easy to make people like you in front of the cameras, make yourself look nice and funny when you're not. I don't like racers who, like him, criticise their colleagues.'[5]

For his part, Rossi was delighted that his arch-rival was to finally be on the same bike so there could be no more accusations that Rossi was only winning because he had a Honda. 'Now we will find out who is best,' he said, while choosing to overlook the fact that he would be on the very latest factory bike whereas Biaggi would be operating out of the independent Camel Pro squad on a lower-spec RCV. Or, at least, that was what Biaggi and Honda claimed. Rossi believed otherwise, saying, 'They have said all along that he only has a standard bike but this is not true. His bike is virtually the same as mine.'

In the final six races of 2002, Rossi never finished lower than second place: it was enough to secure the world title in Rio with four rounds remaining. After his team-mate Ukawa crashed out in Rio, Rossi was uncatchable on points and became the first man to win world titles in the 125cc, 250cc, 500cc and MotoGP classes. Thousands crowded the main square in Tavullia to watch the home-town hero take his fourth world title on a giant screen, the church bells rang out and an all-night street party ensued. Rossi also celebrated in style. 'To win four world championships is like a dream,' he said after the race. 'It is very difficult to explain as I am still full of adrenalin. It is an amazing feeling but you will have to ask me how I feel about winning another world championship in a week! I'm sure there will be lots of parties over the next few days.' Still domiciled in London, Rossi flew his friends to the British capital to help him celebrate, but it wasn't long before things turned sour.

In December, Rossi discovered a more sinister side to being famous when his name was included in a letter accompanying a letter bomb that was intercepted at Milan's Malpensa airport. It had been posted to Iberian Airlines and was believed to be the work of an organisation called the 'Five Cs', an Italian anti-capitalist group with links in Spain. The bomb was one of four devices sent to various addresses in Italy, all targeting big-name companies. In Rossi's case it was his team sponsor, Spanish oil giant Repsol, that was the real target. The letter was understood to have warned Rossi to end his association with the company or 'face the consequences'.

All four bombs were defused by the authorities, but Rossi was put on round-the-clock police protection as he went into hiding in London. He was told to report his movements to the police while the ongoing threat was being investigated and was also told not to make any comments to the press. His father Graziano commented in his stead, saying, 'It's not something to be underestimated. I'm a bit worried, but it seems strange to me that something like this is related to sport.' Rossi was also given security advice from military police who also opened all his mail during this period.

The story was broken by Italian newspaper *la Repubblica* on 15 December and it was news to Rossi and his team when they read it. Team boss Carlo Fiorani said, 'We're shocked and stunned by the news. The first anybody knew of this, including Valentino, was when we read an article in a newspaper that said his name was found in a separate message contained in a letter bomb.'[6]

With Repsol being the real target rather than Rossi, it was thought his name was merely used by the terrorists to generate publicity and it certainly succeeded on that front. Rossi pulled out of several public engagements in Italy and, when he did finally speak to the press, said he was living in fear. 'Certainly I have fear because there is nothing I can do to change this situation. I am being accused of having a contract with Repsol but that is absolutely untrue and I have my hands tied. My relationship is exclusively with Honda and I certainly can't choose their sponsors.'[7]

The matter eventually died down and Rossi's life could return to normal, but not before his only period of relaxation in the year had been completely ruined, not only by stress and fear but also by the fact that he could not appear anywhere in public and had to change so many of his plans. It was not a pleasant way to end the year, but as 2003 dawned, it was business as usual. There was, after all, a world championship to defend.

★

The feud with Honda had become serious throughout the 2002 season and it would only get worse in 2003. Yet, with so few other competitive alternatives available to Rossi, Britain's leading motorcycling publication *MCN* stated that 'The chances of him walking away from a [Honda] deal are about as high as yours are of buying a bungalow on Mars.'[8]

The results on track were still there. In the first four races of the 2003 season Rossi never finished lower than second place, but then came one of the longest win droughts of his seven years in Grand Prix racing. After another home victory in the fourth round at Mugello, Rossi failed to win for the next four races in Catalunya, the Netherlands, Britain and Germany. He would recover his form in the second half of the season to take three consecutive victories in the Czech Republic, Portugal and Brazil, and after finishing second in Japan would then win the last three races of the season in Malaysia, Australia and Spain.

While he tied up his fifth world title in Malaysia with two races remaining, it was his next outing in Australia that proved to be one of Rossi's greatest-ever races and seemed to prove there were absolutely no limits to his talents. While Rossi was involved in a close battle at the front with Repsol team-mate Nicky Hayden and rookie Marco Melandri, his pit board signalled that he had incurred a ten-second penalty for overtaking under a yellow flag. After losing his British GP win when a similar penalty was imposed after the race, this was like a red rag to a bull. And this time, Rossi had time to fight back. 'I decided to fight very hard to beat the ten-second penalty,' he said. 'I had already won the championship so there was nothing to lose.'

Rossi's performances had, on occasion, got a bit sloppy in 2003, as there were no other riders really pushing him and forcing him to focus at one hundred per cent. Now he had the challenge he needed and the result was extraordinary. He smashed the lap record on four consecutive laps and totally destroyed the rest of the field to finish 15.2 seconds in front of Loris Capirossi and a further 20 seconds ahead of the best of the rest. MotoGP races are usually won by seconds or fractions of seconds, so for Rossi to show what he could really do when he absolutely had to must have been completely demoralising for his rivals. In the post-race press conference he rubbed further salt into their wounds by nonchalantly admitting that it was the first time he had ridden at his full capacity for a whole race distance. 'I closed my eyes for the last ten laps,' he joked, before adding, more seriously, 'It was incredible – I've never ridden a whole race at one hundred per cent before.'

So this was what he was capable of when he really tried. It was an ominous display for his rivals and his admission that it was the first time he had ridden at his full potential made all the others look very second rate.

After having treated the crowd to an absolute masterclass in motorcycle racing, Rossi then endeared himself to Australians (and Brits) even more on his victory lap by carrying a home-made flag bearing the number 7. It was a tribute to his friend and hero Barry Sheene, an Australian resident for the previous sixteen years, who had sadly passed away from cancer earlier in the year. 'When we came back here I had a strange feeling to realise he has gone,' Rossi said after his emphatic win. 'We made a flag using a sheet from the hotel,' he revealed. 'Sorry, hotel!'[9]

It was the kind of stunt Sheene would have approved of. Before Rossi, he was the most famous and charismatic motorcycle racer of all time and it was he who inspired Rossi to keep his famous number 46, even when he was entitled to wear number 1 as world champion. 'Barry was the first rider that always used the same number – so, number 7 – and this inspired me a lot, and I think inspired also the other riders, like Schwantz, that always use the same number.'

Sheene's best friend and former team-mate Steve Parrish believes Sheene would have inspired Rossi in more ways than one, even if Rossi didn't consciously realise it. 'I've never asked Rossi the question, but I think that Barry Sheene would undoubtedly have been one of his idols when he was a kid because he was the bloke that was at the top when Rossi's dad was racing. I would say that Valentino would have grown up knowing that Barry was the icon of the paddock; he was that flamboyant character who turned up in his Rolls-Royce and had all the girls and was always signing autographs and making himself very accessible and I think some of that must have filtered through to Valentino. Barry and Valentino got to know each other quite well when Valentino moved up to the 500cc class. Barry was working for Channel 10 in Australia at the time, covering Grands Prix, and he spent a lot of time in Valentino's garage and was really in his corner when he switched to 500s.'

In Rossi, Sheene's legacy was in good hands and Sheene

would no doubt have approved of Rossi's decision to buy a sprawling mansion on his favourite holiday island of Ibiza, which he did during the winter of 2002/2003. Rossi had spent a lengthy holiday there with close friends the previous summer and decided he wanted a permanent party and chillout house in the Spanish sunshine. 'Very much happen on that holiday,' he said, tantalisingly. 'Maybe too much.' But not so much that he didn't wish to have a permanent base there...

The performance in Australia, along with his fifth world title, meant Rossi was now universally being spoken of as one of the greatest riders of all time, perhaps even *the* greatest. In 2003, he set 12 new lap records, retained 2 existing records, set 9 pole positions, won 9 races and set a new record for the most amount of points scored in one season (357). His closest rival, Sete Gibernau, finished 80 points behind him. Seldom had a rider been so dominant in the premier class in the modern era.

Despite lifting a fifth world title and having a new mansion to remodel, it was clear throughout the season that the ongoing tensions between himself and Honda, together with the relentless attentions of the media, were now getting to Rossi. 'Racing is certainly less fun now,' he admitted. It has changed and I don't enjoy it as much as I used to... It is true that I have lost a bit of momentum and the taste for racing.'[10]

This was as negative as anyone could remember Rossi ever being and it wasn't just down to the bad luck he had experienced in 2003. In France, he had fallen foul of new rules regarding aggregate race times in a restarted race, and in Britain he had romped home to an easy victory only to be docked ten seconds for passing under a yellow flag. It appeared that the charmed life Rossi had led so far was beginning to unravel ever so slightly and that he had reached a seminal point in his career. The Italian media had also turned on him. After having been the golden boy for so long, there was now as much criticism of Rossi as there was praise. 'Nobody talks any more if I make a great race or some great move to win,' he complained. 'They only talk about my errors. I am under the spotlight and it is really tiring.'[11]

There was no doubt that things were going wrong for Rossi by the mid-point of the 2003 season, but mostly it was the tense and unfriendly atmosphere in the Honda garage that was eating away at the fun-loving Italian. 'It pisses me off that people don't see the real value of what I have done. People have to understand that the Honda RCV is not a bike that became good overnight – I played a fundamental part in its evolution.'[12]

Rossi was tired of Honda taking all the credit for his race wins – tired of the firm's philosophy that it's the motorcycle and not the rider that makes the difference. And he was steadfastly determined to prove otherwise. He was also tired of not being able to have fun. Speaking of the way Honda operated he said, 'There was a rigour, a discipline, which stifled the will to laugh and joke. And I'm just not comfortable in such an environment, one where people are unable even to smile.'[13]

Money was another issue that was driving a wedge between Rossi and his employers. He was understood to be asking for a 30 per cent pay rise that would take his salary up to around £7 million a year – far more than any other rider had ever been paid. In the midst of the negotiations, Honda boss Carlo Fiorani said, 'There is a big difference at the moment between what he is willing to accept and what Honda wants to pay... Valentino's management is aware we aren't about to offer a blank chequebook.'

By late August Fiorani was confident that Rossi would sign

another two-year deal, saying, 'Any talk of last-minute hitches is untrue.' But it *was* true. For behind the scenes, always in the utmost secrecy, Rossi had been in extensive talks with Honda's arch-rivals Yamaha and the most sensational rider switch in Grand Prix history was already well underway.

*

Although the pair still clashed on occasion, by 2003 Rossi had effectively beaten Max Biaggi, both on track and psychologically. His new nemesis, and the second great rival of his career, was a young Spaniard called Sete Gibernau, and no one, not even Rossi, saw him coming. Gibernau had been racing in the premier class since 1997, having ridden for Yamaha, Honda and Suzuki but without ever making much of an impact. In 2002, riding a Suzuki, he had finished in sixteenth place overall in the championship, but after switching back to Honda in 2003 he became an unexpected challenger to Rossi. Initially, Gibernau and Rossi held no animosity towards each other; on the contrary, the two were very friendly and Gibernau had gladly offered Rossi advice when he first moved up to the 500cc class, but that would change as soon as Gibernau started regularly beating his rival.

Gibernau won his first Grand Prix just one week after the tragic death of his Gresini Honda team-mate Daijiro Kato, who crashed out of the third lap of the 2003 season-opening Japanese Grand Prix at Suzuka and hit a wall. The young Japanese rider clung to life in a coma for two weeks before finally succumbing to his injuries. It was a harsh reminder that, despite all the advances in track safety and protective riding gear, motorcycle racing was still a very dangerous, and sometimes fatal, sport. Multi-millionaires they may be, but the top MotoGP riders are still risking their lives every single time they go out on track.

The 2003 season was a particularly harsh one for the motorcycling world. In March, Barry Sheene had lost his battle with cancer, and in June, the Isle of Man TT's biggest star, David Jefferies, had lost his life following a crash in practice for the closed public-roads event that was no stranger to fatalities. Another TT great and British Superbike Champion, Steve Hislop, was killed in July when the helicopter he was piloting crashed in a remote field in southern Scotland. But the first tragic fatality of 2003 was MotoGP rookie Kato and, as it had been a full ten years since the last death in Grand Prix racing, the paddock took it hard. Gibernau, though, seemed to find a new focus after losing his team-mate, and won in his honour next time out in South Africa. After this inspiring victory, the Spaniard then inherited the full factory bike of the late Kato (to replace the customer bike he had been running) and from that point on Gibernau would be Rossi's toughest competitor over the next three seasons. And, just as with Max Biaggi, it would all get a bit ugly.

Gibernau was a very different character from Biaggi but, at the hands of Rossi, they both came undone. The grandson of the founder of Bultaco Motorcycles, Paco Bulto, Gibernau was a cheery, outgoing and friendly type before being psychologically beaten down by Rossi. But for now, at least, they were friends (and would even get together socially in Ibiza, where they both had homes), even though the Spaniard took four race wins from Rossi during the 2003 season and finished second to him in the championship. The racing between the two was close but still cordial; however, all that would change in 2004.

Ahead of the final round of the championship in Rio de

Janeiro, Rossi had still not announced his plans for the 2004 season but it certainly appeared that his future did not lie with Honda. Japanese motorcycle manufacturers have traditionally been very diplomatic and reserved in any statements regarding their riders, so it was very telling when Honda boss Suguru Kanazawa released a statement in September 2003 that read: 'If Valentino chooses to ride for another manufacturer we will try to build a better machine that would beat and destroy him.' It was fighting talk that not only showed how upset Honda was at the prospect of losing the best rider in the world, but was also a statement that underlined the company's belief that it was the bike, not the rider, that won world championships. It was an arrogance that did not appear to be shared by fellow Japanese manufacturers, Yamaha. 'Championships are won by exceptional riders,' said Yamaha's Lin Jarvis. 'We have some very good riders but he [Rossi] is exceptional.'

By October, Rossi had become more and more vociferous in his attacks on Honda, making it seem increasingly less likely that he could remain within the camp. Speaking of his four-month contract negotiations he said, 'They are very difficult. A disaster. I don't know if all Japanese are like this but the Japanese at HRC are incredible. They behave in a very strange way.'

Max Biaggi inadvertently gave his rival even more motivation to switch camps when he said. 'He says he wants to change but he'll never leave Honda. They treat him too well there and he doesn't have the balls to accept the Ducati challenge.'

Biaggi was referring to persistent rumours that relative MotoGP newcomers Ducati had offered Rossi an £8-million-a-year deal to ride its increasingly competitive Desmosedici.

Rossi had gone so far as to visit the Ducati factory in Bologna and believed that Ducati 'were streets ahead of Yamaha', but there were several issues on which he and the bosses of the Italian factory differed. Ducati's outlook and approach to racing seemed to Rossi to be too similar to Honda's, with an overwhelming emphasis on the machine and the technology and less importance attached to the rider. Rossi shied away.

That meant the only realistic option left open to him was to sign for Yamaha. But just how realistic was it? The firm's M1 machine had only scored one podium in 2003 and Yamaha hadn't won a premier-class world title since Wayne Rainey lifted the 500cc crown in 1992 in what had been a completely different era. The firm had thrown millions of pounds at its M1 in 2003 but it still failed to deliver any serious results in the hands of Carlos Checa and Marco Melandri. Could Rossi turn the entire project around if he signed for Yamaha? It seemed a very tall order.

By contrast, between the start of the new era of MotoGP in 2002 and the end of the 2003 season, Honda's RC211V had won twenty-nine of the thirty-three Grands Prix. If Rossi wanted to continue winning in the premier class he would surely have to remain with Honda, however deep the gulf between the two parties. Marco Melandri certainly thought so. A close friend of Rossi's and the reigning 250cc world champion, he had already spent a year on the Yamaha in MotoGP and was convinced that even his friend's mercurial talents could not turn the M1 into a winner. 'If Valentino did come to Yamaha at least he would be able to give them some direction with development,' he said, 'but he would not have a chance of winning.'[14]

And then, in a press conference at the final Grand Prix of the year, came the bombshell. 'I have done everything with the Honda,' Rossi said. 'Win in the dry and the rain, win at my best track, win at my worst track, so I feel I have finished my work with this bike. I've had an incredible four years with Honda – three world championships and thirty-three wins from sixty-four races. Maybe my choice seems a little bit crazy but we will see next year.'

Rossi had signed for Yamaha and would be taking his trusted Honda crew with him; the crew that, as things transpired, effectively saved his career. Knowing he could no longer ride for Honda and believing that riding for Ducati would be a very similar experience, Rossi later revealed he had been ready to retire from racing if he could not build the perfect team around him at Yamaha. He was serious too: if racing couldn't be fun, he had no interest in taking part. But with his trusted crew chief Jerry Burgess and most of his other team members from the Honda garage agreeing to defect with him, Rossi had the crew he needed, not only to win but also to enjoy his racing. It was a heartening display of loyalty and something of a risk for all involved. 'When I announced to the mechanics that I was going with Valentino they said, "I'm coming too,"' Burgess later explained. 'Some of those guys were leaving very secure jobs and taking a big gamble.'[15]

It was the most sensational signing in Grand Prix racing anyone could remember. Throughout his career Rossi had always had access to the best and most proven motorcycles and had always made the right choices when it came to signing contracts. But this seemed a bridge too far. Could he really climb onto such an inferior bike and hope to hand it to his former employees? Valentino's ultimate test was about to begin.

CHAPTER 8

YAMAHA

'No one, and I mean *no one*, could believe
what he did in that first race.'
ANDREW SMITH

'In 2003 we were over in Japan for our annual product evaluation, trying out the following year's models, and we had dinner with Takashi Kajikawa who was vice president of Yamaha,' says Andrew Smith who, at the time, was sales and marketing director for Yamaha UK. 'We were talking about how we could get Yamaha back to the top as we had been going through a challenging time both on track and off. It was a round-table discussion and we started talking about motorsport and said, "Why don't we go for Rossi and get him to come to Yamaha?" because one of our Italian colleagues had heard through the grapevine that Rossi was becoming a bit frustrated and maybe needed a new challenge, where he becomes more of the winner, rather than the manufacturer.

'We agreed that, if we could get him, we'd build a bike around him, and that's ultimately what we did. The guy who'd been in charge of our MotoGP project was moved sideways and Masao Furusawa came in and took over the project. He was instrumental in talking to, and convincing, Rossi.'

By the end of 2003, after Rossi had made the official announcement that he would be riding for Yamaha, the morale boost within the company was astonishing to behold. 'It was incredible when we learned that Rossi had actually signed for Yamaha,' says Smith. 'It was so exciting but I honestly thought it would be a year of learning and the following year we could get back to winning. I was convinced it would take a year for Rossi, the bike and the team to get up to speed. The hope was for some podiums towards the end of the season and then be ready to challenge for the championship in 2005.'

Alison Forth had at this point been global press officer for the Factory Yamaha Racing Team for several years and says the lack of success was beginning to have an effect on morale within the squad. 'I'd say spirits were a bit low in the team. We'd had the years with Max Biaggi and Carlos Checa, and Biaggi was the closest we came to having a victorious rider. We had the occasional race win but, really, poor old Carlos had the habit of falling off and Max was... sporadic, let's say. Rossi and Honda ruled the roost up to that point, so while the mood amongst the Japanese and the European racing hub – headed up by Lin Jarvis – was not entirely deflated, it was clear that something had to change.'

Rossi's signing with Yamaha was such a closely guarded secret that even most of the team didn't know about it until just before the official announcement. And as excited as Forth was about their new star signing, there was some sadness too: as part of the deal Rossi brought most of his crew with him from the Honda team and that meant some of the Yamaha staff had to go. 'When the news first came through everyone was in disbelief,' she explains. 'Spirits were great but obviously with the news of the incoming team came the sad news that quite a lot of the old crew, dating back to the Wayne Rainey era, were having to leave. The team had been quite British up to that point but Rossi brought in a lot of Australians and Italians, so, culturally, things were really shifting. But from a marketing perspective it couldn't really get any better than having Rossi on your team. We thought we'd lucked out getting Biaggi and Checa, who were prominent racers in Europe, but to get Rossi was just really exciting because he was a true global brand.'

Honda and Yamaha have been major rivals since the 1960s, so the poaching of Rossi was seen as a major triumph within Yamaha. Andrew Smith: 'It was seen as a great coup because all the benefits and motivation Rossi brought to us when he signed for Yamaha, well, we knew the reverse would be true at Honda when he left. But, to be fair, they probably coped with losing him better than we did some years later because their attitude has always been "We're Honda – our bikes can win anyway." That attitude was one of the biggest motivations for Rossi joining Yamaha in the first place. After he left Honda, I think he was basically written out of their books.'

As commercial manager for Honda's World Superbike team, Chris Herring witnessed first-hand the clash between Rossi's way of doing things and Honda's way of doing things and wasn't surprised at his decision to leave. 'I think Italian riders just need to feel a little bit more love than they got at HRC. They look for that personal, human connection within the team and I think that's what Valentino was missing at HRC at that time.'

Herring also says that Rossi had witnessed the way his Suzuka 8 Hours team-mate Colin Edwards was unceremoniously dumped despite winning the 2002 World Superbike championship for the firm and thinks that might have contributed to his decision to leave. 'Valentino was with Colin when Honda told him his services would not be required in 2003 because they were pulling out of World Superbikes. Maybe that woke Valentino up to Honda's way of operating, seeing Colin getting dropped like that. At that time HRC's director was Koji Nakajima and he was the guy who told Edwards he had lost his job – even though he went on to win the WSB title for Honda at the final round that year. That's the bizarre thing about HRC and the way they operate. Nakajima also came very close to losing the Repsol sponsorship for Honda's MotoGP team. He issued so many demands to the Repsol people and basically told them, "This is what we want and we want it now."'

There was a strange culture within HRC at that time in terms of how riders and plans were being dealt with, Herring explains. 'Ending Honda's involvement in WSB after nine years or so was just one example. I suspect that the people at Yamaha knew this and that's why they approached Valentino about riding for them in MotoGP. There's always been a bit of a stand-off between the Italians and the Japanese. I had a conversation in 2003 with an Italian guy from Honda Europe and he thought it was a bit of a giggle that Honda was not only going to lose Valentino to Yamaha but that he was also taking all his crew with him!'

Honda's loss was Yamaha's gain and the thrill of signing Rossi could be felt throughout the company. 'Everybody was really excited when he signed and everybody was hopeful that we'd be back to getting lots of coverage and that Valentino would transform the bike and the team and we would be back to winning ways soon,' Smith says. 'But no one, and I mean *no one*, could believe what he did in that first race.'

Even before the legendary first race in South Africa, Alison Forth had seen Rossi's potential and had dared to dream. 'Right from the first tests we realised very quickly that he could do things on that bike [Yamaha's much-maligned M1] that had never been done before. So, the mood around testing was like "Oh my God! This is really exciting!" But in our wildest dreams I don't think anyone thought he could win that very first race.'

It was apparent from the outset that Rossi was the boss at Yamaha and that everything was geared around him. In essence, he got whatever he wanted. 'Yes, totally,' Forth admits. 'It was clear from day one when we started testing that Rossi was in charge. Everywhere he went he had his manager, Gibo Badioli, and one or two others that worked in his management team with him and they would call the shots on everything and we would have far less access than we'd been used to with other riders. That passed over to the mechanics and the way the team was run – it was all centred around Valentino.'

There were good reasons for this: as well as being a phenomenal rider, Rossi's developmental skills are exceptional, as he would prove when he helped turn around Yamaha's ailing M1. His ability to assess precisely what was working on a motorcycle and what was not, his accurate feedback on new parts and his ability to feel even the tiniest change in settings have impressed many of his mechanics, crew chiefs and team members over the years. When he was still with Honda, Carlo Fiorani noted, 'He has some kind of amazing link system which allows him to think "I like this" and "I don't like this," so he can test many different things at the same time without getting confused.'[1]

Years later, his long-time mechanic at Yamaha, Alex Briggs, would compare Rossi's analytical brain to a supercomputer. When asked what made Rossi different from other riders he said, 'I suspect it's like buying a computer; some are just faster than others, some have bigger CPUs and more memory. He is the equivalent to the fastest computer that you can buy that keeps regenerating![2]

Rossi's first race on the Yamaha M1 would be at the Phakisa Raceway near Welkom, South Africa, on 18 April 2004, and it would prove to be, even according to the man himself, the greatest race of his life. His embittered former employers at Honda had refused him permission to test the Yamaha until his contract was up on 31 December 2003, which immediately put Rossi on the back foot compared to his rivals. It may have been petty but Honda was within its rights to do so, even though most manufacturers do not usually hold so rigidly to such clauses (Aprilia, for example, had allowed Rossi to test the NSR Honda in 1999, despite still having a contract with him). But after such a bitter split Rossi could expect no favours from Honda, nor was he granted any. The pettiness of the decision still angered him, however, and he knew the lack of testing time would ultimately hinder his race programme. 'Their attitude pissed me off,' he admitted. 'It will cost me four races, but I always knew things would be like that.'

It didn't matter. By the time of the South African Grand Prix he and his crew had worked their magic on the M1 and, helped by a new engine, got it up to fighting speed. Not as fast as the Honda or the Ducati, but fast enough and well mannered enough to allow Rossi to take the challenge to them. He topped the final pre-season test at Catalunya and then set pole first time out in South Africa. The move to Yamaha had, according to Rossi, always been a two-year plan: develop the bike in year one and try to challenge for the title in year two; a year to learn, a year to win. And yet here he was on pole position at the first attempt. And this time there was no doubting it was Rossi the man, not the machine, that was making the difference. It was obvious to the naked eye: he was having to ride out of his skin to make the bike competitive, sliding the rear wildly out of corners, hopping and skipping on the brakes on the way into every corner, bucking and weaving down the straights... He rode the M1 like a man possessed from the moment he got on it and would do so all year long.

The race in South Africa was once more against his old rival Max Biaggi, still riding for Honda but still in a satellite team rather than the official Repsol squad. Rossi's soon-to-be new nemesis, Sete Gibernau, was also in the mix and also on a Honda. By mid-race distance, all Gibernau could do was follow the other two and, with six laps to go, Biaggi passed Rossi and tried to make a break. He couldn't. But forced to ride every bit as hard as his countryman, Biaggi also started running wide and making mistakes. Both riders were at one hundred per cent, giving absolutely everything, holding nothing back. So much was at stake. Biaggi had spent so long complaining that Rossi was only winning races because he was on a Honda and had repeatedly said his rival couldn't do the same thing on a Yamaha. And yet here they were, Biaggi on the supposedly unbeatable Honda and Rossi on the inferior Yamaha and still Biaggi couldn't break him. Rossi was never more than half a second behind. With three laps to go it was his turn to slam a block pass on Biaggi at the penultimate corner and attempt to break away, but he couldn't gap Biaggi by any more than three-tenths of a second by the start of the final lap.

No one, not even Rossi's Yamaha employers, had expected that he could challenge for the win first time out. Television commentators, trackside spectators, the teams and officials in the paddock, and the millions watching the live broadcast across the globe could not believe what they were seeing. They were, by now, convinced that they were watching the greatest motorcycle racer who had ever lived. It was simply inconceivable that any other rider could do what Rossi was doing.

One lap to go, 2.63 miles, and just one man and one bike – Max Biaggi and a Honda – were preventing Valentino Rossi from pulling off his greatest-ever triumph. It wasn't really a fair fight; with motivation like that to spur him on, it was as if Rossi had been given another gear. He bit the screen of his M1 in one last all-in effort, buried his gangly frame beneath the Yamaha's paintwork to gain any tiny aerodynamic advantage he could, timed his gear changes to perfection, got on the throttle that little bit earlier, pulled on the brakes that little bit harder, skirting and skimming the very limits of physics and adhesion as he poured every ounce of his ten years' experience into that one final lap; concentrating so furiously that the outside world, and the dangers it contained, simply did not exist for him. Rossi saw his chance to add to his legend, to cement it for all time and, most importantly, to prove to Honda and the world that it was *him* who made the difference, that *he* was the magic ingredient.

In what was, to all intents and purposes, his final destruction of Max Biaggi, Valentino Rossi crossed the finish line of the South African Grand Prix one-tenth of a second ahead and won on the Yamaha M1 at the very first attempt. It was, without doubt, the greatest performance of his life and his antics on the victory lap showed that he realised this, too. There were no gags, no costumes, no elaborate silliness; instead a simple display that was far more emotional and powerful because of its spontaneity. He rode his M1 onto the grass, rested it against the trackside fencing, climbed off and, with helmet still in place, mimicked kissing the front of the bike. He then sat on the ground looking utterly exhausted, his shoulders starting to shake noticeably. He seemed to be in floods of tears, unable to believe what he had just achieved, and this is what the motorcycling press reported at the time. He had risked everything in jumping ship and signing for the underdogs and it had all paid off. But in fact, Rossi wasn't crying; he wasn't crying at all. Quite the opposite. 'I was laughing,' he later admitted. 'Laughing because of the incredible feeling of pride, relief and happiness which had overcome me.'

Yamaha's Andrew Smith watched on in disbelief before realising Rossi's win had just left him out of pocket. 'Just before the weekend of the South African Grand Prix we were fighting to meet our monthly sales targets and I sent my usual email round to all our staff in the offices and out on the road and promised that, if Rossi won, I would personally buy every single person in the company (Yamaha Motor UK) a big cake to celebrate. That meant around ninety people and ninety big birthday-size cakes, but that's how confident I was that Rossi *wouldn't* win that first race! When he won and then pulled the bike to the side of the track and got off and patted it and kissed it – it was what dreams were made of. It was just magical. And then I got about ninety emails saying, "Can't wait for the cake!"'

Even Rossi couldn't believe what he'd just managed to do. 'Ninety days ago even I didn't think this was possible,' he said afterwards. I think this was the best race of my career. I can't believe I won. A race like that was a miracle.'

Like everyone else in the Yamaha team, Alison Forth was utterly astonished at her rider's achievement. 'It was absolutely incredible. I was in a mobile unit during the race along with the other marketing people and all the cooks and people who ran the hospitality unit, and the atmosphere got so heated, then when he crossed the line we all ran up to the pit garage and it was pure mayhem. The media scrum was incredible – a total bunfight. The Italian media in particular went completely berserk. We were all staying in the same hotel with the Japanese mechanics who aren't usually known for their displays of emotion, but that night we all ended up in the swimming pool with our clothes on. The Japanese had to wear the same clothes the next day for some reason and they were trailing through the airport with squelching wet socks!'

Carlo Pernat, who was the first man to sign Rossi way back in 1995, still considers it Rossi's greatest-ever victory. 'For me, his greatest race was when he won on the Yamaha first time out after Yamaha's results had been terrible for so long. This was an unbelievable race because it proved that the rider was more important than the bike – and that is the exact opposite of what Honda believed. Valentino proved that, even with an inferior bike, it was *him* who made the difference.'

The point was not lost on Rossi either: 'I proved that the rider is what counts in motorcycle racing... In the past it has been said that when I win it is because I am on a good bike. I always knew that was not fair and this race proves it.'[3]

His case was given further credence by the performances of the other Yamaha riders in the race: Norick Abe was ninth, Carlos Checa was tenth, and Marco Melandri was eleventh. The three were, on average, forty seconds behind Rossi at the chequered flag.

Koji Nakajima, the man who let Rossi go from Honda, looked devastated in the aftermath of the race, as he crouched alone between hospitality units drawing on cigarette after cigarette. Apart from being humiliated by Rossi he had to face the fact that there were no Hondas on the podium for the first time since 2001. 'I'd like it if he was still riding for Honda,' was all he managed to say to the press. 'It was a pity that Valentino left Honda.'

His counterpart at Yamaha, Masao Furusawa, on the other hand, could not contain his delight. 'It's absolutely fantastic,' he said. 'I'm really, really happy. It is an unbelievable day for Yamaha. What happened was beyond expectations. Valentino really is a genius behind [sic] the bike.'[4]

That race win meant Rossi became the first rider in history to win two consecutive races in the premier class on two different makes of bike. Even Biaggi (who, to his credit, was the first to shake Rossi's hand on the cooling-down lap) had to admit he was impressed. 'He made a great race. Mutual respect, after such a race, is unquestionable.'

With the opening chapter of the fairy tale over, the MotoGP circus headed to Jerez and Le Mans where Sete Gibernau took back-to-back victories while Rossi struggled to fourth place on both occasions. It was the first time he had failed to find the podium in two consecutive races since his debut in the 500 class in 2000. He was also third in the championship behind Gibernau and Biaggi. Had the South African result been a fluke? Was the Yamaha really going to handicap him as so many thought it would? Not likely. An ecstatic home win over Gibernau at Mugello was followed by another in the Spaniard's home race at Catalunya and yet another in Assen, putting Rossi back at the top of the championship – albeit in a dead heat with Gibernau.

Rossi's performance in treacherously slippery conditions at Mugello had impressed even the mercurial Troy Bayliss. Eventually a three-time World Superbike champion, Bayliss was riding for Ducati in MotoGP in 2004 and was known as one of the hardest racers around. But even he was awed by Rossi's performance on that day. 'You really have to hand it to Valentino,' he said. 'He puts it on the line – he was going like a maniac.'

With both Rossi and Gibernau crashing out of the Brazilian Grand Prix, they remained on the same points going to Germany but this time Biaggi won with Rossi fourth and Gibernau crashing out, meaning Rossi now had a one-point lead in the championship over Biaggi. Back on winning form at Silverstone, Rossi then had to give second best to Gibernau at Brno and deal with the fact that both Gibernau and Biaggi were given full-factory machines from this round onwards, such was Honda's determination to beat Rossi. So Biaggi finally had what he'd always wanted – a full-factory Honda; the bike he'd always insisted had an advantage over all the others and the reason why Valentino Rossi had won so many races. It didn't seem to be the magic bullet Biaggi had been hoping for, however: he finished third.

Portugal went Rossi's way but local rider Makoto Tamada won the Japanese round for Honda (at the Motegi circuit, which is owned by the firm), beating Rossi into second place and giving his ex-bosses something at least to feel a little smug about.

Rossi was by now riding the Yamaha as if he'd been on it for years, as Neil Hodgson, who was riding an uncompetitive Ducati in MotoGP that year, saw at first-hand. 'I was on track with him every weekend, so every weekend I'd get glimpses of him up close, either when he came past me or when he was on an out-lap and I could get in behind him and try to hang onto him for as long as I could. Because it was Rossi, I'd always try and get as much time behind him as possible just to observe what he was doing.

'The standout thing I saw was that, for such a skinny individual, he could muscle that bike into places on the track that really took strength but when he did it always looked effortless. I don't know if that was the way he used the throttle or the way he used his arms and legs as long levers, but he could just place that bike anywhere he wanted to with minimum effort. He never looked ragged either. I mean, he did in his early days on a 125, and even on a 250 and a 500 until he got used to them, but by the time I saw him up close it just looked easy. It was annoying, really. Annoying, because you know you can't do it. I'd try to follow him into a corner and would end up out on the edge of the track, having to close the throttle, and by then he'd gone, so I'd think, "So much for that tow then."'

In Qatar, Rossi's hitherto friendly rivalry with Gibernau came to a crashing halt under the most unusual circumstances. With the track being completely new and therefore rather 'green' and slippery, Rossi's crew took a scooter out to his third-row start position on the night before the race and performed a few burnouts, leaving a mass of grippy rubber on what was effectively going to be Rossi's launch pad. Rossi was not present and Jerry Burgess did not inform Yamaha boss Davide Brivio of what he and the team had done.

Spotting the black rubber on his rider's grid position, Brivio reported it to the circuit manager, thinking that someone had tampered with Rossi's slot. Then Honda became aware of the melodrama and Gibernau's team boss Fausto Gresini filed an official protest, claiming Rossi's team was trying to gain an unfair advantage.

It all seemed rather petty and, while the Yamaha team was not found guilty of breaking any specific rules, race organisers decreed that it was 'against the spirit' of the sport and slapped Rossi with a six-second penalty, which meant he had to start the race from the back row of the grid. Max Biaggi, incidentally, was handed the same penalty after his own crew had been caught sweeping his grid slot (an action that *was* quite specifically forbidden in the rules). Rossi immediately made his position clear: 'I've been looking for an excuse not to talk to Sete. Today he gave me one.'

In the event, Rossi crashed out of the race while Gibernau won and closed the title gap to just 14 points. But Rossi solely blamed his rival for the protest and the goodwill between the two was at an end. 'Sete was the one who was behind all this,' he said. 'He has acted like a child. It is like a knife has been pushed into my back.'

From here on in Gibernau would be the new Biaggi, the new nemesis, the new motivation for Rossi to dig deeper in order to beat him. And that made Rossi even more dangerous, as Jerry Burgess pointed out: 'Valentino is the sort of rider I wouldn't want to get angry. He can take you apart on the track.'

At the following round in Malaysia, Rossi began the mental destruction of Gibernau. After vowing never to speak to the Spaniard again he blanked him at the pre-race press conference to such an extent that Gibernau appeared genuinely shaken. While giving his rival the cold shoulder, Rossi joked with the world's press after setting pole position, saying, 'This was a very important pole position because at least we know exactly which part of the track we have to clean.'

After beating Gibernau by more than twenty seconds in the race, Rossi then refused to shake hands when the Spaniard tried to congratulate him on the slowing-down lap. Then he stopped and started sweeping up the track with a broom before donning a T-shirt boasting details of his new fictional cleaning company, La Rapida. 'We clear out rats,' he said. 'We disinfect, clear drains and clean starting grids.' Then, in a direct reference to his six-second penalty in Qatar, he added, 'We also do night jobs – all done in six seconds.' It was a classic example of Rossi's mind games: while the gag was funny to everyone else, the words were carefully chosen to wound and belittle those they were aimed at, in this case Gibernau, who Rossi clearly viewed as a 'rat'.

At the post-race press conference in Malaysia, Rossi rammed home another jibe at the Spaniard who had only managed to finish seventh in the race. 'For me, Sete did the best race of the season,' he said. 'He has given me a lot of points, which is like a big present. I am really grateful.'

In short, Rossi made it perfectly clear that Sete Gibernau was now persona non grata in his world: the gloves were off and no quarter would now be given. Rossi was going to take him apart in any way he could and his rival seemed to know it.

Nonetheless, Gibernau came out fighting like a Spanish bull in the next round in Australia and gave Rossi an epic race for his money. But no matter how hard he pushed, Rossi pushed more and stole the win by a tenth of a second to take his sixth world title and Yamaha's first in twelve years. The firm's last champion, Wayne Rainey (who had been paralysed in a crash in 1993), was full of praise for his successor and could see that Gibernau had been mentally beaten. 'He's just got Sete beat,' Rainey told *MCN*. 'Rossi knows he can just about blow on Sete and he will fold. It just so happens that Sete is the only guy with the speed to take the challenge to him. Mentally though, he's much weaker than Rossi.'[5]

Rossi's title win for Yamaha had consequences that reached far beyond the racetrack. Andrew Smith explains: 'It was incredible when he won the title at the first attempt. It was so motivational for the staff and, equally importantly, for the dealers. At a time when our product line-up was, at best, challenging, it gave us a whole new lease of life. I wouldn't say his title directly affected bike sales but it did wonders for the brand, and people were talking about Yamaha and we were getting much more press coverage. It was like a snowball effect – Rossi winning meant more Yamaha coverage, more interest, people coming into the dealerships talking about Rossi winning on a Yamaha... As far as generating coverage and enthusiasm for the brand, no one – and I mean *no one* – could have done more than Rossi did.'

It was only the second time in history that a rider had won consecutive premier class world titles on two different makes of bike. The first had been Eddie Lawson when he took the 1988 500cc world championship for Yamaha then repeated the feat on a Honda the following year. Rossi had done it the other way round, switching from Honda to Yamaha, but it was this achievement, above all others, that had the motorcycling press calling Rossi 'the greatest ever'. It was a title that would stick, though it would eventually morph into the GOAT – the Greatest of All Time.

Australia's Wayne Gardner, the 1987 500cc world champion and a contemporary of the aforementioned Lawson, happily ate humble pie after Rossi had pulled off the feat that Gardner never believed possible. 'I said he couldn't do it and he proved me wrong. He has just gone up ten levels in my book. I think he is probably the greatest rider in history. He is by far the best I have seen.'[6]

★

'Hijo de puta! Hijo de puta!' 'Son of a whore! Son of a whore!'

Rossi was accustomed to hearing his name being chanted at race meetings, but this was something entirely new to him. This was undistilled hatred – and he was on the receiving end of it. Thousands of Spanish fans joined in the insulting chant as he completed his victory lap at Jerez, the opening round of the 2005 MotoGP season.

Rossi had always been the beloved one, the charmed rider who could do no wrong, who counted every race as a home race. Adored wherever he went, he could always be assured of looking out on to grandstands filled with tens of thousands of fans dressed in his own brand of Rossi yellow. Now the love had turned to hate as the Spanish crowd bayed for his blood.

Local hero Sete Gibernau had led all but three laps of the 27-lap Jerez Grand Prix, but if he believed Rossi had calmed down over the winter and would now forgive and forget what had happened at Qatar the previous year, he got a rude awakening on the final lap of the race. It was Gibernau's home Grand Prix and he was desperate to win it and start the season with a victory. He very nearly managed it, too, and had he not riled his rival so much in 2004 Rossi might just have conceded defeat. Instead, he waited until the last corner of the last lap of the race before ramming his way up the inside of the Spaniard, clattering into his Movistar Honda, and knocking him off the track and into the gravel trap while he himself went on to win the race.

The pair were so far ahead of the rest of the field that Gibernau managed to get back on track and finish second, but the damage had been done – and it was extensive. Rossi, so accustomed to fans cheering his name, now had to get used to another chorus as tens of thousands of Spanish fans booed and chanted vitriolic slogans.

To his credit, Gibernau acted like a gentleman throughout the aftermath of the race. Unlike Rossi at Qatar, he accepted his rival's handshake, however stern his expression while doing so. The normally placid Spaniard was clearly furious, his body language speaking volumes both in parc fermé and on the podium, but Rossi remained unrepentant. 'There was enough space for me to pass him in the final corner,' he said at the post-race press conference. 'It was the only place where I could pass. We touched but motorbike races are sometimes like this. I know Sete is not happy, but there are going to be sixteen more races this year and there will be many more hard battles.'

Gibernau maintained a dignified silence, refusing to make any comment on the last lap, no matter how many times he was asked for his opinion. Perhaps he had learned from the Rossi/Biaggi feuds that there was little to be gained by making an enemy of the most popular man in racing: if you turned on Rossi, you turned on at least 60 per cent of MotoGP's fan base.

Whichever camp one was in, it was hard to deny that Gibernau had been treated roughly: deprived of a home win by what was, at best, a harsh move by Rossi and, at worst, a dangerous and unfair one. So the Italian's overly joyful celebrations on the podium did not sit comfortably with many and Rossi's squeaky-clean image became ever so slightly tarnished. It was the only time in his career that Rossi was booed during the podium ceremony.

But then, in a sport where the winning margins are so miniscule, each and every tiny advantage must be pursued and that includes gaining a psychological edge over your rivals and mentally upsetting them if the chance presents itself. Rossi was no fool; he had already been through this with Biaggi and had seen the demoralising effects of his constant jibes towards the Roman to the press. He and Gibernau had not started out as natural enemies, but as soon as the Spaniard became a legitimate threat on track – as he had over the last year – then Rossi sought to neutralise that threat in any way he could. Psychological dominance is part of the arsenal of weaponry at Rossi's disposal that has helped him become the greatest motorcycle racer of all time. What was becoming increasingly clear was that beneath the perma-smile, the curly locks, the post-race antics and the seemingly laid-back approach to life, Rossi was in fact a ruthless, driven and determined motorcycle racer. Of course, no sportsman reaches the top of his game without these attributes, but in Rossi they were so well disguised that it came as a bit of a shock when they revealed themselves. He was a smiling assassin – and all the more dangerous for it.

On the podium at Jerez, Sete Gibernau had looked like a beaten man, and he was. After the grid incident at Qatar, Rossi had reportedly vowed that Gibernau would never win another race (although he later denied saying this), and the Spaniard never did, despite racing in the top class for another two years. Rossi's work, by fair means or foul, was done. He had neutralised another threat to his continued dominance of MotoGP.

In fact, Rossi's second year on the Yamaha was even more dominant than the first, as dominant as he had ever been on the supposedly unbeatable Honda. In Rossi's absence, and without his highly rated development skills and feedback, Honda seemed to have lost its way, with neither Max Biaggi nor his team-mate Nicky Hayden able to take the lead in developing the bike to keep up with Rossi's Yamaha. By season's end the Yamaha was widely considered to be a better bike than the Honda, something unthinkable just two years before.

In 2005, Rossi took 11 wins (including six wins from the first seven races), 5 pole positions, 6 fastest laps, and finished the season a massive 147 points ahead of his nearest challenger, Marco Melandri – another all-time record. He won in the wet in China (his first wet race win on the Yamaha) and in Britain, and he took his fourth consecutive home win at Mugello, where he sported a mortar board on the podium in reference to the honorary degree in Communication Science that had just been bestowed upon him by the Carlo Bo University in Urbino, much to the chagrin of several Italian academics. He had just one non-finish all year (when he crashed out in Japan) and would finish on the podium in every other race, proving he was now devastatingly consistent as well as devastatingly fast. He also became the first Yamaha rider ever to win five Grands Prix in a row, and in Germany he equalled the late, great Mike Hailwood's tally of 76 wins to put him himself joint third in the all-time GP winners list. Only Giacomo Agostini (122) and Ángel Nieto (90) had more, but both those riders raced in more than one class, as was the norm back in their respective eras. In a respectful touch that was appreciated by Hailwood's family, Rossi posed with a poster he had made up that read

Above: A baby Valentino with his father, Graziano Rossi.   © *Olycom/Rex Features*

Below: Rossi, Sr and Jr.   © *Mondadori Portfolio / Getty*

Left: On the podium at
the French Grand Prix
in Le Castellet, Southern
France, 1997.

© *Florian Launette / Rex Features*

Right: Valentino waves to the
crowd while riding a victory
lap at the Malaysian Grand
Prix, 1997.

© *Mike Fiala / Rex Features*

Left: Riding with his hero,
road racing legend Kevin
Schwantz . . .

© *Kevin Schwantz*

Right: Kevin and Valentino
pose again with rally driving
legend Colin McRae (left).

© *Kevin Schwantz*

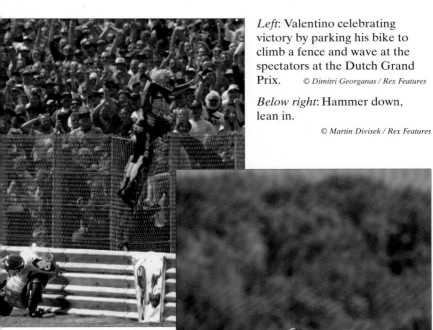

Left: Valentino celebrating victory by parking his bike to climb a fence and wave at the spectators at the Dutch Grand Prix. © *Dimitri Georganas / Rex Features*

Below right: Hammer down, lean in.

© *Martin Divisek / Rex Features*

Below: Jorge Lorenzo, Valentino Rossi, Jack Miller, Marc Márquez and Andrea Iannone pose during a photo opportunity in Valencia. © *Getty*

Left: Rivals: Showing down against Max Biaggi (in yellow) in 2004.

© *Enric Fontcuberta / Rex Features*

Right: And here taking on arguably an even fiercer rival, Marc Márquez (left), in 2019.

© *Ahmad Yusni / Rex Features*

Left: With friend and fellow racer, the late Marco Simoncelli. His death affected Rossi deeply. This was taken before the second day of testing at Sepang Circuit in Kuala Lumpur, on 23 February, 2011.

© *Mirco Lazzari / Getty*

Going. . . going. . .
gone… The thrills
and spills of life as
a MotoGP rider.

'Scrubs up alright':
Valentino Rossi's
private life can be a
closed book, but he
has dated a string
of beautiful women,
including Francesca
Sofia Novello (above)
and Linda Morselli
(right).

© NurPhoto / Miguel Benitez /
Getty Images

Left: Rossi is almost as good on four wheels as on two, and at one stage weighed up the possibility of a competitive switchover. Pictured here at the WRC rally in Hamilton, NZ, in November 2006.

© *Brendan O'Hagan / Getty*

Right: Rossi passes Gareth Jones after the latter crashed at the Wales Rally GB in 2008.

© *Carl De Souza / Getty*

Left: Rossi taking a spin at an F1 training session in Valencia, 2006. He would test for Ferrari a number of times over the years, apparently once causing Michael Schumacher's jaw to drop with amazement!

© *Sipa / Rex Features*

Above left: Popping a wheelie!

Above right and below: The hero returns to his hometown of Tavullia – and a sea of yellow support. Forza Rossi!

'76 Rossi, 76 Hailwood, I'm Sorry Mike'. As much as he could upset a crowd, like he did in Spain, he still knew how to charm one. 'I made a special flag to apologise to Mike Hailwood for matching his seventy-six wins because when another rider arrives at your level it's always disappointing,' Rossi said. 'Mike is one of the greatest riders ever and now I am beside him on the all-time winners' "podium" in Grand Prix, which is a fantastic achievement.'[7]

Sadly, Hailwood himself was not around to appreciate the gesture: he had been killed in a car crash in 1981, along with his young daughter, when struck by a truck performing an illegal U-turn.

By winning eleven races in the season, Rossi had not only equalled his best tally with Honda (set in 2001 and 2002) but had become the first Yamaha rider to win so many races in a season. And, in the firm's fiftieth-anniversary year, he handed his employers not only the rider's world title but also the team and constructor titles, the latter of which is most important to the manufacturers. Rossi's seventh world title, and his fifth consecutive title in the premier class, was secured in Malaysia with three rounds to spare. Happy and relaxed in the Yamaha team, Rossi resumed his post-race gags, this time joining fan club members dressed as Snow White and the Seven Dwarfs trackside – one for each title.

Gibernau had raced Rossi hard in 2005 and had come agonisingly close to taking wins but on every occasion that looked likely, Rossi had found the extra motivation to dig deeper and deprive him, if only to hold good on his supposed vow that Gibernau would never win another race.

The season simply could not have gone any better for Rossi. Win after win, record after record, he seemed completely unstoppable and made the greatest riders in the world look distinctly average. Marco Melandri probably summed up the 2005 season most succinctly when he noted: 'This championship is between Valentino and Rossi.' The rest were racing for second place.

In 2005, Rossi also became the first motorcycle racer to feature on the Forbes rich list, thanks to his previous year's estimated earnings of £24 million. What's more, his 'celebrity rating' saw him placed just behind former US president Bill Clinton. A motorcycle racer almost as well known as an American president? It would have been unthinkable before Rossi's time that a minority sport could produce such a household name: this was new territory for both Rossi in particular and MotoGP in general.

The demands on Rossi's time were by now overwhelming, as press officer Alison Forth witnessed first-hand. Forth had worked with top riders like Max Biaggi and Carlos Checa before, but when Rossi signed for the team the whole nature of her job changed. 'It was like being hit on the head with a sledgehammer!' she says. 'In the past we'd been very proactive in our marketing so we were always looking for coverage and there was quite a bit of demand for interviews with our riders, but when Rossi came in we were being approached by media titles that we could only have previously dreamed about, like *Rolling Stone* magazine [Rossi appeared on the cover of the Italian version of the magazine dressed as Elvis Presley under a title that read 'The King']. It opened up a whole new world of dealing with entertainment publications as opposed to just sporting ones.'

And the attention was truly global, whereas previously the demand had mostly been from the countries their riders came from. 'Suddenly we were being approached by titles from every single country. We had to turn a lot of requests down and my job became more like a press secretary rather than doing anything creative – it became like a booking agency job! We had to turn so many people down, even journalists that we'd previously been very friendly with, so you had to grow a thick skin because it didn't matter how nice they were to you, they had to get in line with everyone else.'

In her years working closely with Rossi, Forth found her charge to be professional and respectful, but she also sensed a shyness at the heart of him. 'I always found Valentino to be extremely professional to work with. He was so good in dealing with the media once an interview had been arranged. But I think he was quite guarded. We all see a certain version of Valentino on television and he is very self-assured, but I would almost go as far to say I think he's possibly a bit shy. That was my take on him, anyway. He was always incredibly respectful towards me and once we got him into position for an interview it ran like clockwork – there was no need for me to do anything as he ran it all himself: he's a very smart guy. But the demands on him were such that to get him into position was a nightmare. He was always running late because he couldn't physically get anywhere without being mobbed and held up. That put a lot of pressure on me because I was constantly having to back up and delay the interviews.'

Steve Parrish was covering MotoGP for the BBC at the time and remembers Rossi's desperate attempts to evade the madness that surrounded him. 'Uccio Salucci would ride the scooter through the paddock, with Rossi on the back, at breakneck speed so that they didn't get stopped by people. You'd always see the pair of them doing about 40mph everywhere so they didn't get stopped and pestered, but that's the kind of life Valentino had to lead after he became famous.'

Parrish also remembers that even the BBC had to get in line for an interview with Rossi. 'He was always great to work with and always very accessible, but we still only got a couple of one-on-one interviews per year and we always had to go through his press officer to arrange them at the start of each year – that's how much demand he was in. But you could talk to him all you wanted in the hospitality areas and you always got a good comment from him. He always had something sensible and interesting to say and never pulled any punches. So many of the other riders just gave you the same old corporate answers but he was never like that.'

Neil Hodgson raced against Rossi in MotoGP in 2004 and has been a presenter with BT Sport since 2014, so he's seen the constant demands on Rossi's time over many years of both racing against him and working with him. 'Week in, week out, there's always a horde of people standing near the Yamaha trucks trying to get a glimpse of him and you don't see that with any other rider. They all just want a glimpse of him and maybe a little wave – it's like getting a blessing from the Pope! I mean, those people will tell their grandchildren that they saw Valentino Rossi. You see fans dressed up like him, covered in Rossi tattoos – he has a fanatical following, more like a rock star than a motorbike racer. I mean, for me, the equivalent would be seeing Elvis Presley – I'd have felt the same way about seeing him.'

There were less obvious side effects of Rossi's fame too, as Andrew Smith remembers: 'The balancing act we faced was that, whenever Rossi attended a Yamaha product launch, he completely stole all the attention away from the product! He attended many new bike launches and when the president of Yamaha said some words on stage he would get a polite smattering of applause, but when Rossi would come on stage he would bring the house down like a rock star. We had to explain to the various presidents over the years that it wasn't the fact that they weren't popular or appreciated; it was just the Rossi effect. I remember Colin Edwards saying he'd come out of the garage when he was Rossi's team-mate and would hear the fans getting all excited and then he'd hear them saying, "Oh, it's only Colin."'

Amidst all the madness and chaos, Rossi still had to try to focus on doing his real job – winning races and championships. But it was becoming more and more difficult with all the distractions and the constant demands on his time. In 2006, he would take his eye off the ball and would lose his world title. He would finally be defeated.

CHAPTER 9

DEFEAT

'He is not a tax evader and the proof
is in his decision to pay.'
Lucio Monaco

Only four riders other than Rossi had won races in 2005:
Marco Melandri, Alex Barros, Loris Capirossi and the
young American, Nicky Hayden. With pop-star looks, long
hair, an all-American smile, impeccable manners and a
deep Kentucky drawl, Hayden was a sponsor's dream and
was being groomed as Repsol Honda's new boy wonder.
He was universally popular, second perhaps only to Rossi
among MotoGP fans. Hayden had won the AMA (American
Motorcyclist Association) Superbike championship in 2002
and made his debut in MotoGP the following year. After
being named rookie of the year in 2003 with fifth place
overall, his upward trajectory stalled somewhat in 2004 and
he only finished eighth, but he took his first win in 2005 at his

home round at Laguna Seca en route to third position in the championship, and by the start of the 2006 season Hayden was ready to challenge for the world title. He would be the first man to dethrone Rossi in the premier class since he took his first 500cc title in 2001.

Throughout his career Valentino Rossi had never truly tasted defeat. Of course he had lost races, and even championships, but the latter case scenario had only ever happened in his first year in each respective class – 125cc, 250cc and 500cc. After a learning year he always won and, since 2001, had kept on winning. In the six seasons he had spent in the premier class, he had won for five consecutive years. And then the wheels came off – or at least they started chattering.

'Chatter' is the name given to a little-understood clash of vibrations or frequencies between a bike's engine, its chassis, and the tyres the bike is on, and it causes the front wheel of the bike to stutter harshly under braking, leaving the rider with no other option than to slow down until the motorcycle stabilises again. It's severely restricting for a rider and there's no easy cure, just a long process of set-up changes and a step-by-step elimination of possible causes.

The 2006 Yamaha M1 suffered from chatter at certain circuits and made the opening of Rossi's season something of a rollercoaster ride. He suffered a very dangerous-looking crash at the first corner of the first round in Jerez, having been rammed by local rider Toni Elias, and was lying on the track as the whole pack surged past him just inches away. Uninjured, Rossi remounted and rode his badly damaged Yamaha to a heroic fourteenth place and two precious points. It wasn't the opening defence to his title he'd been hoping for and chatter was largely to blame: because of it, Rossi had only managed to qualify in ninth place, so in the race had found himself trying too hard to make up positions into the first corner when he was clipped by Elias. And yet, even after being knocked off his bike and scoring just 2 points, Rossi still maintained his sense of humour. 'His [Elias's] bike touched my helmet and I thought, "Fuck, now we have another ten behind!" But these things happen. Toni apologised after the race but I told him to don't worry… only to remember to brake next time and, if it is too late, to hit another bike instead of me!'[1]

But it wasn't just chatter that hindered Rossi in 2006. After winning in Qatar with a new chassis that helped the chatter issue, he then suffered tyre failure in China that robbed him of a finish, and in both France and America his engine blew up meaning he had three non-finishes in one season – not the kind of consistency that wins championships.

There would only be five victories in 2006, compared to eleven the year before, but Rossi still managed to turn a fifty-one-point deficit to Nicky Hayden into an eight-point advantage going into the final round at Valencia. All he needed to do was follow the American home in that final race and an eighth world title would be his.

Despite winning only two races Hayden had led the championship all year, thanks to more consistent finishes when he hadn't been able to win. Rossi only took the championship lead after the penultimate round in Portugal where Hayden had scored no points after being knocked off by his Repsol Honda team-mate Dani Pedrosa. It was, most people agreed, the only time anyone had seen the perpetually cheery American get angry. Rossi was pipped to the line in Portugal by Toni Elias and robbed of 5 points that would prove crucial in the outcome of the championship. It was Elias's only victory in MotoGP and he was absolutely no threat in the championship, but the repercussions of his one-off victory would be huge.

So it was one race to decide the championship. The whole season would be concentrated into just 30 laps or 74.67 racing miles. Rossi started from pole position while Hayden started on the second row in fifth place. The two men collided in the first corner of the first lap and Rossi was forced out wide but managed to avoid crashing and recovered to seventh place. But something was wrong; he was having tyre problems again, struggling for grip even so early in the race and, on top of that, the temperature gauge on his M1 Yamaha was climbing alarmingly. Was the engine about to blow up for a third time in the season? Whatever the problem, it was robbing Rossi of about 15 per cent of his bike's normal power output. He was caught in a classic catch-22 situation: badly needing to get in front of his rivals so his bike could suck in clean air to help cool the engine, yet so robbed of power he couldn't pass anyone and consequently was stuck behind a host other machines and the 'dirty' warm air they left in their wakes.

Then the unthinkable happened. Unthinkable, at least, for the usually dominant Rossi. At turn two on lap five he crashed and the championship seemed to be over. Unsure as to why he had crashed, Rossi managed to remount and rejoined the race at the back of the pack and out of the points. It was still mathematically possible to win the title but it would depend on where Hayden finished, on how many riders currently in front of Rossi retired from the race, and on how many he could manage to pass on his under-performing bike.

Randy de Puniet's crash out of thirteenth place promoted Rossi by one position, as did Alex Hoffman's crash on lap ten. Rossi managed to power past the even slower bikes of Garry McCoy and James Ellison, and then Chris Vermeulen crashed out and José Luis Cardoso pitted: four more places. Rossi was fourteenth and in the points but Hayden was running third – enough to win the title. With a gap of eight seconds to the next rider in front of him, Rossi could ultimately do no more than finish in thirteenth place while Hayden pulled off the shock of the season by finishing third, taking the MotoGP world championship, and becoming the first man to inflict a title defeat on Valentino Rossi since the beginning of the decade. He won the championship from Rossi by the slender margin of 5 points.

No one grudged Hayden the win. As one of the most popular men in the paddock, both with fans and riders, he was universally respected and loved in equal measure and conducted himself in a gentlemanly manner with everyone he encountered. He was also modest enough to know that luck had played a part in stealing the title from Rossi. 'I may not always have been the fastest but every race I've tried my hardest' he said after an emotional victory lap saw him ride helmetless in floods of happy tears. He also paid tribute to his friend and former Honda team-mate, Rossi. 'I have a ton of respect for Valentino Rossi. As we know, he's the GOAT [Greatest of All Time]. He's the one, in my opinion, who has done so much in our lifetime for MotoGP and put it at the level that it is. To be the guy that beat him... it wasn't easy. I had a couple of breaks. Everything went my way and to be able to beat him certainly made it extra special.'[2]

Rossi took the defeat well, at least in public. He'd had a hugely challenging season but had ridden magnificently to make up for all the points lost because of poor tyres, blown engines, chatter problems, and other riders knocking him off. It was the kind of year that tested a rider's real mettle and Rossi showed that, in defeat as well as in victory, he could learn and become stronger. 'It was a difficult race and we had some problems,' he said after the final round. 'I made a mistake off the start and another on the slide. I don't understand why I slid, but when you crash it is always a mistake. It's a big emotion this year, positive and negative. We were able to gain fifty-one points from Brno to arrive in front at the last race but, unfortunately, we lost. We did a lot of incredible victories but in life it is always possible to lose. Great congratulations to Nicky – he did a great job. He's a good guy and a great rider. He won. He's the best and I'm very happy for him.'[3]

But then Rossi and Hayden had always been, and would always remain, friends, so the defeat, as hard as it was to take, was perhaps made a little easier to swallow. Only years later did Rossi confess to having been a touch complacent during the 2006 season, of taking his success a little too much for granted. 'When you win five titles you think a sixth will happen,' he said. 'It is natural. I did not give my all in 2006.'[4]

Speaking some thirteen years after the event, Rossi still cited that Valencia race as the biggest regret of his career. It still pained him. 'Valencia in 2006, if I stayed calm and didn't crash, I would have won.'

Racing is full of 'ifs' and 'buts' and there were those who pointed out that Rossi would have won the title if only Toni Elias had not deprived him of those 5 points at Estoril in Portugal (Rossi would have then finished equal on points with Hayden but had more race wins, so would have taken the championship). Elias had also knocked Rossi off in Jerez earlier in the season, depriving him of even more points. And the Spaniard feels Rossi has never forgiven him for this. Speaking fourteen years after the event, Elias said, 'When I meet Valentino – I see him every year in Austin – I can see that he still has [Estoril, 2006] stuck in his heart; he has not forgiven me. It's over, it's time to be friends, but it is not possible. He is so competitive he will never forgive me!'

Nicky Hayden would never again truly challenge for the championship, but Rossi's next big rival would be a very different prospect and a very different character. In 2007, Rossi would have his first championship head-to-head with a young Australian rider who had already showed some promise on a satellite Honda in 2006. His name was Casey Stoner.

★

Born in Tamworth, New South Wales, in 1985, Casey Stoner was a straight-talking Aussie who had been racing motorcycles since he was four years old. He had climbed the ladder to MotoGP the hard way, his parents moving to England with him when he was just fourteen so he could get a foothold on the European racing stage. He had dominated the schoolboy dirt track scene in Australia but made his road-racing debut in the UK in the one-make Aprilia RS125 Challenge in 2000, winning the series at his first attempt. Money was scarce – his parents had sold up everything to take their son to Europe and the small family lived in their race truck, parked in the back yard of a friend's house – but that only made the gritty young Stoner even more determined. By 2002, he had earned a ride in the 125cc world championship and four years later was riding a satellite LCR Honda in MotoGP, taking a podium in only his third race. It was the kind of rapid career progression that Valentino Rossi had made and Stoner made it perfectly clear that he was a rider to watch, but when he switched to ride for the factory Ducati team in 2007 he reached another level, winning first time out in Qatar with a bike that made the most of the new MotoGP regulations.

Fearing the 990cc bikes were too fast and therefore too dangerous, MotoGP bosses brought in a lower capacity limit of 800cc for the 2007 season and Ducati engineers got the jump on their rivals by capitalising on the new regulations better than any other manufacturer. The Desmosedici was easily the fastest bike on the grid, able to blast past all its rivals on the longer straights. The Bridgestone tyres used by the team added another advantage and made for an overall package that was often unbeatable.

With less power than the previous MotoGP machines, the 800cc bikes had to be ridden more precisely and that meant there was only one ideal line around any given racetrack, since different lines through corners would affect acceleration out of them and the bikes didn't have enough grunt to overcome any shortcomings on the rider's part. The ruling made for more processional races because riders, all attempting to stay on that one perfect line, were less able to overtake. Consequently, most riders were not enthusiastic about the enforced change in regulations, but Stoner and the Ducati found an advantage and he hammered it home mercilessly, ultimately handing Ducati its first-ever premier class world championship title (and to this day, the only one). He won three of the first four races while Rossi struggled on his slower, though better-handling, Yamaha. By year end Stoner had taken ten wins to Rossi's four and finished a full 126 points ahead of him. Worse still, Rossi lost out on second place in the championship to Honda's Dani Pedrosa, beaten by a solitary point into the worst championship position he had ever finished a MotoGP season in. It was his second championship defeat in two years, to two different riders, riding two different makes of bike, and it looked, to some at least, like the bubble had burst, that the wonder kid had lost his mojo, that Rossi's meteoric career was on the slide. In MotoGP, you're only as good as your last result.

In a rare admission of fear, Rossi later confessed to being scared at times during the 2007 season. 'I took lots of risks because we were not competitive. When you're not fast enough you try to push more and it's dangerous. I was scared. But it's clever to be scared because this job can hurt.'[5]

There were other reasons why Rossi was glad to see the back of 2007. He had been deeply upset when his friend and rallying hero Colin McRae lost his life in a helicopter crash on 15 September. On the following day, Rossi won the Portuguese Grand Prix and dedicated his victory to the late Scotsman. 'Colin is one of my idols and it's because of him that I have my passion for rally,' he said. 'I am glad that I could win for him today.'

After enduring his worst-ever season in MotoGP and suffering the loss of his friend, Rossi then found himself in serious trouble with the Italian tax authorities, who had been investigating him on suspicion of tax evasion. At the heart of the dispute was Rossi's claim that he was genuinely domiciled in the United Kingdom when he appeared to spend so much time in Italy. 'Everybody in the world knows I have lived in London, an extraordinary city, since 2000,' Rossi said in his defence. 'Naturally I go back to Italy to see my family, friends and to take holidays.'[6] But as evidence to the contrary, the Italian tax authorities cited the fact that Rossi owned a villa in Tavullia, an apartment in Milan, had eight cars insured in Italy and a boat moored on the Adriatic coast near Tavullia. They also questioned his application for a broadband connection at his villa in Tavullia, a seemingly trivial but actually important matter: if he was living in London, why did he need a broadband connection in Italy? The outcome was a demand that Rossi pay €110 million in taxes for the period 2001–2004. During that time, the agency calculated he had avoided paying €43.7 million in personal income taxes, business taxes and VAT payments, meaning that, together with fines and interest, he had accrued this overall bill.

Even for a man of Rossi's wealth it was a huge sum and, while he protested his innocence on Italian television and in the press, saying, 'The professionals who handle my income declarations have assured me that they respected the rules,' the authorities believed otherwise.

There were very genuine fears that Rossi might face criminal prosecution and even jail after tax inspectors reported him to the public prosecutor's office in his home province of Pesaro. *Italy Magazine* reported that Rossi's residency in London enabled him to take advantage of favourable tax conditions such as only declaring earnings made in the UK and avoiding taxes on his big-money merchandising and personal sponsorship contracts.[7] The Italian tax authorities pointed out that Rossi had only declared earnings of €500 in Italy in 2002 and stressed again that while he was resident in London, he was not domiciled there.

Among the 'professionals' Rossi referred to was Luigino 'Gibo' Badioli, who had been his manager since 1997. An old family friend and former furniture salesman from Tavullia, Badioli managed Rossi under the umbrella of his Great White London management company and had also declared himself domiciled in the UK. He was also placed under investigation for tax evasion amounting to €10 million. Of that sum, the court alleged that some €7 million was reinvested in Italy through various trust companies. Badioli appealed but lost his case and in February 2014 was sentenced to three years in prison.

Valentino, on the other hand, came to an arrangement

with the tax authorities and agreed to pay a total sum of €35 million. At the press conference held in Pesaro after coming to the arrangement, Rossi said the earlier figure of €110 million was merely 'a threat to start talks' but stated that he was satisfied with the outcome, however big a dent it made in his personal fortune. 'I am happy with how this issue has been resolved. It is a high figure, but it is more important to be calm, serene and happy.'

Italy's junior economy minister, Vincenzo Visco, who was at the time leading a government crackdown on chronic levels of tax evasion which was destroying Italy's economy, said of the case, 'I'm a great fan of Rossi and I'm sorry about this but the law is the law. A singular situation has been created in which it is enough, on the basis of British law, to create a more or less fictitious residency in London in order to avoid paying taxes in one's own country.'[8]

During the investigation it emerged that Rossi was paid €12 million by Yamaha and earned a further €25 million from sponsorship and merchandising deals, easily making him the highest-paid motorcycle racer of all time. His €35-million settlement with the tax authorities was not the only damage caused by his financial indiscretions – he had also tarnished his hitherto angelic public image.

Rossi's lawyer at the time, Lucio Monaco, told Italian newspaper *Il Resto del Carlino*, 'He suffered too much because of this story – a lot more than people can imagine. He is not a tax evader and the proof is in his decision to pay: he didn't want a war but a fair agreement.' His business consultant Victor Uckmar added, 'It's a sacrifice Rossi has done for the sake of his career. He didn't want the oppression of the tax office investigation to go on for a decade. If not for his racing, he's done it to leave these worries behind.'[9]

In February of 2008, after the case was finally settled, Rossi moved back to Tavullia full time, declared his taxes in Italy from then onwards, and set up his now famous VR|46 business, which acted as his own management company and was to be administered by Rossi himself. From now on he would be his own manager.

The tax case had been a hugely expensive interlude and a serious and highly stressful distraction which most observers agreed must have affected Rossi's performances on track. But Steve Parrish believes he would have mostly been able to put it out of his mind once he was on the bike. 'I think a good rider can put anything out of his mind during a race, whether you're going through a divorce or the loss of a loved one or whatever. I mean the tax thing would no doubt have been an aggravation for Rossi *before* he got on the bike and that probably didn't do him any favours, but once you get on a 500cc bike or a MotoGP bike it doesn't matter what's going on in your normal life – you're forced to focus. It might affect your build-up to the race but once the visor's down and you're away, nothing else matters. It must have been very awkward for him having to deal with all that, though.'

Back at home in his beloved Italy and with the tax problem under control, Rossi could prepare to face his racing rivals with a new focus in 2008. After losing out on the title for two consecutive years, speculation that had already been rife for some time reached a crescendo: Rossi would quit MotoGP and drive for Ferrari in Formula One. As fanciful as it sounded, it was in fact a very real possibility. Rossi had started his racing life on go-karts and had often said that his future would probably be on four wheels, but it had initially appeared that those four wheels would be on a rally car rather than a Formula One car.

While he had competed in the annual Michelin Race of Champions event in 2000 and 2001 and had also beaten several established rally stars in the Bologna Rally Sprint in 2001, Rossi's first foray into a proper world championship rally came in 2002 when he entered the Rally of Great Britain. His debut on the world stage didn't last long, however; he crashed out just fifteen minutes and ten miles into the second stage and got his Peugeot 206 wedged on a tree stump. So bad did Rossi feel about his early exit that he almost gave up any further idea of car racing. 'The way I feel at the moment I'm not sure if I will come back next year,' he said when he could finally bring himself to speak.

Completely disgusted with himself, Rossi was already driving back to London when Michelin – the tyre company that had secured his drive – tried to arrange some television interviews with him. In fact, he was so keen to exit stage left that he even left his mobile phone in the Peugeot.

The late world rally champion Colin McRae had been sympathetic at the time. 'Conditions out there were pretty difficult, even for experienced guys,' he said. 'I ran off and a couple of others also had problems. It wasn't the easiest day to be making your debut.'

In fact McCrae, a big bike-racing fan, had warned Rossi that the Welsh stages were among the most treacherous and difficult of the year and far from ideal in terms of making a debut, but with Rossi's schedule being so tight it was the only round he could contest. Once he had got over his disappointment, Rossi hinted at a future on four wheels for the first time. 'I love rally so maybe it's possible I could come and do the world championship,' he said.

There were positive signs, however. He had finished twenty-seventh in the Cardiff Special Stage, just eight seconds behind McRae and, in the rally itself, his co-driver Carlos Cassina had been impressed before the crash. 'Everything up to that point had been brilliant,' he said. 'He had not made a single mistake.'

Rossi's early exit from the race did not dent anyone's belief that he would be as natural on four wheels as he was on two. John Surtees remains the only man to have won world championships on two wheels and four (he took seven motorcycle Grand Prix titles between 1958 and 1960 and won the Formula One world championship in 1964) and there was great excitement at the prospect of Rossi trying to emulate the Englishman's feat. So when, in 2002, Rossi announced his plans for a test drive in the Honda-engined BAR F1 car, even F1 mogul Bernie Ecclestone got excited, spotting the potential for an immediate boost of F1's global image and appeal. 'Teams and sponsors manipulate the image of drivers and flatten them out, controlling them too much,' he said. 'Characters don't emerge – we need someone like Valentino Rossi.'[10]

Even Surtees himself had faith in the Italian. 'Rossi will have a lot to learn but you either have natural speed or you don't,' he said. 'I think Valentino has the speed and he'll know straight away if he wants to do it.'[11]

Ultimately, the BAR test never happened but the prospect of an F1 test reared its head again when Rossi signed for Yamaha in 2004, this time with Toyota, a firm that had close links with Yamaha. But as things turned out, Rossi got his first taste of an F1 car not in a BAR or a Toyota but in a Ferrari F3002 – and he kept it secret from his team, from his sponsors and from Yamaha. After Rossi's stance against tobacco sponsorship had softened (money ultimately talks), his Yamaha team was was sponsored by Gauloises in

2004, whereas the Ferrari sported Marlboro colours. It also ran on Bridgestone tyres rather than the Michelins Rossi was contracted to use in MotoGP. Failing to inform Yamaha of the test would have resulted in most riders facing the sack (especially as Toyota owned five per cent of Yamaha and wanted him to test its car), but the fact that Rossi could apparently do as he pleased proved just how much power he now had in the MotoGP world and how much Yamaha was prepared to bow to his every whim in order to keep hold of the goose that laid their golden eggs. It seems inconceivable that Honda would have been so lenient with Rossi, but Yamaha team boss Davide Brivio meekly said, 'We weren't aware Valentino was going to test the car... But there is nothing to stop him driving any car in his free time, which he sometimes does for training purposes.'

An odd statement, given that at no time in history had a motorcycle Grand Prix rider ever used a priceless F1 Ferrari for 'training purposes'. And it wasn't just any Ferrari, it was six-times F1 champion Michael Schumacher's car – and the very one he would use to take a seventh world title later that year. Rossi even wore Schumacher's helmet in a vain attempt at disguise.

The test took place at Ferrari's private Fiorano test track in Italy, shielded from the press and spectators and, having swapped 230bhp for 900bhp, Rossi spun the Ferrari a couple of times (the first time being on the very first corner of his opening lap) but completed around twenty laps and posted a time around three seconds off Schumacher's best. No mean feat for a first attempt, especially given that Schumacher had lapped the Ferrari test track thousands of times. While the bike-riding German was impressed with Rossi's pace, he maintained reservations about whether he could make it to the very top of the sport. 'It took him a while to get used to it but he was very impressive by the end of the day,' he said. 'He has great ability. I would probably say he would come in at a certain level, which may be competitive, but to reach the final bit is usually difficult.'[12]

There had been a very realistic chance that Rossi would switch to F1 after his contract with Yamaha expired at the end of 2005. After all, what more was there to achieve in motorcycle racing? Rossi had always relished the challenge of moving up classes, changing bikes, switching manufacturers and moving from two-strokes to four-strokes. He would still only be twenty-six years old when his Yamaha contract expired; young enough to work his way up in F1, a sport that is not quite as youth-obsessed as MotoGP tends to be. Rossi, however, downplayed the test, claiming it was only to 'understand what a Formula One car is like'. It was the downforce and braking capabilities that impressed him most. He said, 'On a bike you feel like you have more space and you feel more free but in the car it feels like you are in prison. In the car, what impresses more is how it feels like it is being sucked to the track – and the braking capacity is incredible.'

Rossi had another test in the Ferrari in the middle of 2005 and claimed he was beginning to understand the handling of the car. Then, in a pre-season test in 2006, he finally appeared in public and against a whole grid of top F1 drivers too, including Schumacher, Fernando Alonso, Jenson Button, Felipe Massa, Nico Rosberg and Mark Webber. By now, after just two short tests spread over the course of two years, Rossi was impressively up to speed, lapping just 0.7 seconds off Schumacher's pace – and that was in an older-spec car with an older-spec engine than the F1 legend's. Even Schumacher seemed to be getting nervous, saying simply, 'I didn't give him any advice – he doesn't need it.'

Of the fifteen drivers who participated in the test, Rossi finished with the ninth fastest time, ahead of big names like Mark Webber, David Coulthard and Jarno Trulli – all Formula One race winners. It was a seriously impressive performance and Schumacher was now telling the press that Rossi could move to F1 immediately and be competitive.

Graziano Rossi said his son came 'very, very close' to switching to a full-time career in F1 in 2006 but the closest he actually came to racing for Ferrari was when its driver, Felipe Massa, was injured at the 2009 Hungarian Grand Prix and ruled out of the Italian GP at Monza. Ferrari bosses were quick to spot the publicity potential of fielding Rossi in a one-off drive. An Italian motorcycling legend driving the most famous Italian car in the Italian Grand Prix at Monza? It would have been the greatest dream of all for the hordes of Tifosi and would have garnered more column inches for Ferrari around the world than any other move they could have made. But Rossi only races to be competitive and he knew that, without testing, he could easily have looked very average and damaged his hard-earned reputation. He said no. 'I talked with Ferrari about racing at Monza,' he admitted, 'but without testing it would not have been logical. We already decided that to enter Formula One without testing is more risky than fun. You can't go there and do everything to understand the car in three days.'

Rossi would drive a Ferrari again – in 2010 he tested a 2008-spec car – but never quite so seriously. His future, he decided, was on two wheels where he had more control over his racing. 'Formula One drivers are like robots,' he complained. 'They operate under instructions from the engineers over the radio. I prefer motorcycles. When I race, I like to make my own strategy and my own decisions.'[13]

It had been a very near thing, though. 'I really thought about going,' Rossi later said. 'I had a great test in Fiorano, about a second off the lap record, and that made the decision difficult. Then I went to Valencia and drove alongside the other F1 drivers, experiencing the atmosphere and the media pressure, and I made my decision.'[14]

Having decided against a switch to F1, Rossi nevertheless continued to race rally cars from time to time and enjoyed some considerable success behind the wheel. Colin McRae showed Rossi the ropes when he first expressed an interest in rallying and in 2006 the pair competed against each other in the Monza Rally and Rossi came out on top in his Subaru Impreza, proving yet again that, should he decide to commit himself fully to either F1 or rallying, he could be genuinely competitive. In fact, his victory over McRae started a host of new rumours that he would switch to the World Rally Championship in 2007 when his second two-year deal with Yamaha came to an end, but the lure of bikes and MotoGP was too strong and his future rally appearances would be in addition to his bike racing, not in place of it.

And very impressive appearances they were too. In 2006, Rossi came eleventh out of thirty-nine competitors in the Rally of New Zealand driving a Subaru Impreza WRC04, and in 2008 he completed the British WRC round in twelfth place in a Ford Focus RS WRC07. 'I have always loved rally, ever since I was little,' he said. 'It is one of my great passions and it is great to do one when I have the time and the chance. I always enjoy it a lot and, when I have given up the bikes, I will do more.'[15]

The Rally of Monza had become an annual outing for

Rossi and in 2018 he took his seventh win after clean-sweeping all nine stages. He is now the most successful driver in the event's history, two victories clear of Le Mans 24 Hour winner Rinaldo Capello. But as much as he enjoys driving a rally car, and as much as he treasured the experience of testing an exotic F1 car, Rossi's heart has always been in motorcycles, and at the end of 2007 he signed another two-year extension on his Yamaha deal. He was staying in MotoGP after all. He wanted his title back. The only problem was that the man he had to wrestle it from was Casey Stoner and, unlike Max Biaggi and Sete Gibernau, he was made of sterner mental stuff and was immune to Rossi's psychological warfare. Making matters even more difficult was the fact that Stoner's chief motivation to hold onto his world title was a simple one: he really didn't like Valentino Rossi. 'It is important to me that people realise I always have a lot of respect for all of my competitors but I can't say that about Valentino because I feel he shows none in return,' Stoner wrote in his 2013 autobiography, *Casey Stoner: Pushing the Limits*. 'He rarely accepts when he has been beaten by the better man on the day; if he gets beaten it's because the other rider's bike is better.'[16]

Against a hardened and determined foe like Stoner, the 2008 season would prove to be one of the toughest Valentino Rossi had ever faced and he would have to dig deeper than ever before if he was to come out on top.

CHAPTER 10

INVICTUS

'I'd have preferred a bit of a cleaner battle.
I've lost a bit of respect for him.'
CASEY STONER

*T*hings had started to get nasty in MotoGP in 2007, especially if you were Casey Stoner. When Nicky Hayden took the world title from Valentino Rossi in 2006 there had been no bad feeling towards him among most Rossi fans; he was a friend of Valentino, so there was no bad blood. The same could not be said of Stoner when he deprived Rossi of the title in 2008.

Because of the dangers involved in motorcycle racing the fans have always shown great respect for all the riders who are out there quite literally risking their lives. That started to change in 2007, as Stoner explained: 'Around that time I became the target of a lot of hatred, especially from Valentino's many followers,' he wrote in his 2013 autobiography. 'The first signs of it began to show in 2007 when I started beating him. Mum used to get some nasty emails.'[1]

At the 2008 Day of Champions event (an annual charity bash that runs ahead of the British Grand Prix), Stoner, like all the other riders, gave up his own free time to make a public appearance and help raise money for the good cause. But as Rossi's main rival, he was booed when he came onstage. This was new territory for motorcycle racing and it left a bad taste in many people's mouths, not least Stoner's who refused to participate in any future events.

But there was worse. After crashing in practice for the British Grand Prix that same year, the Australian was being given a ride back to the paddock on the back of a scooter when he suddenly found himself under attack. 'There were people swearing and spitting at me, a couple of them even jumped in front of us trying to make the guy riding the scooter lose control or crash.'[2]

These were scenes more reminiscent of football matches where tribal loyalty is everything and the 'us and them' mentality prevails: it had no place in motorcycle racing. Stoner had, after all, been doing his bit for a life-saving programme in Africa in the first instance and had just survived a potentially lethal crash in the second. Yet there was an element amongst Rossi's vast fan base who hated Stoner simply because he was as fast (and even faster, on many occasions) than their hero. Of course, Rossi himself could not be blamed for the behaviour of others, nor did he condone such behaviour, but it reflected badly on him nonetheless – if only because the protagonists were all wearing Rossi merchandise. 'For so many years Valentino had been their hero,' Stoner said, 'and anybody who came along to challenge him was the bad guy, whether it was Max Biaggi, Sete Gibernau, Jorge Lorenzo or myself.'

If the Rossi fans hated Casey Stoner, they would soon learn to hate Jorge Lorenzo even more. At just twenty-one years old, the Spaniard was already a double 250cc world champion and had been signed as Rossi's Yamaha team-mate for his debut season in MotoGP in 2008. Like Biaggi, he was another intense character; egotistical and volatile, he was no stranger to losing control in the paddock, to taking a swing at his mechanics or to throwing his helmet around and stomping off in a mood if things weren't going his way. Lorenzo had been groomed to be a MotoGP rider from a very young age by his domineering father, who schooled him in every aspect of the sport – even going so far as conducting fake interviews with his son to prepare him for the later attentions of the press. And then there were the acting classes: Lorenzo understood that Rossi had moved the goalposts in the entertainment stakes and that he would need to offer something more than just race wins if he was to become anywhere near as popular. To that end, he took drama classes in London in order that he could appear to be more engaging, flamboyant and theatrical. To cite just one instance of his eagerness to appeal, Lorenzo had gone to the trouble of tracking down and gaining permission to borrow the actual costume worn by Russell Crowe in the movie *Gladiator* for his podium appearance after winning the 250cc world title in 2007 .

Perhaps more importantly to Rossi, whose theatricality came completely naturally, Lorenzo was a huge Max Biaggi fan. 'He was the first person I was watching,' the Spaniard said. 'I really like him, you know, and I want to become like him.' It was only a matter of time before the harmony that had existed in the Yamaha garage when Colin Edwards was Rossi's team-mate was shattered. Rossi and Lorenzo were clearly not going to get along.

Lorenzo's debut in the MotoGP championship was hugely impressive. He set pole position in the first three rounds, was second and third in the first two races and then won the third: better even than Rossi had managed in his debut season in the premier class. A series of heavy crashes dented his championship challenge, however, and he would finish the year in fourth place without taking another win. But the speed was there and once the consistency was too, Lorenzo would prove to be a formidable competitor. And for that reason alone he also experienced the uglier side of a certain element of Rossi's fan base. 'There are these other scumbags – disrespectful and bad-mannered people – who are Rossi fanatics and get enjoyment out of insulting us,' he said. 'They almost want me dead!'[3]

Lorenzo did, however, acknowledge that Rossi himself did all he could to address this nastier element amongst his fan base. After the Misano race in 2009, Lorenzo said, 'On the podium he tried to hush the fans who were whistling at me.'

There would be some serious clashes with Lorenzo in the future but for now Rossi had his hands full with Casey Stoner as the two fought tooth-and-nail for the 2008 MotoGP crown. And Rossi was under no illusions about how good his rival really was. 'Stoner has a great talent and sometimes it's impressive how fast he is. In three laps he make the lap record and you say, "Fuck! Impressive!" But if you work step by step it's possible to fight with him.'

First blood went to Stoner in Qatar while Rossi came home fifth, struggling to adapt to the Bridgestone tyres he had elected to run since they had worked so well for Stoner on the Ducati the previous year. Next time out at Jerez it was Dani Pedrosa's turn to win on the Honda with Rossi second and Stoner struggling to eleventh after running off track and fighting his way back from last place. Lorenzo took his debut win at round three in Portugal with Rossi third and Stoner sixth. It wasn't until China that Rossi finally found his form and took his first win of the season while Stoner claimed third. A further win in France saw Rossi move to the top of the championship points table for the first time in the season. It was his ninetieth Grand Prix victory and placed him second equal with Ángel Nieto in the all-time winner's list; only Giacomo Agostini now had more wins. To mark the occasion, Rossi took Nieto for a pillion ride on his victory lap. 'To arrive at ninety wins and equal Ángel's record is a dream for me,' he admitted. 'I had quite a lot of pressure because Ángel was waiting with the special leathers to join me on the bike so I really needed to win! It was great to ride with him.'[4]

Nieto had been a thirteen-times world champion in the 50cc and 125cc classes between 1969 and 1984 and was still heavily involved in the Grand Prix paddock as a team owner. Sadly, he was killed in 2017 following a road traffic accident in Ibiza. He was seventy years old.

Another home win in Mugello – his seventh in succession at the Italian circuit – allowed Rossi to pull a forty-six-point lead over Stoner in fourth place. The Catalan Grand Prix went Pedrosa's way, with Rossi and Stoner finishing second and third respectively, while Stoner ruled the roost at Donington and had to endure the aforementioned abuse from certain Rossi fans. Rossi finished second at Donington, but Stoner had moved up to third in the title standings and after Rossi could only limp home in eleventh place at Assen after a first-lap crash (Stoner won the race), he dropped to second in the standings, 4 points behind Pedrosa, with Stoner just 25 points behind him. Another win for Stoner in Germany reduced the points gap to just 20 and then came the American Grand Prix and one of the most audacious moves that Valentino Rossi ever pulled off.

Struggling all year to match the top-end speed of Stoner's Ducati, Rossi was forced to get very creative in his overtakes at Laguna Seca, so much so that he pulled a move no one had ever seen before, let alone thought possible. The race was an all-time classic battle between youth and experience, between the outright speed of Stoner and the superior race craft of Rossi. The levels of aggression throughout the tussle proved that Rossi was not too old and over the hill as some were suggesting, and the race ultimately decided the 2008 MotoGP world championship. And after so many overtakes throughout the thirty-two laps it all came down to one outrageous move at the Corkscrew.

The Corkscrew is a notorious piece of racetrack; a steep, downhill, left-right chicane that drops 18 metres in just over 450 metres of track length – equivalent to the height of a five-and-a-half-storey building. Rossi forced his way past Stoner on the entrance to the left-hander but was carrying too much speed and ran over the kerb onto the inside of the track at the right-hand corner that immediately followed, his Yamaha M1 kicking up dust and stones and bucking and weaving as it tried to find traction. When Rossi rejoined the track he ran out wide, taking Stoner with him and forcing him to the very edge of the track. It was enough to gain a slight advantage and Rossi was never headed again. Stoner later suffered a slow-speed crash of his own making but was still so far ahead of the rest of the field that he was able to remount and finish second. But he was far from happy with Rossi's riding and made no secret of it. After refusing to shake the Italian's offered hand in parc fermé, Stoner said, 'I've been racing for many years but for me some passes went past the point. I was disappointed by the way he was riding. I frigging nearly went into the gravel so many times. I'd have preferred a bit of a cleaner battle. I've lost a bit of respect for him.'[5]

Rossi disagreed that he had ridden over the edge of acceptability. 'I am sorry that Casey thinks some of the passes were a bit strong but I really don't agree. I passed only on the brakes, I braked in the same places every time and we never touched. Of course, this was an aggressive race but it was definitely a fair one.'[6]

Rossi was ecstatic, not only because he had beaten Stoner, but because he had finally mastered the new tyres that had proved to be such a headache for him. 'In 2008, I switched to Bridgestone tyres,' he said. 'It was one of the greatest challenges of my life, after switching to Yamaha, and Laguna was the race where all my efforts paid off.'[7]

For more neutral observers than Casey Stoner it ranked as one of the greatest victories of Rossi's career and it marked the turning point of his season. After crashing out at Laguna (though still managing to remount and finish), Stoner had another two falls at Brno and Misano while Rossi not only won in America but in the next four rounds as well. His fifth consecutive win came at Motegi in Japan and it was enough to secure his eighth world title with three rounds to spare. It was his sixth premier-class world title and his haul of nine wins in 2008 put him clear of Giacomo Agostini at the top of the all-time winners list in the premier class with sixty-nine wins to Ago's sixty-eight. Since the inauguration of the Grand Prix world championships in 1949, no rider had won more 500cc/MotoGP races than Valentino Rossi – and he had won those races in an era of fierce competition and evenly matched motorcycles, whereas Agostini, for many of his wins, had the luxury of running the only factory machine on the grid and was therefore often able to lap most of the competition, such was his advantage.

Agostini had been the only rider to ever regain the premier-class title after having lost it for two years, but now Rossi had repeated the feat and could legitimately lay claim to being the greatest motorcycle racer of all time. And he wasn't finished yet – in the middle of the season he signed another two-year deal with Yamaha. The distraction of perhaps switching to Formula One or the World Rally Championship was over. MotoGP had won: Rossi was coming back for more.

★

Few riders can claim to have been a genuine threat to Valentino Rossi in his prime, but those that were fast enough, almost to a man, noted how the Italian's attitude towards them changed. While he had never liked Max Biaggi, Rossi had been friendly enough with Casey Stoner before the Australian started beating him regularly. 'As soon as I became a fierce competitor everything was different but it wasn't me who changed,' Stoner said. Marco Melandri, who had been a close friend of Rossi's for years before he started winning races in 2005, noted the same shift in attitude: 'When I started to race well with him he changed a lot. When we were growing up we were very good friends. Valentino plays games with everybody… the way he talked to the media – he tries to never say something good about you.'[8]

Sete Gibernau was another rider who had started out as a friend but eventually became an enemy when he was fast enough to pose a threat and, following the incident at Qatar in 2004 when Gibernau's team protested Rossi's team for cleaning his grid spot, the friendship was over. 'He blamed me but it was nothing I did. Of course I didn't report him – I didn't even see what happened. I'd had a very good relationship with Valentino for many years but after that it just came around,' Gibernau said.[9]

Rossi's new-for-2008 Yamaha team-mate Jorge Lorenzo would become another classic example. Rossi had taken great umbrage at Yamaha's decision to sign the Spaniard, a clear indication that he viewed him as a serious threat. He had supposedly managed to block the manufacturer's plans to sign Casey Stoner in 2006, but Lorenzo's deal with Yamaha had reportedly been done before Rossi knew anything about it. Colin Edwards had been a safe team-mate for Rossi in the Yamaha camp between 2005 and 2007, never threatening him for the title and failing to score a race win, but he had been a good number two rider, maintaining a good relationship with Rossi and ensuring there was always harmony in the garage. That would all end with the signing of Jorge Lorenzo.

While the two were never close enough to be called friends, Rossi and Lorenzo had at least managed to be civil towards each other in 2008, despite the fact that there was a dividing wall down the centre of their garage at every race meeting. It had initially been erected because Rossi was running Bridgestone tyres (having had issues with Michelins for the past two seasons) while Lorenzo was on Michelins, so the rival companies quite naturally wished to protect their respective secrets. But in 2009, MotoGP switched to a one-tyre rule – with Bridgestone as the sole provider – in an attempt to keep costs down and to give every rider the same level of tyre support. And yet the wall in the garage remained firmly up – at Rossi's insistence. 'It was Valentino's decision, not mine,' Lorenzo said. 'But now that we are both on the same tyres the wall is not necessary.'

'If Lorenzo wants to, he can pull his side of the wall down,' Rossi responded, 'but I'll be keeping mine.'

In another highly unusual move, Rossi refused to let Lorenzo see his data – something that is standard practice among team-mates so both riders can work towards developing the machine into a better package. While his employers were not pleased about the wall, they nonetheless bowed to Rossi's request for it to stay in place. 'Yamaha was absolutely not happy about the dividing wall,' says former employee Andrew Smith. 'But I think it showed just how much power Rossi had at that time.'

Not all top sportsmen feel the need to hate their rivals but it's far more common than not. Four-times World Superbike champion Carl Fogarty was a classic example. He, like Rossi, had several fierce rivals over the years, but America's Scott Russell was the strongest and therefore the most hated. 'I probably needed to hate him because he wanted to win as badly as I did,' Fogarty admitted years after he had stopped racing. 'The rivalry intensified my aggression and made me a better and more focused rider.'

Rossi clearly felt the same. 'You have to hate your enemy, yes, but it depends in which way. I mean, it's possible to hate your enemy on the track but have a quite good relationship away from the track. Not a good friend, but civil.'[10]

In a sport that is won or lost by split seconds, a rider must use every weapon at his disposal and if hating a rival gave him added aggression and the motivation to push just that bit harder to secure a win, then Rossi was quite happy to hate. Hate made him faster. And in 2009 he loved to hate Jorge Lorenzo, even if the Spaniard did not share this philosophy. 'I'm not one of those who think that just because you are my rival, you can't be my friend,' he said.

Lorenzo would prove to be Rossi's main rival after Casey Stoner was forced to sit out three races in the second half of the 2009 season. The former world champion had to undergo an exhaustive battery of tests before being diagnosed with lactose intolerance, which had led to him suffering from chronic fatigue. He came back and won two out of the last three races but the condition seriously affects Stoner to this day, with the lightest of exercise resulting in utter exhaustion for days afterwards. But in the back-sniping world of the MotoGP paddock it was assumed that Stoner's mystery illness was all in his head and that Rossi had got to him just like he had Max Biaggi and Sete Gibernau.

With the Australian unable to mount a season-long challenge for the title it fell to Lorenzo to pick up the gauntlet and he proved very willing and able to do so. The situation with Lorenzo was a strange one: Rossi was now such a veteran that he was racing against riders who had grown up supporting him, and Lorenzo was one such rider. Despite having been a fan of Max Biaggi, he had openly declared that Rossi was the greatest motorcycle racer of all time and had contributed more to the sport than anyone else: 'He has had more impact than any other rider in history; he's done more than anybody to help the sport grow and he has given motorcycling a whole new dimension.'[11]

As well as studying Rossi's riding techniques and race craft, Lorenzo and his psychologist even went so far as to study Rossi's character in a bid to understand why he was so popular and how Lorenzo could change his own character to become more so. The crucial difference was that Rossi's hugely engaging character was completely natural, not contrived, and any attempt to 'design' such a character must surely be doomed to failure. But it was a compliment, nonetheless. In fact, it wouldn't be too much of a stretch to say that Lorenzo was, initially at least, a Rossi super-fan: 'He's got everything… He brakes well, really hard. He has good corner speed, he accelerates well. He is a great strategist and he wins a lot of races with his head. He's just extremely fast… He's very strong when it comes to a mental battle and he has talent.'[12]

But Lorenzo was fast too and Valentino Rossi knew it, which is why there was no possibility of them being friends as long as they were racing against each other. There was now a psychological, as well as a physical, wall between the two riders, and Rossi's dislike of his team-mate only increased when Lorenzo out-performed him in the early part of the 2009 season. From the first four races Rossi only managed one win to Lorenzio's two and also had to suffer the indignity of coming last in France – the first time he had ever done so.

In fact, the entire French race was a catalogue of disasters for Rossi but he never gave up and never stopped trying. It was declared a wet race, so all the riders (including Rossi) started on wet tyres. Five laps in, as the track began to dry out, Rossi took a gamble and was the first rider to come into the pits to change to his number two bike, which was fitted with slick tyres. No sooner had he rejoined the race than he caught a wet patch and crashed out, snapping the gear lever and smashing the screen on his Yamaha M1. Despondent, he walked away from his bike, only to then change his mind as soon as he calculated that others were likely to crash out and he might be able to salvage some precious points. Remounting his damaged bike, he cruised back to the pits to find his number one bike now fixed and fitted with slick tyres, ready to go. He was delayed further when it was pointed out that the rules did not allow him to rejoin the race unless at least one of his tyres was different to those on which he had entered the pits, necessitating further delays as his crew fitted yet another tyre. And still it wasn't over. In his haste to get back out on track, Rossi forgot to engage the pit lane speed limiter, broke the speed limit, and was penalised with a ride-through penalty which meant yet another visit to pit lane and a painfully slow crawl down it before he could finally get his head down and ride as fast as he could to try and close the gap to the last-placed man in the race. Try as he might, and despite setting the tenth fastest lap of the race, the gap was just too great and Rossi finished the race two laps down, last and pointless. It was a race that proved even the greatest can get it wrong and it meant that Rossi went to his home Grand Prix at Mugello one point behind Jorge Lorenzo after the Spaniard had done everything right in France and taken the win.

Rossi then had to suffer the indignity of being beaten into second place by his much younger team-mate in front of his home crowd at Mugello and found himself 5 points in arrears going to Catalunya which, in turn, was Lorenzo's home Grand Prix. And it was there that the defining moment of the 2009 season occurred.

The 85,000-strong crowd at the Circuit de Barcelona-Catalunya was treated to one of the best MotoGP races of all time and arguably the greatest last lap of all time, despite there being just two protagonists: Rossi and Lorenzo. All race long the Yamaha team-mates had shadowed one another, both making passes but both realising there was no chance of breaking away. Better to stay in position, maintain the pressure on the other rider, and keep the powder dry – and the tyres in good shape – for a last-lap, do-or-die confrontation.

Rossi led on to the final circuit by just 0.09 seconds,

Lorenzo using part of the pit lane exit to grab the inside line for turn one while Rossi ran wide. On a racetrack with very few overtaking opportunities Rossi only had one realistic chance left and that was at the end of the back straight, but Lorenzo defended his line perfectly and should, in theory, have been able to hold his position to the flag; there was simply nowhere else to make a pass. But from his earliest days observers had noticed Rossi's creativity when it came to finding lines that no other riders used: it was one of his strongest points and it would now serve him better than ever before.

In retrospect, Lorenzo admitted he had not defended on the final corner quite as much as he could have because he too considered it practically impossible for anyone to make a pass there. It was a lesson in race craft he wouldn't forget; when racing against an in-form Valentino Rossi a rider could never assume anything, and certainly never assume that he was safe from attack. In a move never seen before, Rossi somehow managed to make his M1 Yamaha fit into a gap that didn't really exist in the final corner, squeeze his way through, and control the exit on to the finish straight, ultimately taking the victory by just 0.09 seconds to secure one of his greatest-ever wins.

That victory was important in many ways. After Rossi had been headed by Lorenzo all season long in the championship, the extra 5 points he scored for winning meant he drew level on points. He had also beaten Lorenzo in front of the Spaniard's home crowd – a further psychological triumph – and he had turned his season around by filling himself with the confidence that he could beat his new nemesis in a straight, last-lap dogfight. Lorenzo was magnanimous in defeat. 'Of course I am sad to have lost because I put my heart on my bike, and in my career I am more used to winning these last-lap fights, but today Valentino was maybe a little bit cleverer or a little bit braver than me at the very end and he was able to beat me.'

Next time out at Assen, Rossi notched up his 100th Grand Prix win, an astonishing milestone that had only ever been achieved once before – and again the record-holder was Giacomo Agostini. Rossi was now just 22 wins short of Ago's all-time record of 122 victories (across all classes – Rossi already had more wins in the premier class than Agostini), but his tally was even more impressive as he had only ever raced in one class at a time while Agostini had raced in the 350cc and 500cc championships at the same time, thus greatly increasing his opportunity to rack up wins. Standard practice back in the day, but Grand Prix racing has now become so specialised and competitive that to race in more than one class is simply unthinkable.

Another major difference in Agostini's era were the circuits he and his opponents had to race on. In an age before every country had purpose-built racetracks with all their in-built run-off areas and safety features, Ago and his contemporaries had to race on many circuits that were nothing more than closed public roads, chief amongst them being the Isle of Man TT where the Italian took ten wins before turning his back on the event in 1972 when his close friend Gilberto Parlotti lost his life on the notoriously dangerous 37.73-mile roads course. Parlotti was just one of over three-hundred riders to have lost their lives on the course since the TT began in 1907. In June 2009, during the two-week TT festival, Rossi joined Agostini on a parade lap of the course and watched some of the racing in person for the first time. He was staggered by the experience. 'The lap is great and impressed me a lot because I know that it's dangerous and also fast,' he said. 'I don't expect a road like this to be a track and it is unbelievable to be going flat out around it on a Superbike. You need to have two great balls!'

Rossi would later tell *Top Gear* magazine that, as much as he enjoyed his visit, he had no plans to compete in the TT. 'I understand why people love this because it's fucking awesome – it's unbelievable, great. But, unfortunately it's too dangerous. Sometimes riders are crazy!'

While he didn't exactly dominate the second half of the season after Assen, Rossi did enough. There were wins in Germany, the Czech Republic and, most pleasingly, at home in San Marino, but Lorenzo, Stoner, Dani Pedrosa and Andrea Dovizioso would also take wins, forcing Rossi to play the consistency game. If he wasn't strong enough to win, he learned to settle for podium positions or even lower placings. In an increasingly competitive series (made more so by the new one-make tyre rule), consistency became key: the old win-it-or-bin-it philosophy simply wasn't good enough any more.

As a result of this more measured approach, Rossi wasn't able to secure his ninth world championship with a win; instead he took it with a safe third place ahead of arch-rival Lorenzo (who had been forced to start from last position after failing to make his grid spot on time) but well behind runaway winner Casey Stoner, who had by now recovered from his chronic fatigue issues, albeit temporarily. Lorenzo admitted that Rossi had quite simply outridden him in 2009. 'Maybe I'm not as ready to beat Rossi as I thought I was,' he said. 'I still wasn't braking as hard as him and Rossi was so intelligent, often beating me with his improvisation. The only way to take points from him was to learn to beat him in direct combat because the racing was so close.'[13]

It had been, by Rossi's own admission, the most gruelling

championship so far and the most difficult defence of his title. Speaking after sealing his fourth world championship for Yamaha, his seventh in the premier class, and his ninth in total, he said, 'It was a difficult year. This race reflected how the season went – very tough, with some mistakes, some disappointing results. But I won six races, I was consistent and it's another world championship.'[14]

As pleased as he was to take another title, Rossi wasn't exactly in the mood for lavish celebrations: he had suffered a personal tragedy on the eve of the third-to-last race of the 2009 season when he was informed that his stepfather, Mauro Tecchi, had committed suicide. Rossi's mother had married Tecchi, an engineer by trade, in 2007 and the two shared a house in Viale Trento, Pesaro. Following an argument with Tecchi, Rossi's mother had left to spend some time in Tavullia but, after hearing nothing from her husband in several days, she returned to the marital home only to find his body on Friday, 16 October. The fifty-two-year-old had committed suicide sometime between Tuesday, 13 October and Wednesday, 14 October with a self-inflicted gunshot wound to the chest. During the police investigation it emerged that Tecchi had left the television blaring and used a pillow on his chest to muffle the sound of the gunshot from neighbours. The 12-gauge shotgun was found by his side. Tecchi left no note and investigators concluded that depression might have been behind the suicide. Rossi, who had always been very close to his mother, was clearly shocked by the news and refused to speak about it other than saying, 'This is a terrible thing – I don't know what to say.'

It was a hideous way to end a year which had otherwise provided many highs, not least the winning of a ninth world championship. From here on in, though, it would be a much harder ride for Rossi. The glory years, or at least the years of domination, appeared to be over.

CHAPTER 11

A BRIDGE TOO FAR

'I think this was the only bad mistake
Vale made in his whole career.'
CARLO PERNAT

While he'd had many rivals for the world title in the past, Valentino Rossi had never had to deal with one in his own garage. It was a new experience for him and one that he really didn't like. He felt it was largely down to himself and his crew that the under-performing Yamaha he had inherited in 2004 had been turned into a serial race – and title – winner and he was furious that an identical bike was being given to his main championship rival, Jorge Lorenzo, in 2008. Rossi expected more loyalty from Yamaha and when the Japanese firm signed Lorenzo again for the 2010 season, the writing was on the wall.

It was clear that, with Rossi now thirty-one years of age, Lorenzo was being groomed as his replacement when he finally decided to retire; he was seen as the future of Yamaha and Rossi strongly objected to the fact that he himself no longer enjoyed the clear number-one status in the team. 'Usually I try to put a lot of work in developing the bike and I usually do it just for me,' he said. 'But now I'm also doing it for my worst enemy. You know… sincerely, I don't think I deserve this after what I did for Yamaha. But this was Yamaha's choice.'[1]

Even Rossi's team manager at Yamaha, Davide Brivio, could understand his rider's objections. 'Sometimes I can feel a little bit of frustration from Valentino. He is developing the machine and, in the meantime, he's preparing the tool for his best rival to try to beat him.'

In a 2009 interview with the BBC, Rossi effectively issued Yamaha with an ultimatum: 'Yamaha have to decide between me and Jorge for 2010,' he said. 'I am not sure one hundred per cent if I will stay with Yamaha. It depends on what happens next year. It depends on my performance and the fight with Jorge Lorenzo and the decision of Yamaha for 2011. I could change bike, ride for Ducati and try to win the world championship with an Italian bike. That would be a great motivation. But I prefer at this moment to stay with Yamaha because the love between me and Yamaha, our relationship, is something special. To change bike would feel unfaithful.'

Ducati. It was the only realistic option, should Rossi choose to leave Yamaha. He had burned his bridges at Honda and the Ducati was the only other bike on the grid capable of winning races. But it hadn't won another title since Casey Stoner took the championship in 2007 and it was becoming clear that the Australian's unique riding style was the key ingredient needed to extract the most from the fast but difficult-to-ride machine. So, while openly complaining about Yamaha's decision to keep Lorenzo as his team-mate, Rossi signed a one-year contract (as opposed to his usual two-year deal) to stay where he was for now and see how the 2010 season panned out and whether his bosses would bend to his will or opt to retain Lorenzo's services.

As things turned out, the 2010 season would prove to be something of a disaster for Rossi and it would also prove his fear of Lorenzo was well founded: the young Spaniard would take his first MotoGP crown while Rossi would suffer the worst injury of his career to date.

For a motorcycle racer, Rossi had been incredibly lucky when it came to injuries. Despite being a prolific crasher in the early part of his career, he had never suffered any serious injuries and hadn't even broken any major bones – something practically unheard of for a professional motorcycle racer, and especially one who had been around for as long as Rossi had. The most serious injury he had suffered occurred in 1994 when he was riding pillion on a scooter with a friend near Tavullia and the pair were struck by a car, resulting in Rossi suffering a broken left ankle and a couple of mangled toes. The ankle continued to give him some discomfort for many years when he was racing, but his record was still astonishing when compared to other riders. At Assen in 2006, he had fractured a bone in the little finger of his right hand during free practice but still managed to race, and the following year he fractured three bones in the same hand during practice for the final Grand Prix in Valencia but again managed to race. It was a record that was the envy of every other rider in MotoGP. But that all changed in 2010 and, after some fifteen years of racing in Grands Prix, Rossi would face yet another major test – how would he cope with a serious injury?

Motorcycle racers have a remarkable attitude towards pain

and injury that is at complete odds with the majority of people. Driven by a manic need to win races and score points, they will, as a matter of course, defy medical advice and go to any lengths in order to ride, even when it seems impossible. Riding with freshly broken bones is commonplace; heavy strapping of wounds and taking multiple pain-killing injections before racing is also just part of the job and accepted without complaint. The only thing that matters is being out there and not handing any advantage to your rivals. Riders on crutches, unable to even bear their own weight, have been lifted onto 220mph GP missiles and left to get on with the business of racing; others have vomited in their helmets mid-race due to the pain they're suffering, yet still they race on. And even when they accept they can't race for a while they will do everything in their power to ensure they can race again as soon as possible. In 1992, facing amputation, Mick Doohan opted to have his left leg stitched to his right leg in order to feed the mangled right leg an adequate blood supply. He returned to win five consecutive 500cc world titles. Barry Sheene suffered life-threatening crashes in both 1975 and 1982, sustaining injuries that required so much internal metalwork that he made mainstream news in the UK and was regarded as some kind of bionic man. He returned to race after both accidents. Franco Uncini was feared dead when he was struck by Wayne Gardner at the Dutch TT and lost his helmet in the collision. After coming out of a coma, he recovered and returned to the saddle just nine months later. There are literally thousands of examples, but Rossi had never been tested in this department. At thirty-one years of age and by now a millionaire many times over, could he really find the motivation to push through the pain barrier and return to action to take the same risks all over again?

The crash happened during practice for his home Grand Prix in Mugello. Up to that point, Rossi had not missed a single Grand Prix in fourteen years. Since he started racing in the 125cc world championship in 1996, he had made the grid for all 230 races. It was an incredible run but it came to an end at Mugello in 2010 during Saturday free practice. Caught out by a cold tyre, he was thrown over the top of his motorcycle in a classic 'highside' crash and broke his right tibia and fibula (the two main lower-leg bones) when he was thrown hard to the ground after being ejected from his bike. The impact was so hard that both bones broke out through the skin and Rossi was clearly in great pain as he writhed around in the gravel trap with his leg bent at a most unnatural angle.

Doctor Claudio Costa of the Clinica Mobile, the mobile clinic that attends all Grand Prix races (and who saved Graziano Rossi's life way back in 1979) was concerned about the complexity of the break. 'It's a more serious fracture than we expected,' he said. 'It's a compound fracture which involves both the tibia and the fibula. I hope there are no complications. It will be at least two or three months for him to recover. It's not the usual break of the bone, it's very serious.'[2]

Already struggling with a shoulder injury picked up in a motocross training accident two months previously, Rossi was now facing a recuperation period of several months, which meant he would not only have to sit out his home Grand Prix but also the British, Dutch and Catalan races. Any hope of a tenth world title disappeared the instant the leg was broken.

As is normal with motorcycle racers, Rossi was back in action well ahead of the timescale predicted by his doctors: two races earlier, in fact – a full month faster than anyone expected. He turned up at the German Grand Prix on a crutch just forty-one days after his crash (having already tested a road bike ten days earlier) and received a standing ovation at the opening press conference. MotoGP hadn't been the same without the main man – Rossi had been missed.

After his leg had been plated and screwed, Rossi had spent fifteen tedious days lying on his back in bed before undergoing intensive sessions in a hyperbaric chamber and long hours of physiotherapy and training to speed up the healing process. Despite his best efforts he was still far from fully fit when he lined up at the Sachsenring, a circuit he had deliberately chosen to make his comeback at because it was predominantly left-handed, meaning he would have to exert less pressure through his still weak and painful right leg. He finished fourth, just off the podium and, in doing so, had passed yet another test of his greatness: he had proved he *was* prepared to come back from injury, he *was* prepared to ride hurt and he *was* prepared to push as much as his body would allow him to get the best result possible. His racing CV now seemed complete.

Former 500cc Grand Prix rider Niall Mackenzie says the injury (which he himself suffered three times) wouldn't have fazed Rossi in the slightest. 'Injuries like that don't affect riders one little bit. If road riders have one crash in their lives it's absolutely traumatising and they will always want to talk about it, but racers are programmed differently. I don't know of any racer that's come back from an injury like that and ridden any slower because of it. If your injuries prevent you from moving properly and riding the bike properly, that's a different thing, but as long as a rider is physically capable then they're not going to be mentally affected by it. There's something in a racer's psyche that means they just don't get affected by stuff like that. They've grown up with crashes and injuries, so it's just part of the job. You get used to the crashing and the injuries and the pain.'

Rossi had won the opening race of the year in Qatar, then finished third and second to Lorenzo in Spain and France respectively before suffering the crash at Mugello. By the time he returned in Germany after missing four races, Lorenzo had taken charge of the championship, winning the previous three races and capitalising fully on Rossi's absence.

It would be another eight races before Rossi would win again, in Malaysia, but it was too little too late and he could manage no more than third position in the championship behind Lorenzo and Dani Pedrosa. His worst nightmare had come true: his team-mate had taken the championship from him. And while he could at least console himself that it hadn't exactly been a straight fight, Yamaha's decision to retain Lorenzo's services in 2011 was the final straw in what had been a difficult year. Rossi announced he would be riding in red the following year. He was switching to Ducati.

★

'It was dreadful when he left,' says former Yamaha man Andy Smith. 'We initially thought it was just a negotiation tactic and that he would finally stay with us. His coming to Yamaha was not just about winning races – it was about the motivation he brought with him, the interest he brought with him to the dealers, which was so important, and what he did for the staff. So when he left it had completely the opposite effect and it was much more significant than if the president of Yamaha, or the managing director, left. Rossi *was* Yamaha.'

Rossi was emotional about the split too and wrote what was effectively a love letter to the Yamaha M1 that had brought him four world titles and, somewhat fittingly, forty-six race wins:

> Many things have changed since that far-off time in 2004 but especially 'she,' my M1, has changed. At that time she was a poor, middle-grid-position MotoGP bike, derided by most of the riders and MotoGP workers. Now, after having helped her to grow and improve, you can see her smiling in her garage, courted and admired, treated as top of the class. Unfortunately, even the most beautiful love stories end but they leave a lot of wonderful memories, like when my M1 and I kissed for the first time on the grass at Welkom, when she looked straight in my eyes and told me 'I love you.'

It wasn't the first, or last, time that Rossi would refer to his motorcycle as being like a girlfriend; of being more than just an assembled collection of metal, titanium and carbon-fibre parts. 'I always feel a personal connection with the bike because I think the bike has a soul,' he told Mark Neale, director of the 2003 MotoGP documentary film *Faster*. 'I always make a personal feeling together – I always speak with the bike. When the bike arrives in January, it's like with a girlfriend!'

Sadly for Rossi, his love affair with the new Ducati would never fully blossom and would end in an acrimonious divorce. By the time he announced his Ducati deal (said to be worth €12 million a year), it was the worst-kept secret in the paddock. He had been at Yamaha for seven years and enjoyed unprecedented success with the firm but his inability to accept Jorge Lorenzo as his team-mate and his need for a new challenge and new motivation meant he had to move;

he had to take a chance. And he would once again be taking most of his crew with him. If, together, they had managed to turn the Yamaha into a winning bike, they were supremely confident they could do the same with the waning Ducati. While Stoner had won ten races on his way to the 2007 title, in 2010 he only took three wins; the Desmosedici had clearly lost its edge.

On paper at least, though, Rossi's new deal seemed too good to be true. An all-Italian team, an all-Italian bike and the most famous Italian motorcycle racer of all time? The Italian press and fans went into meltdown. In fact, the relentless pressure from the Italian media played a part in Rossi's decision, according to the first man to sign Rossi, Carlo Pernat. 'For me this was a decision taken by the Italian sporting world, not by Valentino,' he says. 'All the Italian people, and particularly the Italian media and the fans, even Philip Morris [owners of Marlboro and Ducati's main sponsor] pushed for this to happen. The problem was that Valentino arrived at Ducati in the wrong moment. The bike, at the time, was not a good bike and it was not the right bike for Valentino – it was right for Casey Stoner but not Valentino.'

He continues: 'Before joining Ducati, Valentino thought about it a lot, really a lot, but all the people pressed him so, for me, it was a little bit forced. There was so much pressure for him to sign with Ducati. I would say thirty per cent of Valentino did not want to go and, ultimately, it was not one hundred per cent his decision to go. For sure, Vale could have had some success with Ducati if he had joined them a few years later but it was not possible for him to win with the bike they had at that time. I think this was the only bad mistake Vale made in his whole career – but like I say, seventy per cent of the decision came from the pressure of others.'

Whatever the case, 2011 would prove to be an annus horribilis for Valentino Rossi in more ways than one. It would prove to be the low point of his remarkable career and the first year since he'd started world championship racing that he didn't win a race. He even struggled to get anywhere near the podium most weekends, scoring just one third place across the entire season when wet conditions played to his favour in France. He never qualified higher than sixth place, was outside the top ten in qualifying on nine occasions and, in France, he qualified in a career-worst sixteenth place. He continued to struggle with his shoulder injury from 2010 too. He had opted to have surgery during the winter break and surgeons had discovered much more tendon damage than expected and the lingering pain and restriction of movement further hampered his debut year on the Ducati, more so than many people realised at the time.

By round ten at Laguna Seca, rumours started spreading that Rossi was attempting to buy himself out of the Ducati deal with the intention of running his own private Honda in 2012. It never happened and instead he crashed out of the last four races (in total he crashed twelve times throughout the year – more than he'd ever crashed in the premier class) and finished the season in a lowly seventh place with just 139 points compared to champion Casey Stoner's 350. Stoner, who had switched to Honda after feeling Ducati had lost its way, took great delight in seeing his rival fall from grace. 'I enjoyed watching Valentino struggle on the Ducati as he'd made it very clear that, before that happened, he thought the reason for my success was the bike. Even when that bike wasn't working I put it on the podium and they [Rossi and his team] were nowhere near it, unless a bunch of riders crashed or it rained.'³

Speaking of both Rossi and Burgess, Stoner told *Moto-course*, 'I think they had a lot more expectations of what that bike was and maybe less respect for what I was doing than they should have. When they got on it they realised that maybe I'm a little better than they thought I was; maybe I used less electronics than they thought I did.'[4]

Honda bosses were enjoying Rossi's discomfort, too. If, as Rossi had so vehemently pointed out when leaving Honda, it was the rider and not the bike that made the difference, then 'Now it is time for him to prove it,' quipped HRC boss Shuhei Nakamoto.

Any lingering respect that Stoner might have had for Rossi evaporated completely in just the second round of the season at Jerez. In wet conditions and in only his second race on the Ducati, Rossi made an overly ambitious move on Stoner from a long way back going into turn one. Unable to stop in time for the corner, Rossi slid out and took the Australian with him. The blame was entirely his and, to his credit, he did immediately make for Stoner's garage to apologise, but it wasn't enough to appease the fuming Honda rider. Rossi failed to remove his helmet and was also followed by a television crew, both factors that led Stoner to think the apology was insincere. The Australian, already changed back into his team gear, faced Rossi down and was heard by millions to say, 'Obviously your ambition outweighed your talent.' It was an audacious comment to make to a nine-times world champion when Stoner himself only had one title to his credit, but it proved he was not mentally affected by the aura of Rossi. 'Of course, I took another hammering from the press, who accused me of disrespecting a great champion, but I stand firmly by my comment to this day,' Stoner wrote in his autobiography. 'There was never a truer word said. It doesn't matter about

Rossi's past achievements or seeming greatness, at that moment in time his ambition outweighed his talent, simple as that. That is why he crashed instead of making the pass.'[5]

Rossi, as ever, laughed it off. 'I don't think he likes me very much,' he said afterwards. He wasn't wrong.

Former World Superbike champion turned BT Sport MotoGP commentator Neil Hodgson says Stoner was central to Rossi's decision to sign for Ducati. 'There were a few issues there and they start with Casey Stoner – I think everybody underestimated how good he was, including Valentino Rossi and Jerry Burgess. They thought they could go to Ducati and get it winning again quite easily, even though no other rider had managed to do so after Stoner. I think Burgess said something like, "Oh, we'll fix the Ducati in two weeks." That was the first time Rossi experienced losing a bit of confidence, because he jumped on the bike, made some radical changes, and it didn't solve anything – we still see now that the Ducati doesn't turn properly. And then he started crashing. He crashed the Ducati more than any other bike, and he's a human being after all, so he started questioning himself. That was the first time it had happened in his career, so it was a new experience for him. Even the great Valentino Rossi lost a bit of confidence.'

Rossi went so far as to admit that he'd been fooled by Stoner's success on the Ducati. 'Casey's performance fucked us a little bit, and this is the truth,' he said before the Malaysian Grand Prix at Sepang. 'A lot of people thought the Ducati is fast because Stoner was in front, but maybe sometimes Stoner make some stupid mistake and crashed a lot of times. So people always thought it was a problem of Stoner. But it is not true because the problem is the bike is very difficult to ride and Stoner is very fast.'[6]

And then, just as it seemed his season could not get any worse, came the Malaysian Grand Prix.

Rossi's closest friend in the paddock was Marco Simoncelli. From the village of Coriano, just a stone's throw from Tavullia, the gangly Italian with the huge leonine hairdo was seen as something of a successor to Rossi. A former 250cc world champion, Simoncelli had graduated to the MotoGP class in 2010 and had set two pole positions and scored two podiums in his second year in the class. As flamboyant on the track as he was off it, Simoncelli was accused of wild riding on more than one occasion and had been penalised in France for causing Dani Pedrosa to crash. He had also had more than one run-in with Jorge Lorenzo, who also considered his riding to be out of control.

But the fans loved the happy-go-lucky attitude of Simoncelli and Rossi had taken him under his wing and become a mentor of sorts. The two would ride dirt bikes and train together as well as hang out together socially; for Rossi, Simoncelli was a little bit of home in every paddock he went to. Which made what happened next even more devastating for him.

The Malaysian Grand Prix at Sepang was the penultimate round of the 2011 championship and Marco Simoncelli had just scored his best-ever MotoGP result with second place in Australia. The Honda rider was looking for his first win; everyone knew it was coming, it was just a matter of when. Lying in fourth place on lap two, Simoncelli suffered a loss in traction in his rear tyre in turn eleven and he was thrown out of the seat of his bike but was still tangled up with the machine when, in a completely freakish incident, the rear tyre gripped again and veered Simoncelli right across the track in front of a chasing Colin Edwards's and Valentino Rossi. Neither rider had the slightest chance of reacting in time. Edwards' machine struck Simoncelli's lower body while Rossi's Yamaha struck his friend on the head with such force the impact tore Simoncelli's helmet off.

While Rossi fought to regain control of his Ducati, Edwards sat dazed by the trackside with a dislocated shoulder and some small breaks, staring at the immobile and helmetless body of his colleague, hoping, praying, that it wasn't as bad as it looked. It was. Simoncelli was removed from the track and taken to the circuit's medical centre. At 16:56 local time, less than one hour after the crash, Marco Simoncelli was pronounced dead. He was twenty-four years old.

Like the rest of the paddock, Rossi was devastated. At first too upset to speak publicly about the incident he instead posted a short tribute on Twitter: 'Simoncelli for me was like a youngest brother. So strong on track and so sweet in the normal life. I will miss him a lot.'

Later explaining the crash on the eve of the final race of the season, Rossi said, 'I remember being behind Colin at this turn and in the next moment Simoncelli was in the middle of the track at an impossible angle. It is like someone pulling out in front of you at a junction. There was nothing I could do.'

The true extent of Rossi and Simoncelli's friendship was revealed in an interview with Italian newspaper *La Gazzetta dello Sport* when Rossi explained: 'We were very good friends. We were together almost every day, at least five, six days a week. Almost always after training we went to dinner... Being involved in the accident was devastating and difficult to overcome but I never thought of quitting.'[7]

Although Rossi and Edwards were clearly in no way to blame for the death of Simoncelli, it would have been impossible for them not to wonder, while alone in bed at night, if there wasn't perhaps something they could have done differently; something that could have led to a better outcome; something that could have saved their friend. It's human nature to replay such tragic incidents over and over in the mind; it was a horror that Rossi and Edwards could not unsee. Wayne Gardner, the 1987 500cc world champion, had been involved in a similar incident that left Franco Uncini in a coma, fighting for his life, though the Italian thankfully made a full recovery. 'I have a pretty good idea about how they'll be feeling,' Gardner said of Rossi and Edwards in the aftermath of the incident. 'But it simply wasn't their fault. There's nothing they could have done. Both will be replaying the event in their mind over and over again, wondering if they could have veered to the left, the right, braked harder. But, while a small consolation, the TV footage of the accident – now and in the years to come – will show them they had absolutely no time to avoid the collision. It was, sadly, just a case of being in the wrong place at the wrong time.'

Kevin Schwantz says that while Rossi's ability to deal with such a tragedy was admirable, he will carry the scars forever. 'Marco was a really close friend of Valentino's, much like he was mine. You know, we all ride and race and we realise that it's a dangerous sport and stuff like that can happen, but when it happens that close to you and it's somebody that's such a close, personal friend, it definitely has an impact. But it's just one more hurdle that Valentino has found a way to get over and he continued to perform at the very top level.

'So he's very strong-willed and I think he realised that Marco would probably have wanted him to continue racing and to go on to win some more races and maybe even a championship. And I think that's what Valentino's done. It's not easy as a rider to deal with someone – especially that close to you – dying but, like I said, we're racers, we're professionals as much as we possibly can be, but the impact is always gonna be there. And you'll always have that with you – it's something you'll be carrying around for the rest of your life.'

Rossi had experienced fatalities in racing before. Daijiro Kato had been killed at Suzuka in 2003, and in 2010 Japanese rider Shoya Tomizawa had lost his life at Misano following a crash in the Moto2 race. But Simoncelli had been a close friend and many wondered if Rossi, who was already experiencing the worst year of his career, would continue to race.

But continue to race he did. After attending Simoncelli's funeral and spending a lot of time with the grieving family, he was back at Valencia less than two weeks later to line up on the grid and risk his life again.

Another crash (his fourth in the last four races) perfectly summed up his train-wreck of a season. Despite Ducati, at Rossi's insistence, wheeling out four new versions of their Desmosedici during the season, nothing seemed to work and Rossi admitted he just couldn't challenge for wins on the Ducati: the bike simply didn't suit his riding style and he had known it from the very first test. 'I understood straight away that riding the Ducati was very difficult,' he said. 'I understood immediately that this bike had some problems exactly in the best point of my riding style. Usually my best part is braking and entering the corner but on the Ducati it is the weakest point, so I was worried for that reason right from the start.'[8]

Only now did it become apparent that Casey Stoner had managed to find a way to ride the Ducati that no other rider could replicate. And he had every right to feel smug now when Rossi was forced to eat humble pie. In 2010, Rossi had gone on record saying that it was impossible to know how good the Ducati actually was because Casey Stoner wasn't trying hard enough on it. Only after trying to race the bike himself did

Rossi realise it was in fact Stoner's incredible talent that was flattering the bike and not the other way round. It was a bitter pill to swallow but swallow it Rossi had to – he had signed a two-year deal and had to see it through. And there were no signs that the 2012 season was going to be any easier.

★

With his confidence shot, his reputation on the slide and the knowledge that he had no chance of winning on the Ducati, Rossi had a grim time in 2012. 'I have some moments when I am down,' he said mid-season. 'I try to resist but it is very difficult.'

A new chassis didn't help. A new 1000cc engine (in compliance with the new-for-2012 regulations) didn't help. Rossi even tried to change his riding style to be more like Stoner's in a desperate bid to get the best out of the Ducati, but he admitted that, at thirty-two years of age, it was perhaps too late to reinvent himself. Ultimately it was a persistently 'vague' feeling from the front end of the bike that Rossi and Ducati could never resolve. And if he was expecting the front wheel to wash out from beneath him at every corner, he was never going to be able to challenge for race wins. And with every crash, his confidence suffered even more. 'I am not used to crashing like this in one season,' Rossi said of his twelve crashes in 2011. 'I think one of my best points is that I only crash four or five times in one season. But with this bike, when you push more, you crash. So with every crash you lose some feeling and confidence, and to come back is difficult.'[9]

In his second year on the Ducati Rossi finished one position higher in the championship in sixth place. He took two podiums: one in wet conditions in France (just as in 2011) and the other in the dry at Misano – mainly because practice had been hit by bad weather so no other rider had a perfect race set-up, while Rossi had just completed a private two-day test at the circuit and had a set-up ready to go. But these were the only highlights of another dire year on the Italian bike while Rossi's former team-mate, Jorge Lorenzo, romped to another world title on the beautifully handling Yamaha M1. For a rider of Rossi's calibre to score just three podiums in thirty-five races was a shock to everyone and clear proof that Ducati had lost its way with the Desmosedici. It also proved that Rossi was not a magician, that he wasn't invincible; like any other rider, he needed his bike and team to be a competitive overall package if he was to be able to win. He could only ride around problems up to a certain point and no further.

The only success story for Valentino Rossi in 2012 was the formal launch of his VR|46 merchandising company. Based in Tavullia (where else?) it would eventually grow to employ more than thirty people and would cash in on the still rampant demand for Rossi merchandise. Always with a keen eye for spotting financial opportunities, Rossi soon expanded his company to produce merchandise for other riders, providing everything from the design stage through to manufacture and global marketing strategies. Five years later, the VR|46 company was producing merchandise for twenty-five other riders, netting Rossi further millions to add to his already considerable wealth.

But that aside, for the first time in his career, Valentino Rossi had been forced to admit defeat. He and Jerry Burgess could not transform the Ducati into a winning bike and Rossi himself was unable to change his riding style enough to make a difference. His two years at Ducati had been a frustrating and expensive failure and would mark a definite watershed in his career. Things would never be quite the same again for him and the move to Ducati was one he lived to regret. 'This for me is one very bad thing,' he later admitted, 'and one of the things I am the most sad about because in my career I have been able to ride every type of bike.'[10]

It came as no surprise to anyone when, during the summer break, Rossi announced he was leaving the Italian factory. With all bridges burned at Honda, the only realistic option now was to return to Yamaha, but he would soon discover that the shoe was now very definitely on the other foot. When Rossi had first joined Yamaha he was the undisputed king of MotoGP, he was in huge demand, he was the most famous motorcycle racer on earth and he was the only man capable of turning the M1 into a winner. First time around, Rossi had been in charge and had the factory at his beck and call. Not so any longer. Now the M1 was sorted and Yamaha had a new double world champion in the shape of Jorge Lorenzo. The future would be all about him – Rossi was, after all, getting old by MotoGP standards. He also had nowhere else to go and Yamaha knew it. If Rossi wanted a bike capable of winning, he had to ride for Yamaha and that placed all the cards firmly in the manufacturer's favour.

The key to Rossi being accepted back was team boss Lin Jarvis. 'His relationship with Lin Jarvis remained quite good because Lin understood why he wanted to go to Ducati,' says Andrew Smith. 'So they stayed in contact and I think the "Can I come back?" talks started because of his relationship with Lin.'

But when he did return, Rossi would find his power had diminished significantly. 'Up until he left at the end of 2010, I would say Yamaha gave Rossi pretty much anything he wanted,' says Smith. 'But when he came back in 2013 my understanding was that he had to come back very much on Yamaha's terms because it was *him* asking *us* to come back. Before he left he was the main man and everything that the team did was, first and foremost, for him, and rightly so – not just for the results but for the marketing he was doing in Indonesia, Thailand and Vietnam, because in those countries it was still very much "Win on a Sunday and sell bikes on a Monday." At that time, that market was where most of Yamaha's profits were coming from. We were struggling to make money in more mature markets like the UK and America.'

Yamaha had been up and down a bit when Rossi left, he explains. 'And when he came back he said he wanted a two-year contract but that he also wanted to become Mister Yamaha – an ambassador – so he became more flexible to work with. When he left at the peak of his career he could have demanded that he would only do four promotional events per year. They would still ask him for five, but he would never do it. But when he came back he was much more flexible.'

There was a lot of pride to be swallowed and Rossi appeared to be genuinely humbled by the experience. 'It was a mistake to go to Ducati because I was annoyed with Yamaha,' he admitted. 'Because after having won [the title] with Yamaha in 2004 and 2005, after so many years in which Yamaha had been struggling, Yamaha decided to bring a very strong team-mate and then I got really annoyed at it. But now I understand I was wrong.'[11]

Rossi would have to accept a huge pay cut (rumours suggested Yamaha paid him only half of what he'd earned at Ducati) and, to add salt to the wound, Rossi would also have to accept that his team-mate was earning more than double what he was. What's more, he was told by Yamaha that he would not be the lead development rider for the team as he always had been before. Now the focus was on Lorenzo as the one most likely to challenge for the title, so the bike was to be built around his preferences and Rossi would have to just get on with it. 'In development, Lorenzo will decide the direction for the bike,' admitted project leader Kouichi Tsuji. 'He will lead but Valentino will assist.'[12]

Even though he wouldn't be leading development of the M1, Rossi knew that at least Yamaha's technicians would listen to him and carry out any changes he asked for – something which had not always been the case at Ducati. In an online interview for motorcyclenews.com, he explained: 'When you speak with Yamaha, and also with Honda, and you say something about the bike – something wrong about the bike – for the Japanese engineer it is not something bad, it is something positive, because they understand the way to improve the bike. Sometimes with Ducati it doesn't happen. When you say the bike has a problem the Ducati guys... first they don't trust you one hundred per cent and, secondly, they are quite angry because you say that the bike has a problem. Ego, maybe, I don't know.'

Being Yamaha's second rider was a bitter pill to swallow but at least Rossi would have a bike on which he could compete again. The Ducati disaster had to be put firmly behind him: it was time to start winning again. But a new rider would join the championship in 2013 and his rivalry with Rossi would outdo any that had gone before. His name was Marc Márquez.

CHAPTER 12

THE REVENANT

'It's so unusual for any sportsman to go on
for that long at that level.'
NIALL MACKENZIE

It took him seven races. Seven races to readjust to riding the
Yamaha. Seven races to regain the confidence he had lost
after so many crashes on the Ducati. Seven races to finely hone
his race craft to be better able to duel with the very fastest
men in MotoGP. Seven races to win again, and to prove that
it had been the Ducati, and not himself, that had failed.

It happened at Assen, a track where Rossi had enjoyed
much success in the past, but this win felt greater than any
that had gone before. It had been almost three years and,
ironically, forty-six races, since he had last stood on the top
step of the podium on 10 October 2010. It was now 29 June
2013 and, at thirty-four years old, Rossi was back at the very
top of the world's most elite motorcycle racing championship.

'This is one of the most special victories of my career,' he said after the Dutch race. 'It is one that I wanted rather than expected. I put this race on the podium of my wins because it is so long since I won... Sincerely, I wasn't sure if I could win again because it is a long time since my last victory in Sepang, but also a difficult time. I had two very difficult seasons, very frustrating with a lot of bad results.'

Finishing behind Rossi at Assen was the man who would become arguably the greatest and most bitter rival of Rossi's career: Marc Márquez. Born in 1993, in Spain, when Valentino Rossi was already racing in the Italian Sport Production championship, Márquez was only twenty-one years old when he made his debut in MotoGP but had already won the 125cc world championship and the Moto2 world championship, and he had stepped up to MotoGP to replace Casey Stoner in the factory Repsol Honda team. Stoner, at just twenty-eight, had made the startling decision to walk away from racing despite a reported offer of £10 million from Honda to race on for another year. He was disillusioned with the sport, tired of the PR duties required of him, and no fan of the increasing levels of electronics being used in MotoGP. He was an old-school racer at heart and happily walked away from such a lucrative offer, 'to go fishing'.

Another of Rossi's great foes had come and gone while he himself continued to race. But foes didn't come any greater, or any faster, than Marc Márquez. In 2013, the young Spaniard was nothing short of sensational in his debut season in MotoGP, winning in only his second race before going on to win another five times on his way to securing the world championship – the first rider to win in his rookie year since Kenny Roberts Sr in 1978.

Following the old pattern, Rossi was initially cordial with

the new pretender. Márquez had, after all, been a huge Rossi fan as a child and at fifteen years old had accosted his hero in the paddock and asked to have his picture taken with him before presenting Rossi with a model of a rally car. Márquez admitted to having had posters of Rossi all over his bedroom wall as a teenager. He was a fan, but he wouldn't be for long.

On his return to Yamaha, Rossi took one win and a further five podiums to finish the season in fourth place overall, behind Márquez, Lorenzo and Pedrosa. Pedrosa, a serial race winner but seldom a genuine threat for the championship, always maintained a civil relationship with Rossi, largely for this very reason. But Márquez had already broken many of Rossi's records in the lower classes and, by taking the MotoGP title at the first attempt and becoming the youngest-ever premier class world champion, he had even outdone Rossi. If the kid kept doing what he was doing, Rossi's reputation as the greatest of all time might well be under threat, and Rossi knew it. The storm clouds were gathering over their relationship.

It had been a reasonable season for Rossi, certainly far more encouraging than his two wasted years at Ducati, but it was still his worst-ever finish in the championship when not on a Ducati and, for him, that wasn't good enough. He was Valentino Rossi, after all – he was supposed to win. And if he wasn't winning then perhaps something was lacking in his team and preventing him from doing so. At the end of his first year back with Yamaha, Rossi shocked the racing world by sacking his crew chief of the past thirteen years, Jerry Burgess.

'I totally understood that move,' Neil Hodgson says. 'Things hadn't exactly started going wrong for Rossi at that time but it was becoming harder for him, so he clearly thought, "I need to make some changes." As a rider you're constantly looking at ways to be better and changing crew chiefs was one of the things he felt he could benefit from. Riders' egos are huge anyway, but can you imagine what Rossi's must be like? I don't mean he's cocky, but his self-belief must be massive, so when the results aren't quite as you would like them to be then you start looking for reasons why, because you're convinced it's not your own fault – especially if you're Valentino Rossi. With technology changing as fast as it does in MotoGP, he obviously just thought it was time for a change and time to see if a new crew chief could help turn things around for him.'

As a former World Superbike champion, Hodgson has the mentality of a racer and fully understood Rossi's decision, but most people were puzzled by it. After all, Burgess had won thirteen world titles as crew chief to Wayne Gardner, Mick Doohan and Valentino Rossi – there seemed to be no one better qualified as a right-hand man. To some, the move reeked of desperation. But if Rossi could not improve his own riding and could not change manufacturers again (there was nowhere left to go), then changing his crew chief was the only significant step he could take to try to turn his results around. 'I've decided for next year I need to change something to try to find new motivation and to have a boost to improve my level, my speed,' Rossi explained. 'Next year will be crucial and I need new motivation. In the last few races I've felt I wanted to work in a different way. It was a difficult choice to make... He is not just my chief mechanic – he is like part of my family, my father in racing.'

Burgess himself sensed a touch of desperation in Rossi's move, saying, 'I've read many sporting biographies where people coming to the end of their careers make changes like this – like a golfer changing his caddy.' But while he admitted being 'blindsided' by his sacking, Burgess did already have one eye on retirement and a wife in poor health whom he naturally wished to spend more time with, so it was not the blow it might have been and the Aussie accepted his fate with quiet dignity. 'This wasn't quite the way I'd envisaged leaving Europe,' he said. But what really hurt was the way in which Burgess, after so many years of loyal service, learned of his sacking. Rather than being told in person by Rossi, as one would expect, the news was leaked by a member of Rossi's inner circle and Burgess learned of his fate in the press. It was an undignified end to a partnership that had yielded 7 world titles, 80 Grand Prix race wins, and a further 66 podiums.

The man Rossi chose to replace Burgess with was Silvano Galbusera, a crew chief with decades of experience in Grand Prix, Superbike, Supersport and even the Paris-Dakar Rally but, while having had experience with 500cc two-stroke Grand Prix machines, he had never worked on MotoGP bikes before. One of the biggest advantages in working with Galbusera, according to Rossi, was sharing a common language. While Rossi's English is good, speaking complex technical jargon in a second language is never ideal, so he could now at least discuss the intricacies of setting up a MotoGP bike in his native tongue.

There were other problems for Rossi to consider, too. During his wilderness years at Ducati and on his first year back on the Yamaha, a new generation of MotoGP riders had come to the fore: Jorge Lorenzo, Dani Pedrosa and Marc Márquez had become the new benchmarks of the sport that Rossi had once dominated. The now retired Casey Stoner believes that, had Rossi faced such fierce competition in his earlier years, he would never have achieved as much as he did. 'I genuinely feel that if he had come through during a more difficult era, like the one myself, Dani, Jorge, Dovi [Andrea Dovizioso] and Simoncelli came through, he wouldn't have enjoyed the same level of success early in his career and he wouldn't have developed into the same rider as a result.'[1]

Rossi was now the elder statesman of the class. The younger riders had learned from him and then gone on to push the limits even more, to such an extent that Rossi would now have to learn from *them* if he was to have any hope of keeping up. In an interview for motogp.com, Rossi explained just how dedicated this new generation was: 'The next generation is always stronger. They are more professional, they put more effort in, they make a perfect life, they eat in a good way, they don't drink, they go to sleep early, they train every day from the morning to the night... I come from an era where the riders drank beer and smoked cigarettes!'

Technology had moved on, too, and that also meant a more scientific approach to racing was called for. 'For me now the preparation is crucial,' Rossi said. 'It is not double, but ten times more, compared to 2003. Now, everybody see the video, you have a lot more support from the technology, you have people with a camera in all the corners so you know exactly the way your team-mate rides or also a rider from another manufacturer. Before, you see the race, you follow the other riders but, at the end, the preparation was ten times less than now.'

Marc Márquez in particular had brought a whole new riding style to MotoGP; as much a revelation as the pioneers of the knee-dragging style of the 1970s, the young Spaniard was now riding with his elbow skimming the tarmac, effectively acting as a stabiliser should the front tyre begin to slip away. He hung the whole upper half of his body off the side of the bike in a way that hadn't been seen before and Rossi, in his mid-thirties, had to work hard to change the riding style that had served him so well during his entire career. 'I've worked a lot on my riding style,' he said. 'After a year with the Yamaha I've tried to change my riding style to make it more modern and adapt to the new tyres, which have less edge grip. Now you need to use your body more and move yourself more when leaning.'

Rossi was very much aware of the changing of the guard and admitted: 'Until 2010 the others learned from me but from 2013, and after Ducati, I have learned a lot from others.' In an interview for the Dorna documentary *Racing Together*, he explained how he had to change his style to meet the new challenge in MotoGP. 'After Gibernau, Biaggi and Capirossi, who I had some great battles with, I think my rivalry with Biaggi was most fiery. But I was always the one that could push that bit further so I could go into battle with a more positive outlook: I could do whatever I wanted. Then when Stoner arrived – also Pedrosa and Lorenzo and then Márquez – they were even stronger, so I had to change my approach and also try to watch them and learn how I could be even better.'

Like changing the way you walk, changing a riding style is not an easy thing to do – in fact, some riders find it impossible – but such was Rossi's determination to extend his career and get back to winning ways that he did, at least in part, succeed. 'I know I couldn't change my riding style and most other people can't either,' says Neil Hodgson. 'If you look at most riders, they have about a five-year window when they're in their prime and then the younger generation comes along and starts doing things differently and the older ones just can't change and can't keep up. I'm sure that in Rossi's case it's helped him being able to train with younger riders, just being around them every day and seeing how they do things, but he's also like the Peter Pan of racing – he's not married, he hasn't got kids. Most people, by that age, have a couple of kids and their wives are moaning at them, asking, "Are you going to spend this weekend with me or are you going to be riding your bike again?" But Rossi doesn't have any of those distractions and that has to help.'

But there was no getting away from it – Rossi *was* getting old by MotoGP standards. He had to train harder in order to compete with the much younger competition, he had to learn a new riding style in order to try and emulate the lap times being set by Marc Márquez, and he had to learn to master the increasingly complex electronics packages that now played such a crucial role on a MotoGP bike, something that former Grand Prix rider and BBC presenter Steve Parrish thinks may have been particularly difficult. 'He would have found it harder to trust electronics than some of the younger riders who had been brought up on them. For him to trust technology that he wasn't raised with – I suspect that's where he lost some of his speed in the later years.'

Kevin Schwantz agrees that getting to grips with electronics and learning to trust them is not an easy process. 'I think Valentino changed his riding style to adapt to the electronics, but absolutely, one hundred per cent, when I did the Suzuka 8 Hours in 2014 and 2015 that was one of the things that I struggled with the most. Going around Dunlop corner while the bike was moving at both the front and rear and the guys were telling me to just trust the electronics and go and roll smoothly on through the throttle and it'll pick up itself... So, it IS difficult to adapt to electronics. But for Rossi to have come through the 125cc class, the 250cc class, the 500cc class and the early MotoGP years when they had some electronics but nothing like they do now? That's an extra tip of the hat from me – to be able to adapt to complex electronics and to change riding style and change focus and to do what your mind tells you you shouldn't be doing… He obviously got to grips with that pretty well.'

Rossi also had to dig deep to find the motivation to continue travelling around the world and to deal with the incessant attentions of the fans and the media. With millions in the bank and no need to worry about his financial future, he must have asked himself if it was worth it all, especially since his chosen sport was so dangerous. 'I have no idea how he's managed to do what he's done for so long,' Hodgson says. 'And not only managed it but managed it while also being Valentino Rossi. It was easy for me – I can go wherever I want and not get hassled by fans or the press, but it was far worse for him. I saw a fan having a selfie taken with Vale just the other day and thought, "God, how many millions of those has he patiently done?" And yet he always smiles and makes sure he looks happy in the picture. People at home switch on their TV on a Sunday and watch the riders at another circuit somewhere in the world but they don't appreciate the travel involved in getting there each weekend. It's relentless, especially if you're a factory rider and have to do all the PR commitments as well. It's not just nineteen rounds of racing, it's all the testing and public appearances on top of the racing.'

Money certainly wasn't the motivating factor, as it may be for some riders entering the twilight of their careers. 'A lot of racers I know, when they're past getting their best results, still race on for a couple of seasons just to tick some more boxes – sort out a pension fund and get some extra money in the bank – but we all know that Valentino doesn't need any more money. So to still have the drive and determination to race on as long as he has, and to put up with all the downsides of the sport, is so impressive. And he still has to race the best riders on the best bikes in the world; he has never dropped down to a lesser championship. I mean, people say he's had some disappointing years of late, but I'd have cut my left arm off to have been as successful as he was in his most disappointing years!'

Niall Mackenzie is also impressed with Rossi's determination to keep on racing. 'I think it's just incredible that he's still riding. He has all the money, all the success, all the women, all those records in MotoGP, and yet he still wants to do it. It's just phenomenal, really. He obviously loves riding bikes so much and that's why he keeps going. He has nothing left to prove but he has no wife or kids or anything in his life that's more important than racing. Most riders evolve into family men and try to get a bit of security behind them but he has a clean sheet so he just keeps going. But the thing that's impressed me most about Rossi over the years has been his consistency – being fast and keeping his chin up in public when things are obviously not going well behind the scenes. He always seems to be upbeat and seems to enjoy himself so much and is always up for the challenge. He just comes out year after year after year, at the very highest level, and is always competitive. It's so unusual for any sportsman to go on for that long at that level.'

It's Rossi's undying motivation to keep on going year after year that impresses Kevin Schwantz the most. Schwantz raced in Grands Prix for ten seasons while Rossi has been at the top level for twenty-five years (as of the 2020 season) and counting. 'Could I imagine racing at the top level for twenty-five years? Absolutely not,' Schwantz says. 'Between all the pressure from the media, from sponsors, from everything involved in the sport, it wasn't hard for me to decide to walk away. Injuries were a bit of it, yeah, but I had given all I could give and I didn't have anything else. But apart from the work side of it, for me Sunday afternoon was what I lived for. It was all the other stuff – it was all the travel, all the media stuff, all the stuff for sponsors, travelling here, travelling there, going everywhere to do stuff… It's all part of the job but it does wear on you, that's for sure. Even if I had been healthy, how do you find motivation every day that you have off to try and go out and better yourself? If you'd done what Rossi has done – he's won, he's dominated – so where does he find the motivation during the winter to just go and chase that dream again?'

Rossi has himself admitted that motivation is everything. 'Motivation is the key. More than training, more than experience or age, motivation counts. You have to ask yourself: "Why am I racing?" I race because I like it, because I'm really enjoying it. I like to set up my bike and ride it on track… I'm still highly motivated. Everything else is a consequence.'[2]

Schwantz says the buzz of winning a Grand Prix cannot be replicated in any other way and believes this is the reason Rossi continues to race. 'Winning a Grand Prix is a lot of fun and, absolutely, it's a buzz. Coming back to the garage afterwards and seeing the team all celebrating and everybody happy – sponsors, friends, family, team members, team members' families, it's an amazing feeling and, typically, it's a pretty big whoop-up that night. It's always really enjoyable after you win a race – there's nothing else that feels like it. It's one of those things that you wanna keep doing 'cos you think that the next win is maybe gonna be at the next race. But at a certain time, you have to realise that maybe that's not gonna happen so you have to step back and let somebody younger get on the bike. You can still be part of the sport as a team manager or owner and you can still get some satisfaction out of it but not nearly the same that you would get as a rider.'

In 2013, Rossi had had to settle for fourth best, having struggled with braking on his Yamaha M1 thanks to a softer compound front Bridgestone tyre that he felt affected stability. He and his crew tried everything to adjust the set-up of the bike to get around the problem but never quite managed it. The end result was the sacking of Jerry Burgess ahead of the 2014 season but, to the surprise of many, the change in crew chief seemed to work: in his second year back with Yamaha, Valentino looked much more like his old self. After taking one win and a further five podiums in 2013, he took two wins and a far more impressive eleven podiums in 2014. He also took his first pole position since 2010, only failed to score points on one occasion when he crashed out of a wet Aragon race and finished second in the championship – his highest placing since he won the title in 2009. Márquez may have taken his second consecutive championship but Rossi had ridden as well as ever, proving to be more consistent than his (often faster) team-mate Jorge Lorenzo and also proving that experience could be just as important as youth in the world's premier motorcycle-racing championship. By beating Lorenzo, Rossi also gained more standing within the Yamaha team, an accomplishment that must have been particularly satisfying. He put that new-found power to good use too: when Yamaha tried to sign him on a one-year deal for 2015, he insisted on his usual two-year deal. He clearly wasn't intending to hang up his leathers any time soon.

But what to do about Márquez? In a truly astonishing display of riding, the young Spaniard won the first ten races of the 2014 season, something that even Rossi had never achieved (his most successful run being seven consecutive victories way back in 2002). It was clearly going to take something very special to beat the Spaniard and perhaps sheer speed was not going to be enough. Few would argue that, by this point, Márquez was the faster of the two riders on any given day, all other things being equal, but he still lacked the vast experience Rossi had at his disposal, nor did he have a history of out-psyching his rivals, either on or off the track. Rossi would have to employ every single weapon in his armoury if he was going to take an elusive tenth world title to cap a magnificent career, and in 2015 he came out of the traps fully locked and loaded, ready to fight with everything he had, by fair means or foul, for the greatest prize in motorcycle racing.

CHAPTER 13

EVERYTHING OR NOTHING

'Valentino's reaction exceeded the limits and
it is not what we want to see.'
ANDREA DOVIZIOSO

In his twentieth season of Grand Prix racing, Valentino Rossi
came out fighting like a tiger, determined to prove that he
wasn't too old, that he wasn't past his best, and to show the
new generation of MotoGP stars that he was still the boss. And
to achieve this, he knew he would have to beat the greatest
rider of that new generation: Marc Márquez.

Rossi was in his third year back at Yamaha and the bike
had been dramatically improved for the 2015 season. At the
same time, Márquez was having untold trouble with his new
Honda, which had taken a step backwards compared to the
previous year's machine. Rossi saw his chance: it was now or
never; everything or nothing.

First blood went to Valentino in Qatar after having to

fight off a rejuvenated Ducati in the hands of fellow Italian Andrea Dovizioso. Márquez could only limp home in fifth place on his evil-handling Honda. While the Spaniard somehow managed to win the next round in America, Rossi came home third to maintain his championship lead. And then the fireworks started.

In Argentina, Márquez opted for a harder rear tyre which offered more grip but less durability. His race strategy was to pull out as much of a lead as he could in the early part of the race in the hope that he would have enough in hand when his tyre eventually went off. By half race distance he had built up a 4.15-second advantage and even Rossi, in second place, thought the Spaniard had the race in the bag. But he wasn't about to throw in the towel. 'I had to try,' he said. 'I concentrated only on my own speed. I had to catch him – or scare him.'

Rossi dug as deep as he ever had, riding like a man possessed, lap after lap, in a bid to put so much pressure on Márquez that he would be forced into making a mistake. By the penultimate lap, Rossi had closed the gap and managed to overtake his rival in the second corner. Márquez, worn tyre or no, came straight back at him. At the end of the back straight Rossi once more fought his way past only to be counter-attacked again in the tight right-hand corner that followed. This time Márquez got so close that the bikes touched, but Rossi stayed ahead. At the next left-hand corner the Spaniard tried yet again to muscle his way past but it was now looking like desperation and recklessness: Rossi had the correct line and when the front wheel of Márquez's bike clipped the rear wheel of Rossi's machine it was game over for the Honda rider. He crashed out, allowing Rossi to win the race and increase his championship lead over Andrea Dovizioso to 6 points.

So far, so good. It looked like the old master was back and well on track to win a tenth world championship. But the clash with Márquez in Argentina had started something. Rossi had finally met a man with the same maniacal, insatiable desire to win that he had and, what's more, this opponent had long been a Rossi fan and knew all his tricks; he would not be intimidated by psychological warfare away from the track or by bullying and harsh moves on it. Rossi had been innocent in Argentina but Márquez's hatred of losing was as strong as Rossi's own, so there was no question that he would take the fight back to Rossi with any means at his disposal. It was only a matter of time.

But the 2015 title fight wasn't just about Rossi and Márquez: Jorge Lorenzo would form the third part of the triumvirate that would participate in one of the greatest seasons that Grand Prix motorcycle racing had ever produced. In fact, the drama that unfolded centred around him, or rather, his respective relationships with Rossi and Márquez as the season ebbed and flowed.

Like Rossi, Márquez had also formed a deep dislike of Lorenzo and he too had clashed with him in the past. This meant that for the first few seasons that Rossi and Márquez raced together they had shared a common belief that 'your enemy's enemy is your friend' and had, as a result, been on very friendly terms, often laughing and joking together on the podium while Lorenzo stood aloof and alone. But the dynamics between all three riders would swing and shift throughout the 2015 season as the battle for the world title heated up and it would prove pivotal in deciding who would be champion.

Lorenzo was also reaping the benefits of a greatly improved Yamaha in 2015 and won the next four races after Argentina to close to within one point of Rossi's championship lead. Then the MotoGP circus headed to Assen, the scene of the next Rossi/Márquez brawl. For the first nineteen laps Márquez had shadowed Rossi, never more than two-tenths behind; watching, waiting, stalking, learning his opponent's strong and weak points. On lap twenty, the Spaniard pounced but was repelled by Rossi four laps later in a move that guaranteed a last-lap showdown. Both men had smashed the Assen lap record and were riding so fast that third-placed man Lorenzo was a full fifteen seconds adrift. Rossi led into the final right-left-right chicane but a Márquez move was inevitable and, when it came, it all went wrong. The Honda rider took the inside line on the approach to the first right and smashed straight into the side of his rival, sending him off the track and over the kerbs and dirt. With Márquez's bike being unsettled by the contact, he was forced to run wide and slow down while Rossi accelerated hard over the dirt to rejoin the track in the lead, having missed out the final corner.

Race direction immediately began an analysis of the incident and eventually decided no penalties should be issued to either rider: Rossi may have missed the last corner, but only because Márquez forced him off the track. Naturally, Márquez didn't see it that way and complained bitterly that he had been on the inside line and Rossi had not taken the final corner. But his protests fell on deaf ears and the result stood. The old master had finally defeated the young pretender in a last-lap head-to-head and had extended his championship lead at the same time. Rossi was back, there was no denying it. A tenth world title looked increasingly likely.

The wins over the next seven rounds were shared by Márquez (three), Jorge Lorenzo (two), Rossi (one) and Dani Pedrosa (one), but Rossi had the greater consistency in finding the podium when he couldn't win and by the time the Australian Grand Prix rolled around he had an 18-point lead over Lorenzo. With Márquez a full 86 points behind Rossi after crashing out of five races, he was now out of the race for the championship – and it was that very fact which would later cause so much controversy.

Márquez won the Australian Grand Prix after a ferocious four-way scrap between himself, Lorenzo, Rossi and Andrea Iannone, yet Rossi claimed afterwards that the young Spaniard had deliberately got in his way in order to help his countryman, Lorenzo, gain more points. It was a strange claim, given that Márquez had actually beaten Lorenzo, thereby denying him five vital points. But it was nothing compared to the verbal attack he unleashed on Márquez at the pre-race press conference ahead of the Malaysian Grand Prix, where he not only reiterated this claim but questioned Márquez's own claim that he had once been a Rossi fan. Rossi also accused him of deliberately hindering him on track. 'I think that his target is not just to win the race but also to help Lorenzo to go far and try to take more points on me. So I think that from Phillip Island [Australian Grand Prix] it's very clear that Jorge has a new supporter, that is Marc.'

Jorge Lorenzo certainly found the comments strange, having just been beaten to the win by Márquez. When asked if Márquez had indeed helped him in the race his sarcasm spoke volumes: 'Sure he helped me,' he said. 'Especially on the last lap.'

Was it the old Rossi psychological warfare at work again or was he feeling the pressure of closing in on a tenth title? Were the cracks beginning to show? Rossi's claims didn't seem to make sense, given that Márquez had beaten Lorenzo last time out. And his remarks shocked not only Márquez but every journalist at the press conference. The only difference was that Márquez took the comments personally and inwardly determined that he would do something about them. And at the Malaysian Grand Prix, all hell broke loose.

★

It appeared to take less than four seconds to undo twenty years of hard and dangerous work; to undermine all the sportsmanship and dignity he had always displayed in both victory and defeat; to shatter the reputation he had built up over two decades, and more than half his life, by winning nine world championships and more MotoGP races than any other rider in history.

More than 320 million people around the world watched in utter disbelief as the great Valentino Rossi ran Marc Márquez out to the edge of the Sepang circuit then snapped out his left leg and appeared to kick the Spaniard from his motorcycle, causing him to crash out on the seventh lap of the Malaysian Grand Prix.

MotoGP is a deadly sport. It may be less dangerous than it was in the past, thanks to constantly evolving safety measures, but riders still die in pursuit of victory and no one is more aware of this fact than Rossi himself. It had only been four years since he had lost his great friend Marco Simoncelli at the very same circuit, which made Rossi's actions in Sepang all the more shocking. For while professional motorcycle racers are willing, and prepared, to take risks with their own safety, risking the safety of other riders is never an option. That is the number one unwritten rule in racing. Like soldiers in the front line of combat, motorcycle racers have to be able to trust the men around them with their lives. Riding at over 200mph, so close to each other they're often left with scuff marks or rubber marks from brushing their rivals' bikes or tyres, racers need to be able to trust one another infinitely, even if they are bitter enemies.

If trust and honour are not motivation enough, there is another factor at play: should one rider deliberately run into another, the chances are they would both crash out, so self-preservation also plays its part. Either way, competitors in MotoGP do not kick each other off their bikes. So to see a rider of Rossi's calibre – known for his fairness, sportsmanship, and superhuman levels of control over twenty years of racing – resort to such potentially lethal tactics was shocking.

In the seconds that followed the incident most of the trackside spectators and the millions watching around the world had to have been stunned into silence, jaws hanging open, disbelief writ large on their faces. Surely he couldn't have? Surely he wouldn't have? Surely he didn't?

The silence was short-lived. Pandemonium followed.

Márquez's Repsol Honda team members threw their hands up in disbelief and outrage as they watched the incident unfolding on the monitors in their sweltering Malaysian garage. Team boss Livio Suppo made straight for race direction to lodge a protest. Many of the tens of thousands of spectators at the track bellowed their protests while Rossi's own team looked distinctly sheepish, not quite believing their eyes. TV viewers in every country from Argentina to Australia howled at their screens, social media lit up on a global level – and not just with race fans, but with the mainstream public joining in too. After all, everyone loves a bit of controversy; a chance to take sides and to voice opinions, no matter what sport is involved. In the sixty-six-year history of Grand Prix motorcycle racing there had never been a moment like this – or at least, not one that was captured by cameras in its entirety and beamed around the world live, later to be subjected to endless slow-motion replays from various angles. For the two protagonists there was absolutely nowhere to hide: they would have to stand or fall by a split-second decision, made in the heat of battle, as adrenalin was surging through their bodies and the 'red mist', so often referred to by motorcycle racers, clouded their vision. Was Rossi to blame or had Márquez frustrated him past the limits of endurance by deliberately getting in his way to prevent the faster Rossi from giving chase to Jorge Lorenzo?

Even Rossi's fiercely loyal army of fans watched in stunned disbelief at their hero's actions. No true fan of motorcycle racing wants to see riders getting hurt. It happens too often as it is; deliberately dangerous actions are indefensible, no matter who commits them.

Márquez managed to remount his factory Honda RC213V after the incident, but it was too badly damaged for him to be able to rejoin the race. Instead, he rode slowly back to his garage and was quickly hidden from view as the doors came firmly down to shield him from the media frenzy that was already erupting. Rossi finished the race in third place behind Dani Pedrosa and Jorge Lorenzo, meaning he had to go through the same process that all top-three finishers are required to do: he parked his motorcycle in the winners' enclosure, spoke to the TV crews and mounted the podium to accept his trophy and bottle of cava. Only after he had completed this standard routine did he have to face the greatest fallout of his long and distinguished career – and the one that threatened to define him.

With Márquez being out of contention for the 2015 title, he might have been expected to stay out of the way of the two title protagonists – Rossi and Lorenzo – in Sepang. That's another unwritten rule of racing: not that you will roll over and let others win, far from it, but that you should not unduly interfere with those who have everything to play for while you yourself cannot win the title.

Of course, Márquez had sponsors to keep happy and wanted to finish the season with as many wins and points as possible. That goes without saying. He had every right to fight for position on track, but most riders would only overtake title contenders if they could do so cleanly and without unduly impeding their progress or risking a crash that could knock them out of contention. Had Márquez possessed a much faster pace on race day than Rossi, Lorenzo and Pedrosa, and had cleared off to win the Sepang race, nobody would have complained. It was the manner in which he would repeatedly attack Rossi once the flag dropped that provided Rossi with a defence of sorts.

While Márquez was criticised for choosing to ignore this unwritten rule, it should be remembered that Rossi himself had also chosen to ignore it on occasion, most notably at Motegi, Japan, in 2010. At that time, he was out of contention for the championship (having broken his leg earlier in the year) while his team-mate Lorenzo had one hand on the trophy. Under the circumstances, Lorenzo might have expected his team-mate not to interfere with his progress, but help from Rossi was not forthcoming. Instead, the Italian hounded the Spaniard and fought him tooth and nail for the final podium place, eventually coming out on top after colliding with Lorenzo several times. So Rossi had already committed the same 'crime' he was now accusing Márquez of.

Lorenzo had been furious after that Japanese race, as were the Yamaha bosses who took Rossi into the team office and had severe words with him. They fell on deaf ears. 'Yamaha asked me to race with more attention,' Rossi said afterwards. When asked what he would do in the event of a similar situation arising with his team-mate again, he smiled and said, 'I will try to beat him again... with more attention.'

Rossi accused Márquez of further plotting too. Despite being fourteen years Rossi's junior, Márquez was already a four-time world champion across three different classes (125cc, Moto2 and MotoGP) and clearly had many years ahead of him to beat Rossi's tally of nine world titles. Even so, world titles are never easy to come by and if Rossi took a tenth crown in 2015, he would be that bit harder to surpass in the record books. Was Márquez really looking that far ahead? Rossi seemed to think so. 'I think Márquez is much compared to me,' he said. 'He wants to beat me on the number of wins, so if I win another world championship he knows he will have to win another world championship to catch up.'

Rossi has always been well known for trying to out-psyche his rivals, forever seeking any slight chink in their armour that would give him an advantage. 'Yeah, he's good at playing mind games and trying to psyche his competitors out,' says Kevin Schwantz. 'But I think what psyched them out more than anything was that, while a lot of guys can talk smack, they can't back it up, but Valentino always backs his talking up. He's been around for a long, long time so he knows exactly how to play those games.'

There were many times when those games worked; when the likes of Max Biaggi and Sete Gibernau had seemed to let Rossi's carefully chosen words germinate in their heads and sometimes found themselves beaten before they had even turned a wheel in anger. But Márquez was made of stronger stuff and had the advantage of knowing about Rossi's modus operandi, so he simply refused to let his rival's words play on his mind. Instead of buckling, he would dig in and fight even harder. Young he may have been, mentally weak he most certainly wasn't.

During the race in Sepang, Rossi had passed Márquez and was trying to break away from him in order to chase down his title rival, Jorge Lorenzo, who was in second place while Dani Pedrosa headed the field. Márquez clearly did not have the pace to go with either Pedrosa or Lorenzo but seemed happy to apply a gargantuan effort to pass and re-pass Rossi, to interrupt his rhythm, and to prevent him from closing in on Lorenzo. In the first seven laps of the race the pair changed places no fewer than seventeen times, with nine of those passes coming on lap five alone. That early in the race, it seemed like madness: two riders constantly disputing position allows other riders to break away (and those behind to catch up) and both Márquez and Rossi were keenly aware of this. So long as they tangled with each other at every corner, Pedrosa and Lorenzo would increase their advantage; one could almost feel Rossi's growing frustration.

If the pair had been fighting for the world title this would be completely normal, but many felt – and Rossi was chief amongst them – that Márquez was deliberately obstructing him and trying to slow him down. The message from Márquez seemed clear: 'You think I was messing with you in Australia? This is what it feels like when I *really* mess with you.'

But then, what did Rossi expect after his very public accusations against Márquez just one day earlier? That he would simply move aside and allow him through? Or that Márquez would be inspired to beat Lorenzo to prove that he *wasn't* trying to help his countryman? This latter scenario may have been what Rossi had in mind all along. He knew he did not have the pace to beat Lorenzo if conditions were dry and the sometimes-fickle Spaniard was on form, so was he trying to play a double bluff? Was he trying to use the sheer pace of Márquez to deny Lorenzo points because he himself could not do so? Was his aim to force Márquez to try even harder to beat Lorenzo just to prove that he *wasn't* helping him?

Whatever Rossi's thinking ahead of the race, his plan backfired once it began, and rather than unsettling Márquez he inspired him to beat Rossi – not Lorenzo – at all costs, even if there was no chance of a race win or world title in it for him.

Frustrated to near breaking point, Rossi threw up a hand up and gesticulated towards Márquez on more than one occasion, clearly bewildered and angered at the Spaniard's tactics. Then, on lap seven, he looked over at Márquez (again, not normal practice in motorcycle racing) and deliberately, and dramatically, slowed his pace as he entered turn fourteen, running wide and forcing Márquez to take an even wider trajectory around the corner. Márquez eventually had to turn in or he would have been pushed onto the dirty and slippery outer limits of the track, or even off of it, and at that point, since Rossi was still drifting outwards, the two bikes collided. In the ensuing tangle, Rossi looked directly at Márquez again then appeared to lash out with his left foot and kick his rival from his bike.

Márquez went down, thankfully unhurt, while Rossi carried on, though he immediately looked over both shoulders to see what had become of his rival. 'At turn fourteen he passed me on the inside, I sat the bike up, he kept going straight ahead and I saw him looking at me,' Márquez explained once he had calmed down sufficiently. 'I didn't know what to do. Then he kicked out at me, knocking my brake lever, and I crashed. I've never seen anything like it – a rider kicking another rider... I hope, for the sake of the sport that this ends here.'

Rossi vehemently denied doing any such thing, yet his denial rang hollow as endless slow-motion replays of the incident on television seemed to clearly show he had kicked Márquez off his bike. It was only when helicopter footage of the incident was played that Rossi fans breathed a huge sigh of relief. The aerial shots showed the bikes becoming tangled and Márquez's right handlebar snagging Rossi's boot. Rossi appeared to free himself by flicking his left leg. It still wasn't clear-cut by any means (there's not much difference between a flick and a kick after all), but it did at least give the yellow camp a chance at making a defence.

'It's very clear from the images, especially from the helicopter, that I don't want to make him crash,' Rossi explained. 'I just want to make him lose time and go out of the line and slow down, because also in Australia he make his dirty game, you know? When I go wide, wide, wide, I slow down, and I look at him like saying, "Fuck! What the fuck are you doing?" His right handlebar touched my leg and I lost my foot from the footpeg. If you look at the images from the helicopter it's clear that, when I lose my foot from the footpeg, Márquez has already crashed, so I don't want to kick him. Also, if you give a kick to a MotoGP bike, it doesn't crash – it's very heavy.'

Graziano Rossi stood by his son's side throughout and, unusually, was even prepared to voice his opinions to the press. 'Valentino didn't lose his head,' he insisted. 'It would have been serious if he kicked Marc, but this didn't happen. He did the only thing he could do – call Márquez's attention to the fact that, while they were passing and re-passing each other, Lorenzo and Pedrosa were pulling away. From a rider's point of view, it's easy to understand – Valentino couldn't continue to lose time due to Marc's unmotivated passes. He called Márquez's attention to this, but in doing this, Marc touched his brake lever and crashed. This was very unlucky for Valentino. He absolutely didn't want to make Marc crash. A rider never wants to crash.'[1]

In the melee that followed the incident, security had to be called in to prevent Rossi's fan club management from storming Márquez's garage – an unprecedented situation in MotoGP, and not one that was welcomed. Never had the GP paddock been so divided and forced to take sides. Never had it threatened to erupt into violence.

Second-place finisher Jorge Lorenzo made his own feelings on the subject very clear on the podium. When Rossi stepped up to take his trophy for third place, Lorenzo made a thumbs-down gesture, but he was booed by the crowd, the majority of whom were clearly still supporting Rossi. When Lorenzo left the podium before the cava was even sprayed, it was to the sound of further jeering and booing.

Soon afterwards, perhaps sensing that he had yet again not done himself any favours on the popularity front, Lorenzo apologised for his behaviour. 'It was a mistake – the gesture that I made on the podium. I regret that and I want to say sorry, especially to the people who watch on the television, because it's not a sporting example for the people, especially the young people who watch MotoGP around the world. So I'm sorry for this gesture.'

Opinion throughout the racing world was, and still is, split on the Rossi/Márquez clash. Rossi's former rival, Casey Stoner, was one of millions to voice his opinion on Twitter. 'If anyone else had done what Valentino did, we would have been black-flagged immediately, no questions asked.' Britain's four-time World Superbike champion, Carl Fogarty, was of the same opinion, saying, 'I think if it was any other rider they would have been disqualified from the race, for sure.'

Andrea Dovizioso, who crashed out of the Sepang race on his Ducati, saw things differently and perhaps offered the most balanced view of the incident. 'Márquez was racing for the podium, but also to disturb Rossi,' he said. 'Valentino's reaction exceeded the limits and it is not what we want to see. I believe Marc was provoking him and Rossi fell into his trap. Rossi contributed to the rising tension on Thursday and we can say that their relationship is finally over. For sure, Marc was playing with Valentino, but he remained within the rules.'

Others, including former racer turned BT Sport commentator, Keith Huewen, and former MotoGP rider, Alex Hofmann, felt both parties were at fault and should share the blame. 'It's sad that two of the greatest riders in MotoGP resorted to dirty tactics,' Huewen tweeted, while Hofman wrote, 'Both have proved they can race each other fair before but both haven't done that today for whatever reason. Both deserve to be punished.'

Vito Ippolito, the president of the FIM, published an open letter condemning both riders for their behaviour, accusing them of bringing the sport into disrepute. In the end it was Rossi who was punished: he was issued with three penalty points which, when added to the one he had already accrued in Misano for getting in Lorenzo's way during qualifying, meant he would be forced to start from the back of the grid in the final race of the season at Valencia. The decision, in effect, decided the outcome of the 2015 world championship.

'Our opinion was that there was some fault on both sides,' said MotoGP race director, Mike Webb. 'But as far as the rulebook goes Márquez did not make any contact, did not break any rules as such, but we feel that his behaviour was causing problems to Rossi, who reacted. Unfortunately, he reacted in a way that is against the rules. It looked like we were going to have a great race but unfortunately it ended in an incident that's controversial.'

Rossi immediately appealed the decision on the grounds that the penalty was too harsh but the FIM stewards overruled him. He then lodged an appeal with the Court of Arbitration in Sport (CAS) – the highest body any sportsman can appeal to – but the court ruled that the penalty should stand while further investigations took place. Rossi would not hear the final outcome until long after the racing season was over and, in the end, the CAS ruled against him, so it mattered little.

Rossi fans began an online petition to have his penalty overturned and it quickly attracted over 750,000 signatures, but it was also to no avail: Rossi would have to start the final round of the season from 25th place on the grid, though still with a 7-point lead in the championship. With 25 points going to the winner of a MotoGP race and 20 points available for second place, he would have to either beat or finish second to Jorge Lorenzo, or hope that the Respol Hondas of Dani Pedrosa and Marc Márquez could finish ahead of Lorenzo and deny him a maximum points haul. It was safe to assume Rossi could expect no help from Márquez.

The atmosphere at Valencia was more tense than at any other Grand Prix in history and Spanish police declared the meeting a high-alert event. Extra officers were brought in to bolster the already heightened levels of security amidst fears that Rossi fans and Márquez fans would clash. Repsol Honda team boss Livio Suppo admitted in 2020 that he had even suggested to both Márquez and Pedrosa that they should pull out of the race after one lap to avoid becoming involved in the title fight between Rossi and Lorenzo. His advice was ignored.

Rossi fans had issued death threats to Márquez on social media and the Spanish rider and his family were physically threatened at home in Cervera. So high were emotions running at Valencia that the pre-race press conference was cancelled for fear of inflaming the situation and Yamaha even cancelled its sixtieth-birthday celebrations that had been planned for that weekend. It was a mess. But a mess draws crowds. According to official figures 110,000 fans turned up and packed the racetrack to absolute capacity while thousands more materialised without tickets, just on the off chance they might somehow get in. A ticket for the Valencia GP was the most sought-after sporting ticket in the world that weekend.

There's an old expression in motorcycle racing that states 'When the flag drops, the bullshit stops,' and when the starter's flag dropped at Valencia, talk was certainly of no more use. All that mattered was how fast you were and, in this test, Jorge Lorenzo came out on top. He was never headed, leading from flag to flag to take not only the race win but also his third MotoGP crown.

Rossi rode superbly to scythe his way past twenty of the world's best riders and end up in fourth place, but he could not affect the outcome of the championship from there. The conspiracy theorists – and Rossi agreed with them on this – claimed Márquez had acted as Lorenzo's bodyguard for the duration of the race. Despite having swapped places with Rossi seventeen times in seven laps at Sepang, Márquez never once attempted to pass Lorenzo in Valencia and seemed content to sit just half a second behind him, shadowing his every move. Less partial observers pointed out that Lorenzo had won all his races in the 2015 season in exactly the same manner – leading every lap – so why suddenly find the pattern unusual now? When everything is right for Lorenzo he is a perfect automaton, lapping with a precision that is almost superhuman and that makes him exceedingly difficult to pass. Perhaps Márquez simply had no answer for him on the day. Márquez himself pointed out this fact and added that he had been planning an all-out attack towards the end of the race but when his team-mate, Dani Pedrosa, found his own blistering pace in the final laps and overtook him, Márquez lost half a second regaining the position and that was enough to allow Lorenzo to take the win. Such is the global support for Valentino Rossi, however, that Márquez found himself being jeered and booed when he took to the podium. And this at a home race, on his own Spanish soil. Never had the old adage been more clearly illustrated: for Valentino Rossi, every race is a home race, even when it's a controversial one.

It hardly mattered. For Rossi to take the title, it would have been necessary for both Repsol Honda riders to beat Lorenzo and no rider can rely on the actions of others to win championships for them. Rossi had lost and he would have to deal with it. He did so by failing to attend the official FIM awards night, leaving a somewhat sheepish-looking Yamaha team member to take his place on stage in front of a silenced audience. On top of the last-minute cancellation of Yamaha's big sixtieth-anniversary plans – which would have seen top brass flying in from Japan and former Yamaha champions flying in from all over the world – it was an ignominious end to what had been an otherwise fantastic season for the rejuvenated Rossi and for Yamaha in general. They had, after all, just finished first and second in the world championship.

After two disastrous years at Ducati, Rossi had made steady progress since his return to Yamaha and was now as competitive as he'd ever been since his glory years of dominance in the mid-2000s. So there were positives to take from the 2015 season but, as yet, Rossi wasn't taking them. 'The championship had the potential to be one of the best but in the last three races something happened that nobody expected – Márquez decided to protect Lorenzo. The problems started at Phillip Island. I knew already my championship was finished before this race [Valencia] because I knew Márquez would finish his work.'

Rossi hadn't won a title since 2009 and must surely have seen 2015 as his last great chance to take that elusive tenth championship and perhaps retire more comfortably. It was a bitter blow and the bad taste did not leave his mouth over the long winter break. When he and Márquez rejoined battle in 2016 they were still sworn enemies and not on speaking terms: they didn't even acknowledge each other on the podium, in press conferences, or in parc fermé. And then at Catalunya, on 3 June 2016, Moto2 rider Luis Salom died during free practice 2 when he struck the trackside wall at high speed.

It was another cruel and sobering reminder that Grand Prix motorcycle racing is still a very dangerous sport. The young Spaniard's death saw the paddock united in grief and loss and suddenly the spat between Rossi and Márquez seemed childish and irrelevant. After another close duel in which Rossi came out on top to claim victory from his arch-enemy, the two found themselves in the winners' enclosure together at Catalunya, only this time the hatred was buried. There were more important things to consider: an untimely death had once again forced the MotoGP paddock to bury its simmering animosities and to realise that this was a very dangerous game they were all playing; a game that required respect. Feuding in the face of the great and tragic loss of one of their colleagues would have been unthinkable. Instead, Valentino Rossi and Marc Márquez looked each other directly in the eye, congratulated each other on their respective rides, and shook hands firmly.

It was over. For now, at least.

CHAPTER 14

AFTERMATH

'Rossi shouldn't have done what he did on track.
He fucked it up.'
NEIL HODGSON

Yamaha had taken first and second in the 2015 MotoGP world championship with Jorge Lorenzo and Valentino Rossi, but the celebrations were not what they should have been, as former Yamaha employee Andrew Smith explains: 'I think there was frustration because we won the world title, but it was a shame the way that it had been won and all the aggro that it had caused. My personal feeling is that pretty much everyone within Yamaha and everyone who wasn't a committed Honda fan wanted Valentino to get that tenth world title. But with the way that Lorenzo won it and with all that had gone on, I think Yamaha was in a no-win situation. If they had really celebrated and promoted Jorge's title it would have been rubbing Rossi's nose in it even more. Yes, we were world champions, but we certainly didn't milk it like we should have done and we certainly didn't get anywhere near what we would have done if Valentino had won it.'

But for all the awkwardness within the Yamaha camp, the popularity of Rossi had clearly not been irrevocably damaged by the bitter end to the 2015 season. 'In 2016, Yamaha had its first-ever Pan-European dealer conference for over 2,300 people in Barcelona,' Smith recalls. 'It had taken eighteen months to arrange and all the top management from Japan were present too. Lorenzo had won the championship, Vale was second, but they had fallen out big time. There were threats that they were going to put another wall up to divide their garage, so we decided it would be impossible for them both to be in the business meeting in the afternoon but that they could come to the dinner in the evening. We had to have Lorenzo on the stage at the business meeting because he was the world champion, but he got booed by the Italian dealers, which was pretty unfair and pretty embarrassing.

'In the evening we knew we had to have a reasonable entrance for Rossi but we were careful not to overshadow the world champion. So there were 2,300 people sitting down to dinner, all in formal black-tie dress, with all the bosses from Yamaha Japan, and they suddenly hear an R1 with a very loud Akrapovic exhaust on it being revved up outside the building. Then the back doors to the venue opened and in rides Rossi, revving it like crazy. This was all captured on the massive screens around the room and there was suddenly a stampede. I would say the average age of the dealers was about fifty – and these are professional business people – but they lost their minds like teenagers at a rock concert! They were out of control.'

Things didn't quite go according to plan. 'The plan had been for Rossi to sit down and have dinner then do an interview on stage,' Smith continues, 'but it was clearly going to be impossible to do that as the crowd was out of control. As I was the MC, I had to repeatedly ask everyone to return to their tables and sit down so that we could interview Vale on stage. They reluctantly sat down, still cheering "Vale! Vale! Vale!" So now we had to do the interview first and then rearrange the time when everybody could be served food later. But as soon as things got settled a bit, people started rushing the stage again – hordes of them – all trying to get a photograph, and it was out of control again. When we eventually got Rossi off stage and sat him at his table of eight for dinner, we quickly realised it was going to be impossible. He was completely swamped by people and they just wouldn't leave him alone. In the end we had to sneak him out and take him to a hotel for dinner. That night really showed me just how much power Rossi has.'

While Rossi still had the vast majority of fans on his side after the ugly scenes in 2015, not everyone was convinced he was innocent of all charges. 'I actually think that incident tarnished Rossi's image,' Neil Hodgson says. 'If you're a Rossi fan you'll just see it through your blinkered vision but, within the industry, I think his reputation was a bit tarnished by it all. I was there when it happened and I'm not exaggerating when I say I felt physically sick when I saw it unfold. I'm a massive Rossi fan but that was like a schoolyard fight that he started. He threw the first punch with the comments he made at the pre-race press conference. We all knew that, with the way Márquez is, he was going to come back scrapping, and that's exactly what happened. Everybody at that press conference was like "Eh? Where did that come from?" when Rossi came out with those comments. I interviewed Rossi immediately afterwards and he didn't back down a single bit. He stood by what he said. Rossi shouldn't have done what he did on track. He fucked it up. Like I say, I'm a huge fan, but with the job I do I'm paid to be honest and that's how I saw it.'

Yet while Hodgson points the finger of blame at Rossi, he acknowledges that Márquez came out of the situation the worst. 'I think Márquez was on his way to becoming quite popular until the 2015 season when he went up against Valentino. That ended his chances of picking up some of the Rossi fans once Rossi retires. No Rossi fan will ever support him after that – they hate him. I speak to so many Rossi fans who tell me that, but I always tell them Marc's actually a really nice bloke.'

Rossi's competitiveness in 2015 convinced both him and Yamaha that there was life in the old dog yet and a fresh two-year deal was signed that would see Rossi racing through to the end of 2018. Lorenzo had also been offered a deal at the opening round of the 2016 season in Qatar, but the Spaniard had stalled for time and, four rounds into the championship, it became clear why: he had signed for Ducati.

Seemingly as keen to get away from Rossi as Rossi had been to get away from him in 2010, Lorenzo was clearly not put off by the fact that Rossi had failed to win a single race on the Ducati. But then, the Italian bike had come a long way since then and both factory riders, Andrea Dovizioso and Andrea Iannone, took wins in 2016. Whether either rider could mount a serious championship campaign was open to question, however, hence Ducati's rumoured £25-million offer to Lorenzo for a two-year deal. It was a payday that would even have raised Valentino Rossi's eyebrows, but it would prove to be a bittersweet venture: Lorenzo also struggled on the Ducati and was so frustrated by his lack of progress in his second year on the bike that he signed a new deal to join Honda – just as he started winning on the Ducati. But it was too late to back out; a deal was a deal, so Jorge Lorenzo became another big-name rider who failed to win a championship on the Italian bike.

Seeking to gain any slight advantage he could in the face of such fierce opposition as Marc Márquez, Rossi tried a new tactic in 2016 – he employed former 125 and 250cc world champion and 500cc Grand Prix race winner Luca Cadalora as his 'spotter'. Cadalora's role could be likened to that of a riding coach; an observer who would stand trackside and see how Rossi was taking each corner in comparison to his rivals. It was not a new idea but it was the first time in his twenty years of Grand Prix racing that Rossi had felt the need for such assistance. 'I don't give any advice, I don't allow myself to say, "Do this or do that," Cadalora said of his role. 'I think about what I have seen and then speak, then Valentino decides to use those words as he sees fit. I go around the circuit with my scooter and study the track. I observe. I try to "feel" the circuit and watch how Valentino and the other riders interact with the track. And afterwards, by studying the times, perhaps he can discern whether it is better to use this or that line.'[1]

Cadalora noticed something inside Rossi's pit box, too – the way he interacted with every member of his team and brought the best out in all of them. 'Valentino always has the right word for everyone, from the crew chief to the cook, and with this empathy he gets the most out of each member of his circle.'[2]

Hiring Cadalora seemed to pay off. The 2016 season was another good one for Rossi, especially considering how many years he was now giving away to the competition, but he didn't win as many races (two, compared to four the previous season), though that was more a measure of just how tight and competitive MotoGP racing had become: in 2016, there were a record eight race winners from eighteen races. Rossi might have added another home win at Mugello had fate not intervened. He set off from pole position and was fighting for his first home win in eight years when his engine blew up. It was his first mechanical failure since 2007 and couldn't have come at a worse time. In what was an embarrassing weekend for Yamaha – Jorge Lorenzo's engine also blew up – but at least it was only in practice, not in the race itself.

Rossi would finish second in the championship again, 49 points behind the champion, Marc Márquez, despite having four non-finishes (his worst record since his first year in the 250cc class in 1998). He did, however, beat his team-mate, Lorenzo, and, when Lorenzo announced he was leaving to join Ducati, Rossi found himself the undisputed number-one rider at Yamaha again. It was a status that would last too, because Lorenzo's replacement was the relatively inexperienced Maverick Viñales and he would need time to learn his way round the Yamaha after two years on a Suzuki. Rossi, for the time being at least, would lead development on the Yamaha M1.

By now, Rossi had interests in the Grand Prix paddock that extended beyond his own racing. Back in 2010, he and close friend Marco Simoncelli had first discussed plans to build a track for their own personal use, and following Simoncelli's tragic death in 2011 Rossi had vowed to see the dream through. Over the next few years he would develop a 230-acre site just outside Tavullia, owned by his father, building a 2km track of hard-packed sand on a base of half-metre-thick concrete as well as a motocross track and an oval circuit. It would officially open its doors in 2014 as the VR|46 Ranch, named after the famous racing 'ranches' established by American GP legend Kenny Roberts Sr back in the 1980s and based along similar lines to Colin Edwards's Bootcamp in Texas.

Initially the track, based around an old farmhouse and with a backdrop of olive groves and vineyards, was intended for Rossi and his friends to train at, to keep their racing reflexes razor sharp, and to have some fun away from the pressures of a Grand Prix weekend, but it soon grew into something more. In time, Rossi started inviting talented young Italian riders to come and train with him and to learn not only about riding but about everything they would need to achieve successful careers in motorcycle racing, from taking English lessons to learning about nutrition, fitness, merchandising and how to deal with the media. Rossi even makes his lawyer available to advise the riders on negotiating contracts. His ranch had become a riders' academy. With the ongoing Spanish domination of Grand Prix racing, Rossi's ranch provided a perfect infrastructure to guide talented Italian youngsters all the way up through the ranks, ultimately up to MotoGP level. Italy had once dominated the smaller classes in Grand Prix racing but the Spanish had taken over, thanks to MotoGP being owned by a Spanish company and an unrivalled infrastructure in Spain to nurture young talent. Rossi decided Italian riders needed to have the same opportunities and he was the one who could provide them – even if it meant spending his own money.

Rossi's racing hero Kevin Schwantz has visited the ranch and says it's the ideal training ground for MotoGP riders. 'I've ridden at the ranch. It was a lot of fun. I got to ride there on my birthday a few years ago with Valentino and Graziano and Mattia Pasini and some other riders – I forget exactly who. There were other riders at the ranch but they were using the gym and working through their weekly training programmes.

It's awesome and it was a great opportunity to see what it feels like to have a bike sliding sideways underneath you. The track has both left and right turns, it's uphill, it's downhill, it's not just a simple oval. I think it really helps to play a big part in how those young VR|46 riders are progressing like they are. Those guys who are coming through the camp, coming through Rossi's ranch, seem to get on Grand Prix bikes and go a whole lot quicker, a whole lot faster, than the average guys do.

'Dirt-track racing is a great way to train,' he explains. 'It's nice, it's fun, it's sliding the bike sideways and realising how much weighting the outside peg on that motorcycle increases the traction when it does start to spin and so, it's learning at every level, that's for sure.

'It's a huge advantage for Valentino to get up in the morning and have that facility right on his doorstep. Most riders get up in the morning and think, "Well, should I go to the motocross track? Should I go to the gym?" but he can just go to the ranch and do everything! They've got fitness stuff there, they've got the riding stuff, you can play around and get everything accomplished in one simple stop so, no doubt, it's an advantage to have all that just outside his back door.'

Franco Morbidelli was one of Rossi's pupils and would go on to win the 2017 Moto2 world championship before taking the ultimate step up to MotoGP the following year. He waxed lyrical about the benefits of the ranch. 'Being in the academy is like being in Florence during the Renaissance; being an artist or a poet or a writer – it is Florence for riders, with Vale as the teacher who keeps us all right and helps us to learn.'[3]

While the younger riders benefitted from Rossi's unrivalled expertise, the ranch also paid dividends for his own training as he could surround himself with younger riders, learn from their new techniques and keep himself sharp by pitting himself in daily races against a hungry, ambitious and fearless new generation of riders: it went a long way to keeping him feeling young and sharp as he approached his fortieth birthday. 'I must say that all this is very exciting because we train together, we go together to the gym, go running,' he said. 'It's nice to be with these kids. It helps a lot to have a nice atmosphere when you're home and it also makes me feel younger.'[4]

Schwantz believes the ranch has played a major part in keeping Rossi motivated during the latter years of his career. 'I think a lot of it comes from the kids that he has at the VR|46 academy – all those young kids that he's got coming through in Moto3 and Moto2 who train at his academy, he motivates himself by getting up and trying to kick their butts every day. Hats off to him – that's something that's probably made his career last as long as it has.'

It was clear that Rossi had one eye on the future, and the ranch and academy were part of his retirement plan, as was the VR|46 Apparel company, housed in a large, modern glass building just outside Tavullia, which not only makes millions selling Rossi merchandise but also looks after the merchandising of many other riders, including many of his rivals. The VR|46 company even provided Marc Márquez's merchandising until things got nasty on track and the deal ended. It currently employs around thirty people, most of whom were original fan club members and friends of Rossi from childhood.

The town of Tavullia has become a mecca for Rossi fans: his image, his race number and his logos are everywhere. Life-size cardboard cut-outs of Rossi stand on residential balconies, the local menswear shop uses his face on its mannequins, flags emblazoned with the number 46 in garish yellow hang everywhere, posters adorn shops and businesses; then there are the Fiat 500s with Rossi paintjobs, the banners, the framed and signed photographs, the mini models of his race bikes, entire houses painted in Rossi's favoured yellow – the local authorities even change the speed limit signs to 46kph (rather than the usual 50kph) during the Misano Grand Prix week as a tribute to their home-grown hero.

Tavullia is an improvised Rossi theme park that draws 20,000 fans from as far afield as Japan and Australia every year, as Rossi fan club director Flavio Fratesi told the BBC: 'Tavullia is seen as a place of pilgrimage by many fans. Some have even come here during their honeymoon. When they come, they come to see the places where Valentino grew up, where he lives and where he trains.'[5]

In the centre of town is the Ristorante Pizzeria Da Rossi, the Rossi Bar and the Rossi Gelateria, all owned by the man himself and containing many of his old race leathers, helmets, boots, gloves and memorabilia – even a few precious race bikes. Behind his pizzeria is the VR|46 Store where fans can buy anything from Rossi keyrings and mugs to replica helmets, pushbikes, beachwear and even underpants. A short walk away is the global headquarters of the Valentino Rossi Fan Club. No rider in the history of the sport has ever inspired so much love or created so many jobs for his local economy. And yet none of those in Rossi's employ are in it solely for the money: as trusted friends from childhood, they're in it for all the right reasons. 'We are a family,' said the fan club president, Rino Salucci. 'That is important to us. This is not like a business. Everyone here, and the fifteen or so local people who volunteer at the fan club, do it out of a passion for Valentino.'[6]

After establishing his vast and hugely successful empire (in 2019, Rossi's net worth was estimated at £106 million), Rossi decided the next logical step was to form a VR|46 team to compete in the smallest class in Grand Prix racing – Moto3. In 2014, the team was launched with backing from Sky and a stable of KTM machinery (Yamaha does not build a Moto3 bike, so there was no clash of interests). In the team's first year Romano Fenati took four wins and finished fifth in the world championship, an impressive achievement by any standards and testimony to how good the fledgling team – run by Rossi's best friend, Uccio Salucci – was, right from the outset.

Running his own team also helped Rossi in his own race preparations at meetings: 'During a race weekend I like to go on track to watch the guys in the practice sessions. I can help them technically, giving them some advice about lines and so on. Then, on Sunday, I watch the race from the signalling wall. It's the perfect way to enter into the racing mood – it's pure adrenalin even from the other side.'[7]

In 2017, a Moto2 team was added and the following year Francesco Bagnaia won Rossi his first world title as team owner, riding one of the team's own Kalex machines. That same year, Rossi's maternal half-brother, Luca Marini, rode as Bagnaia's team-mate and finished seventh overall.

After divorcing in 1990, Rossi's parents had both eventually re-married and both had children, leading to a rather complex network of half-brothers and half-sisters among the Rossi/Palma clan. Stefania and her long-term partner (though never husband) Massimo Marini gave Rossi a half-brother, Luca Marini, in 1997 but she would not marry again until her ill-fated betrothal to Mauro Tecchi in 2007, which ended in his tragic suicide two years later.

Graziano fathered Rossi's half-sister, Clara, in 1998 with his second wife, Lorena. While Luca Marini had followed Rossi into a career in motorcycle racing, Clara opted to pursue a career in music and began taking singing lessons in 2012 at the Pianeta Musica di Davide di Gregorio school in Pesaro. She has also studied piano and spent ten months attending language school in Wisconsin, USA, to improve her English and therefore broaden her musical appeal (she sings in both Italian and English). In 2015, Clara took second place in Italy's prestigious Gallo D'Oro – a well-respected music competition that acts as a springboard for new talent.

Often attending European race meetings with Graziano, Clara has described her relationship with her famous brother as 'something normal. It never gave me any problems... I know who my friends are and they don't care who I'm sister to. I envy nothing [about Valentino], if anything I admire. I like his ability and the desire to always improve. And then he's nice, isn't he? Ours is a good relationship, I would say – as it can be with a quite older brother with whom you don't live. Sometimes I go to the ranch to see him.'[8]

Luca Marini and Rossi have always been very close and are closer than ever now that Luca races for his brother's team. Being in the shadow of such a titan as Rossi might have caused problems for many, but Marini seems comfortable with his place – and grateful for it: 'I think there are more positive aspects than the negative. I can learn a lot from him. I can speak a lot with him and he can give me a lot of advice and this is very important. So it's just a pleasure. I think that he's the greatest of all time. To be his brother, and just being close to him, I can learn a lot of things – and not just in the motorcycle world, but in all of life.'[9]

In 2018, Marini took his first Grand Prix victory by

winning the Moto2 race in Germany on his way to seventh place in the championship. He improved upon this to take two wins and finish sixth overall in 2019, again riding for the VR|46 team. He may not have set the world on fire in quite the same way as Rossi did in his early years, but Marini is clearly a name to watch and many have tipped him as a future world champion.

Rossi's ranch has helped launch many other careers besides that of his half-brother. Other names to have benefitted from his tutelage include: Nicolò Bulega, Niccolò Antonelli, Dennis Foggia, Stefano Manzi, Andrea Migno, Marco Bezzecchi, Francesco Bagnaia, Lorenzo Baldassarri and Celestino Vietti, all of who have been competitive in the Moto2 and Moto3 classes and have every chance of making it all the way up to the MotoGP class in the future. He may have gained enormous wealth from motorcycle racing, but Valentino Rossi certainly isn't shy when it comes to giving back.

And yet, Rossi's efforts didn't please everyone. In 2018, several of the occupants of premises close to the ranch took out an action challenging the noise levels, operating times, and planning permission for the premises. Thankfully the VR|46 organisation won through and the ranch was free to continue operating in much the same way as before.

Rumours persist that Rossi eventually intends to run his own team in MotoGP and, while he has never confirmed this intention publicly, it would seem a natural step to take – even though he might not always be there in person as a team manager. 'I don't know if I want to go around the world, like now, without riding a motorcycle, because it's quite heavy.'

Should he ultimately decide to do so, it would be the final link in the chain and would make the system complete – Rossi's riders could then progress all the way up the ladder from dirt bike riding to Moto3, Moto2 and MotoGP. He would be a kingmaker indeed.

★

Rossi had been racing in Grands Prix for so long by this point that his career straddled several different eras, from two-stroke 500cc machines to 1000cc four-stroke MotoGP missiles, and he had noticed that the style of racing had greatly changed, too. Speaking at a press conference ahead of the Czech Grand Prix in 2017, twenty years after he had won his first world title, he said, 'Fifteen years ago the passion for the motorcycle and the passion for victory was the same for Biaggi, Gibernau, Capirossi and everyone, but during the years the new young riders raise a lot the level. Our profession has become more serious and the difference is also technical because, in the last few years, it's one hundred per cent from the beginning – from the first corner to the last corner. I think this is the big difference compared to fifteen years ago and also compared to ten years ago. Before I had a lot more strategy because the tyres needed two and a half laps to arrive at the right temperature and in the last four or five laps you raised the lap time by one and a half seconds. Now you race from the beginning to the end, so the focus is more important and also your physical condition and preparation. But the fighting spirit is the same.'

His fighting spirit would be severely put to the test shortly after making this statement. On 31 August, while training on an Enduro bike at his ranch, Rossi crashed and suffered displaced fractures to his right tibia and fibula – almost the very same injuries he had sustained at the Mugello Grand Prix back in 2010. It was the second time he had been injured in 2017, the first incident occurring during another training accident in May when he suffered chest and stomach injuries. Surely, most believed when he re-broke his leg, this was the end; it was finally time to quit. Rossi was fast approaching forty and simply didn't need this kind of pain and aggravation in his life. But once again he proved everyone wrong and, despite having to miss his home round at Misano, was back testing a bike just nineteen days after the accident and racing again three days after that. Doctors had predicted it would take between thirty and forty days for him to recover: it took him just twenty-two. He clearly still wanted it.

At the time of the accident, Rossi had been lying in fourth place in the championship, just 26 points behind the leader, Andrea Dovizioso. The broken leg meant he had to miss the race at Misano but he never blamed the injury for losing out on the title; he blamed the combination of his bike and the Michelin tyres that had replaced the Bridgestones as the control tyre in 2016. 'In my opinion the potential of the bike is not bad,' Rossi said. 'The problem is it doesn't work with the tyres.' The combination was particularly bad in wet, low-grip conditions; so bad that Rossi said the bike was 'impossible' and even 'dangerous' to ride. Yet in the dry the 2017 Yamaha M1 was still capable of delivering results, as he proved with a stunning win at Assen when he beat Danilo Petrucci on the Ducati by just 0.06 seconds with Marc Márquez in third.

It was a significant victory for several reasons: not only was it his first win in over a year, it was his tenth at Assen (more than any other rider) and his 115th overall. It also meant that Rossi set a new record for the longest winning spell in Grand Prix racing with his win coming, as it did, twenty years, ten months and eight days after his first victory on a 125cc machine at the Czech Grand Prix way back in 1996. It also made him the oldest rider to win in the premier class since Jack Middelburg some forty years before. His 115th win put him within reach of the all-time record of 122 wins held by Giacomo Agostini. He had already won more races in the premier class than any other rider, now just eight more would give him more Grand Prix victories overall than any man in history. It seemed within reach; it was agonisingly close.

Following Rossi's Assen win, ninety-five-year-old Don Cesare Stefano proudly rang the church bells in Tavullia to celebrate yet another victory for his boy. Sadly, it would prove to be the last time he would do so. The aged parish priest passed away on 6 July 2018. This time it was Don Cesare himself for whom the bells would toll.

CHAPTER 15

UNDER PRESSURE

'It just got ridiculous – it looked a
horrible way to live for Vale.'
ALISON FORTH

For the last quarter of a century, Valentino Rossi has been followed, harassed and harangued by the Italian media. 'Italy is a nightmare – a nightmare,' he has said. 'I will never be able to live a normal life there.'[1] As a colleague of Rossi's in the Yamaha team, Alison Forth witnessed this intrusion on many occasions. 'It's hard for anyone outside of Italy to comprehend the level of scrutiny that Vale was subjected to by the Italian media. They were incredibly aggressive in their style and that was a real shock to me. On one occasion we were at a test at Phillip Island and Vale had a female friend with him. The Italian press went round all the hotels checking the guest lists to try to find her. That sort of thing was going on all the time, which is part of the reason why he rarely had girlfriends in tow at race meetings. Valentino is a private guy and he likes to stick to his inner circle of friends, so why on earth would he want to let the Italian press anywhere near his love life?

'He was very guarded about his private life and I don't blame him. I don't blame him if he kept me slightly at arm's length too – I was only there to organise team interviews, so why should I know anything about his private life?'

Things could get nasty too, especially if reporters sensed a story was slipping away from them. 'I was once grabbed by the neck and pinned up against a wall by a member of the Italian press,' Forth says. 'Vale was in hospital and I was guarding his room and wasn't allowed to let anybody in. The press people were pushing and shoving to get in with TV cameras and this one journalist went ballistic with me and assaulted me. I was in tears. It just got ridiculous. It looked a horrible way to live for Vale – there was nothing about that side of things that I enjoyed. He must have looked at some of the other racers who were less well known and thought, "I wish I could go back to being like that."'

Even trying to hustle Rossi through the paddock became a major operation and one that often threatened to turn ugly as fans became ever more desperate in their approaches. 'It was indescribable,' Forth says. 'Physically, in the paddock, it was a pain in the arse. You couldn't get where you needed to be and this was before the paddock got a lot more strict with passes and restricted access areas, so you just couldn't get anywhere when you were with Valentino – the only place that was safe was inside the trucks or hospitality units. But even then, fans always managed to infiltrate the hospitality units. Fans could get very aggressive too when Vale was on his paddock scooter. It wasn't uncommon to get knocked off the scooter if you were trying to get anywhere with him. It was crazy.'

There was, thankfully, a lighter side to the mania that surrounded Rossi: some fans went to great lengths to deliver the most unusual, and amusing, offerings to their god. 'One year in Spain there was a female fan hanging around and she would not go away. She grabbed hold of me and showed me this aquarium she'd made for Vale and was carrying around with her. It had real live turtles in it (Rossi has a turtle tattoo on his lower abdomen and used to race with a toy Teenage Mutant Ninja Turtle stuck on his helmet) and she had styled the inside of this aquarium in Rossi's colours and motifs – lots of little 46s and that kind of thing – and she was desperate for Vale to have this thing. I promised her I'd give it to him, so I'm walking around the paddock with this aquarium full of live turtles. I knew Vale was a huge animal lover, so I thought, once I showed him this, he wouldn't be able to say no, but his travel plans didn't allow for it so he gave it to one of his crew who was going back to Italy and asked him to keep it. At the airport we even had to get a special passport for the turtles in order to transport them!'

Trying to maintain a meaningful relationship among such constant attention and demands is not easy and Rossi has always gone to extraordinary lengths to keep his love life private. Much has been made of the fact that he has never been married, that he has never had children and that he is rarely seen with a partner by his side at race meetings. In fact, the apparent absence of women in Rossi's life led some to even question his sexuality, but it is, in fact, testimony to his success in largely managing to keep his personal life private.

In reality, Rossi has dated some of the most beautiful

women in Italy, though he always made sure his racing came first and refused to allow romance to get in the way of it. In the early years of his career he would sometimes take his then-girlfriend Eliane Ferri – a ballerina from the Tavullia area – to race meetings but soon learned it was a distraction he could live without. Speaking after the Malaysian Grand Prix in 1999, Rossi said, 'My girlfriend Eliane came out to Malaysia with me. We've been going out for almost two years now, though she doesn't come to so many races. Women need a lot of attention so having her with me at races is both good and bad... It's not good for me at races, not good for my concentration.'[2]

As his fame, power, popularity and wealth continued to grow, Rossi found himself dating a succession of glamorous women, many of them models, actresses and television celebrities. After all, how could he *not* be seen as one of the world's most eligible bachelors when even Brad Pitt confessed he wanted to be Valentino Rossi? 'We are both in the public eye and it is rare for us to have big heroes,' the Hollywood star told Italian magazine *Riders*. 'But I have one who I put above everyone else – Valentino Rossi. I would give anything to be like him. That guy is a real magician. He could hypnotise me. He's like a ballet dancer – it's pure art. For me, watching him in action is like reading a poem.'

Pitt isn't the only Hollywood mega star who dotes on Rossi: Tom Cruise is another fan, as he proved when he sent Rossi a special message on his thirtieth birthday in 2009. 'Valentino, you are a true champion,' he wrote. 'You keep raising the bar, relentlessly pursuing the next race, the next challenge, the next championship. I also know that the victories don't necessarily become easier. You have to dig deeper, work even harder, become more focused to overcome the distractions.

That's what you do. I, like countless others, know that when you're on that track, anything is possible.'

Cruise had been at the American Grand Prix at Laguna Seca in 2008 when Rossi pulled off his audacious pass on Casey Stoner to win the race, and the Hollywood superstar had clearly been impressed. 'It was my great pleasure to be there at Laguna Seca and see you take that victory,' he added in his birthday message. 'I can honestly say I've never seen anything like it. You certainly don't disappoint! Thank you for all the great races you have given us, and for all the great races yet to come.'

Triple Oscar winner Daniel Day-Lewis was another major star who sent a message to Rossi for his thirtieth birthday and he too had been impressed by Rossi's move on Stoner. Listing his favourite moments from Rossi's long career Day-Lewis said, 'Every race, every win, every championship! Vale the kid in the Portaloo is an old favourite, always irresistible in victory and gracious in defeat – not that he had to prove it very often! But the all-time favourite memory for me would be him at Laguna Seca going inside Stoner through the dirt. Death or glory; the whole race an answer to those daft enough still to have a question. And to have shaken the hand of that man – that I won't forget either.'

By 2002, women were starting to flock to Rossi as if he too was a Hollywood heartthrob. By then he had split with Eliane Ferri and had a brief, but supposedly intense, love affair with Italian actress and screenwriter Martina Stella. A notable success in Italy, Stella was described by the American press as a resembling 'a young Reese Witherspoon' and had a small role in the Hollywood movie *Ocean's Twelve* where she played the assistant of Roman Nagel (played by Eddie Izzard). According to the Italian media, Rossi's relationship with Stella only lasted for a few months, as did his rumoured fling in 2005 with television presenter, pole dancer and Miss Italy contestant, Maddalena Corvaglia. Neither Rossi nor Corvaglia ever confirmed the relationship – a stance which would become standard procedure for Rossi but one that only made the press speculate all the more.

Rossi, at that point, still seemed to favour the bachelor's lifestyle. 'I think it is better to be single, given the lives we lead,' he said. 'It's very difficult to have a relationship when you're always far from home, travelling from one country to another... Of course, there's the option to take your girl to all the races but that's something that doesn't convince me.'[3]

In February 2005, however, Rossi did begin a serious two-year relationship with Arianna Matteuzzi, the daughter of Italian racing car driver Gabriele Matteuzzi. The pair were photographed together on several occasions and she accompanied Rossi to some race meetings, leading the press to speculate that the couple were ready to tie the knot. But things eventually turned sour when Rossi's eye was supposedly taken by another Italian beauty, Elisabetta Canalis. A model, actress, dancer and television presenter, Canalis also took part in the American TV show *Dancing with the Stars* and posed nude for animal-rights charity PETA. She would later date Hollywood heartthrob George Clooney for two years but never did confirm or deny any relationship with Rossi, despite all the speculation.

By 2008, Rossi was being romantically linked to another actress and model, Mandala Tayde. Of German/Indian descent, Tayde was born in Frankfurt and is an award-winning actress who has enjoyed success in both Germany and Italy. She became particularly popular in Italy after appearing in the 1999 movie *Amore a Prima Vista* (Love at First Sight). Yet again, both Rossi and Tayde remained tight-lipped about their supposed affair and neither party officially acknowledged any relationship.

Proving he wasn't just interested in high-profile women, Rossi then embarked on a two-year relationship with twenty-five-year-old dental student Marwa Klebi. The pair started dating in 2010 and this time the gossip websites even speculated that Klebi was pregnant, though, as usual, nothing was ever confirmed or denied. The couple were, however, photographed sunbathing together on a luxury yacht in Croatia in a typically intrusive, long-lens, paparazzi-style shot.

After splitting with Klebi in 2012, Rossi began another serious relationship with Italian model Linda Morselli, whom he had first met at Misano five years previously. The relationship lasted until 2016 when it fell apart amid rumours that Morselli was jealous of Rossi's tight-knit circle of inner friends and the usual problems with maintaining a long-distance relationship. There was also speculation in the Italian press that Morselli was tired of Rossi's endless travel commitments and that he himself wished to have no outside distractions when he was trying to win the world title in 2016. As always, Rossi refused to comment on any of the rumours, including the one that the couple had actually been engaged. Morselli would later date F1 driver Fernando Alonso.

After a brief spell seeing Italian catwalk queen Aura Rolenzetti following the break-up with Morselli, Rossi then started dating Italian lingerie model Francesca Sofia Novello. Some fifteen years his junior, Novello is from Arese in Lombardy and has been the face of several fashion campaigns in Milan. She had formerly been a grid girl for the Leopard Racing Team in the Moto3 championship and had studied law at the Università degli Studi di Milano, so had the brains to match her beauty – a combination that Rossi clearly found irresistible. This time things looked more serious and, after a period when neither party spoke of the relationship, Rossi eventually allowed photographs to be published showing the pair in a romantic embrace and finally seemed happy to acknowledge that he was in a serious relationship.

When asked by *Australian Motor Cycle News* if he was a difficult man to date, Rossi answered: 'From a certain point of view yes, because unfortunately you have to share me with all the people and you cannot have me exclusively. Even when we have dinner together we are never alone. The fan comes, the waiter asks you for the photo, the restaurant owner asks how the bike goes. Apart from that I would say no, I'm quite easy, I'm good, I'm not a pain in the ass.'[4]

One thing Rossi has made clear since he started dating Novello is that he would very much like to become a father – but only when the racing is over. 'I'd like to have children and I think I will, but I'm still taking my time because it's difficult to reconcile my life with that of a father's. I have to find the right woman, but maybe I already have because I have a fantastic girlfriend. I'd like my child to be like my mother, with her character and blue eyes.'[5]

It may well have been pure coincidence, but the more Rossi's thoughts seemed to turn towards retirement and having children, the more his results suffered. The 2018 season was Rossi's sixth back on a Yamaha and it was the first year he had failed to win a race since riding for Ducati back in 2012. Increasingly, as the years rolled by, the voices grew louder that Rossi was over the hill, that he had lingered in the sport too long, that he should hang up his leathers before he made a fool of himself. But that is to not see the full picture. The Yamaha was still not performing as well as the

Hondas or Ducatis and in 2018 the firm suffered its longest losing streak (twenty-five races) since Chas Mortimer took a first premier class win on a Yamaha in 1972. Maverick Viñales would end that streak by winning the Austrian Grand Prix, but it was clear that the team was still struggling to marry the Magneti Marelli electronics with the Michelin tyres and there was little or nothing that Rossi himself could do about that.

In one of the most fiercely competitive eras in MotoGP's history, Rossi still finished the season in third place overall, was top Yamaha rider, and beat his much younger (but now considerably experienced) team-mate Viñales. In the penultimate race of the season he led for seventeen laps before crashing out, so he was clearly still giving it everything he had and, age aside, what made his performance all the more amazing was that the 2018 Yamaha M1 was clearly outclassed by the Hondas and Ducatis in several key areas: Rossi could only use the tools that were given to him and, in 2018, those tools were inadequate.

In fact, so embarrassed was Yamaha about its motorcycles that the bosses in Japan took the unprecedented step of agreeing the firm should publicly apologise to both Rossi and Viñales after a dismal qualifying session in Austria in which Viñales ended up eleventh and Rossi fourteenth. 'We, as Yamaha, owe our riders and also you, the media, an explanation,' said marketing and communications manager William Favaro before handing the microphone over to M1 project leader Kouji Tsuya. 'Today was a very difficult day for us,' Tsuya admitted. 'We are struggling. I have to apologise to the riders for less acceleration performance today... We are struggling and have to say sorry to the riders. Now we are working hard as ever to find the solution.'

It was a move that shocked the MotoGP paddock: no one could remember any of the Japanese factories ever holding their hands up and admitting they had got things wrong. It was also an admission that went a long way to proving that Rossi wasn't quite over the hill yet – after all, if he had finished third on a bike that was so slow its makers had to apologise for it, what might he have done on a competitive machine?

The problem with the Yamaha was that it didn't suit the Michelin tyres and the standardised ECU (Engine Control Unit) that was now compulsory in MotoGP – and nobody had any clear idea how to change the situation. 'We don't know exactly what's the problem,' Tsuya admitted. 'Maybe engine character, maybe electronics, maybe chassis stiffness: something here, there and here.'[6]

It was like the Ducati years all over again for Rossi and, while he tried hard to remain upbeat and optimistic that Yamaha would find a solution, the strain began to show as the season dragged on. Had he been a younger rider it would not have mattered so much, but Rossi was acutely aware that time was running out for him and if a fix for the bike could not be found he would never be able to challenge for another world championship. It was too late in his career to change manufacturers and learn a new bike, so he was forced to rely on Yamaha to find a solution.

Despite all Rossi's problems during this period, Neil Hodgson was still seriously impressed by his riding, even in a season when he didn't win a race. Hodgson's only regret being that Rossi and Márquez (who won the title for the fifth time in 2018) never really got to meet in their respective primes. 'In the latter years of his career,' he explains, 'Rossi has still been amazing, but the problem is he came up against Marc Márquez who's a very special rider but who was also in his prime. Rossi was not in his prime when he had to tackle Márquez, which is a shame because it would have been amazing to see both of them going head to head in their respective primes. Although, deep down, I'd have to say that Márquez would have come out on top. People hate me for saying that but Márquez just does it different. Rossi is aggressive but Márquez is even more ruthless and that skill that he's got of crashing but not crashing is something that no other rider can do.'

But if the 2018 season didn't quite go to plan, then 2019 was an utter disaster. Rossi would finish the championship in seventh place – the same position he achieved in his first year at Ducati and one position worse than in his second year on the uncompetitive Italian bike. The only high points were two podiums early in the season and a fastest lap in Sepang, his first since 2016.

At Phillip Island he did at least mark an incredible milestone by taking part in his 400th Grand Prix, although he could finish no higher than eighth in the race. To put into context just how long Rossi has been racing, the second-placed man on the list of most Grand Prix starts is Loris Capirossi on 328.

But otherwise it was a dismal season, with much of the blame still being directed towards Yamaha. The bike had been improved but not enough to make a difference and Rossi was often as much as 6mph slower through the speed traps than the fastest bikes on the grid. In the French Grand Prix, to cite just one example, his bike was the slowest out of the top fifteen. While the tyre issues he had suffered in 2018 had now been largely addressed, a lack of top speed became the new problem with the M1 in 2019. 'I lose too much in the straight and acceleration from the low-speed corners,' Rossi complained. 'We improve tyre life with some different things on the bike – the bike is very good to ride. Looks like the others made another step, especially Honda, and now the difference is very big in the straight.'

It was a hugely frustrating experience to be forced to acknowledge that yet another year had been wasted. To keep costs down, all the top MotoGP teams are forced to select an engine specification at the beginning of the season and stick with it, so Yamaha engineers had their hands tied when it came to trying to coax more speed out of the M1: Rossi would have to wait until the following season before he could expect any major engine upgrades.

Time was now of the essence: Rossi had turned forty on 16 February 2019, just weeks before the season had started. He celebrated with a dinner for close friends in his own restaurant in Tavullia before moving on to a bigger club in Pesaro which could accommodate 180 guests. Rossi's girlfriend, Francesca Sofia Novello, posted pictures of the happy couple on social media for the first time and the Italian press was not slow to pick up on the fact that Novello was wearing a ring on the third finger of her left hand. Speculation began immediately that the couple were engaged but, typically, neither Rossi nor Novello issued any statement to that effect.

Among the congratulatory messages that Rossi received on his big day were those from football hero Diego Maradona, F1 world champion Lewis Hamilton and tennis stars Roger Federer and Rafael Nadal. Most MotoGP riders, even his former nemesis Jorge Lorenzo, sent good wishes, but Marc Márquez remained silent. If he had once been a die-hard Rossi fan, he was no longer.

Rossi was typically philosophical about reaching middle age and, as ever, he looked for the positives. 'Mentally, forty is better than twenty-five,' he said. 'I'm surer about myself and I have less problems in my life. But for sure it's harder physically, especially if you're a sportsman... you have to train more, you have to put more effort in.'[7]

The birthday celebrations didn't last long, however. As soon as Rossi tested the 2019 Yamaha M1 he knew it hadn't been improved enough to compete with the Hondas and Ducatis and the bike's lack of top speed continued to haunt him throughout the season. His home Grand Prix at Mugello marked a particularly low point: after qualifying way down in eighteenth he had been running in last place in the race before crashing out.

By now, even some of Rossi's greatest admirers and colleagues were saying he was simply too old to be racing in the premier class (even his old crew chief Jerry Burgess said he had 'perhaps hung around a little bit too long') and was running the risk of tainting his astonishing legacy. Marco Lucchinelli, the 1981 500cc world champion, told Italian website tuttomotoriweb.com, 'I think it would have been much better if Vale had stopped before. He can run up to fifty years [in] seventh or eighth. He gets there every Sunday and sometimes he can even be fourth, then maybe every so often can take a podium. The Rossi we knew fought for victories every Sunday. Something important has changed.'

But Rossi was adamant that age was not slowing him or altering his approach to racing. 'It is not true that you are no longer aggressive or able to ride at the limit because you are afraid. But it is true that you try and take less risks in the most dangerous moments.'[8]

Steve Parrish believes that one side effect of age for a rider is that he starts to become more aware of the risks and that Rossi is just as susceptible to this phenomenon as any other rider. 'Rossi is a very, very smart, intelligent man and he must have eventually wondered if he really wanted to keep putting his neck on the line every weekend. When you've raced for as long as he has and you've been bounced up the road so many times and you know that every season you can expect to take at least five or six tumbles – and that, in any one of those, you could snap your neck… I think Rossi just got to the point where his blinkers had come off a bit. When you're seventeen years old the blinkers are on so tight that you can't see any farther than the edge of the track, but eventually you start to see those barriers and you start to see those ambulances sitting trackside. And by the time Rossi was in his forties I think the blinkers were finally off.'

Rossi did, however, admit that the game had changed greatly since he first raced in the premier class in 2000. 'Nowadays, we have to deal with so many more factors that weren't there in the past. It's not enough to be a good rider if you want to finish at the front. The riders have become incredible athletes. In the past, you could manage the race and fight only on the last laps; now you need to train hard, you cannot allow yourself to go on track without being at one hundred per cent. When I am not at the races I train every day. The race rhythm has increased: you need to be fully focused from the first to the very last lap. Physical training has become crucial to achieve such a high level of concentration and precision.'[9]

There was still one year left to run on Rossi's contract with Yamaha and he had no intention of quitting before the 2020 season. He was fully aware that he was no longer the dominant force he had once been but still felt he could challenge for wins when everything went right for him. 'Ten or fifteen years ago I was the fastest and now, many times, not,' he admitted. 'But if I am in good shape and particularly concentrated, I feel I can still be the one that goes fastest.'[10]

One man who did decide to throw the towel in midway

through his contract was Jorge Lorenzo. Having struggled with injuries over the previous two years, he also struggled to adapt to the Honda he had switched to in 2019 and announced his retirement ahead of the final race of the season in Valencia. Rossi had once again outlasted another of his great rivals. Gone was Max Biaggi, gone was Sete Gibernau, gone was Casey Stoner and now gone was Jorge Lorenzo. It was further testimony to the remarkable longevity of his career, and the stats showed that Rossi easily outperformed them all. Biaggi ended his career with just 13 wins in the MotoGP class while Gibernau only managed 8. Stoner's tally was a more impressive 38 and Lorenzo's even more so at 47. But between 2000 and 2017, Rossi won a staggering 89 races in MotoGP. His fiercest rivalries might have given him trouble for short periods in his career but the record books will always show Rossi won far more races.

Despite their history, Rossi spoke well of Lorenzo at the special press conference held at Valencia to announce the Spaniard's retirement. 'I think that Jorge is one of the most important MotoGP riders of the modern era. I think we will lose a very important part of our sport. He is a great champion and he impressed me a lot of times for his speed, concentration, and from when he arrived in MotoGP, from the first moment, he was always very strong; from 2008 – so more than ten years. We were team-mates for a long time. A lot of years together we shared the same box and I think for me, personally, he is one of the greatest rivals in my career. Together I think we did some of the best racing that I remember in my history. It is a great shame that he finished but he is good in the body and he is okay, so I wish him good luck for the future.'

Speaking of his relationship with Rossi and Marc Márquez

shortly after retiring, Lorenzo said, 'It's very difficult to be friendly with a direct competitor, especially when we're all killers in MotoGP. Marc is a killer, Valentino is a killer, I'm a killer; we all want to win and we never want to give anything to the others. That makes it hard to communicate, to spend time together, or to have empathy for the other. You don't hate them but you want them to go as slow as possible and to be able to beat them every time.'[11]

In retirement, Lorenzo's character changed completely and he became a far less tense and far more relaxed and friendly person; he also gave up any lingering animosity he might have held onto regarding his rivalry with Rossi. Another epic rivalry was over and this time the two protagonists were quick and happy to bury the hatchet.

The problem for Rossi was that much younger and, it has to be said, faster, riders were constantly replacing the old hands like Lorenzo and he had to ride harder than ever to try to keep up. Chief amongst the new threats in 2019 was a young Frenchman called Fabio Quartararo. At just twenty years old he was precisely half Rossi's age and had been born when Rossi was already racing in his fourth season in Grands Prix. Quartararo was fast from the off and was doing things on a lower-spec, year-old Yamaha M1 that Rossi could only dream of, setting six pole positions and taking seven podiums during the season, though never quite managing a win. Rossi, by contrast, scored no poles and only finished on the podium twice – and that was on the latest full-factory version of the M1. It didn't look good. And it made some wonder why on earth he was still trying when he had nothing left to prove. Ten years previously, after winning his last world title, Rossi himself had stated that he had no interest in ever riding just to make up the numbers.

'Valentino Rossi must retire at the top,' he had said. 'When I understand it is too strong, too hard, and I have to fight for fifth place... why? It is better to stop before that.'[12] And yet in 2019, a fifth place would have been among his better results. He had either changed his outlook to take account of his age, had faith that the problem was with Yamaha rather than himself and, therefore, could be fixed, or simply could not face up to life without racing.

The second half of Rossi's premier-class career had been blighted by two broken legs, two wasted years at Ducati and the subsequent lack of confidence that ensued; by having to be number two rider at Yamaha upon his return, by getting older every year and facing much younger, and faster, competition. He was still one of the fastest riders in the world – and assuredly the most experienced – but he was past his prime, there could be little question of it and the harsh facts could not be argued with: in his first ten years in the premier class between 2000 and 2009, Rossi racked up 77 wins; in the second ten years, from 2010 to 2019, he scored only 12. In his prime Rossi was winning 11 races in a season but it had taken him a decade to score his last 12 wins.

It also didn't look good that Rossi's Yamaha team-mate Maverick Viñales finished the 2019 season in third place overall. Rossi had never been particularly strong in qualifying but had, in the past, often been able to make up for this with a far better pace on race days. But even this skill seemed to elude him in 2019. Neil Hodgson has a theory as to why: 'The problem is, I believe there's a certain amount of adrenalin in your body that you can fire every weekend and Rossi can't fire it in free practice and qualifying. That's why he became known as a Sunday man who could dig deep into his resources and find a bit left to fire on race day and produce something special, but by then it's already too late. Márquez fires it from lap one of free practice 1 because he seems to have a full tank of adrenalin to use. Will Márquez have that same store of adrenalin at forty though? Probably not.'

In light of the new level of competition in MotoGP, Rossi's old tactics were simply no longer good enough. His answer, as it had been back at the end of 2013, was to change his crew chief. This time he parted company with Silvano Galbusera and replaced him with David Muñoz who, in 2018, had been crew chief in Rossi's own VR|46 Moto2 team. Muñoz is Spanish, however, so one of the reasons Rossi cited for sacking Jerry Burgess and hiring Galbusera back in 2013 (namely, because he and Galbusera shared the same language) now seemed to ring hollow. Rossi admitted he and Galbusera had become 'a little bit stuck' and could not find a way to make the Yamaha work. He hoped that Muñoz would bring in some new ideas to improve the package. This time it was a mutual decision between Rossi and Galbusera, who happily remained with Yamaha to work with its European MotoGP test team.

Rossi did at least have some fun at the end of the season when he found himself behind the wheel of a Formula One car for the first time since testing a Ferrari in 2010. On this occasion he drove Lewis Hamilton's 2017 championship-winning Mercedes-AMG WO8 at Valencia while Hamilton, a keen motorcyclist, tried out Rossi's 2019 Yamaha M1 – and crashed. 'I had one little spin with it,' Hamilton sheepishly admitted afterwards, 'but otherwise brought it back home in one piece. I was just step-by-step learning but it's a very steep learning curve.'

Ultimately, Hamilton posted a time on the Yamaha that was four seconds off Rossi's best while Rossi came within 1.5 seconds of Hamilton's time in the car. 'I was a big fan of

Lewis before but now I am even more,' Rossi said. 'We had a fantastic day, where the two top classes of motorsports not only met but worked together. I felt like a real F1 driver for a day – I didn't want the day to end! I also rode the YZR-M1 on track with Lewis. It was a proud moment for the team to share our passion with him. Technically, Valencia is a hard track and today was windy so, at one point, I thought it would be difficult for Lewis to continue, but he was brilliant on the bike and his position on the M1 was great. I think he had loads of fun, which is the main thing.'

Just days after driving Hamilton's F1 car, Rossi found himself on the podium as winner of the Pro-Am class at the Gulf 12 Hours Endurance Race at the Yas Marina circuit in Abu Dhabi. Rossi drove a Ferrari 488 in a team that included his brother Luca Marini and best friend Uccio Salucci. It wasn't the first endurance race he had contested on four wheels: in 2012, he had finished ninth in the Pro-Am class at the Blancpain Endurance Series at the Nürburgring in Germany, driving a Ferrari 458, this time with Salucci and professional racing driver Andrea Ceccato. Prior to that, Rossi and Salucci had qualified tenth and finished eighteenth in the opening round of the series but were forced to miss the final round due to a clash with Rossi's MotoGP commitments.

In 2013, Rossi drove NASCAR star Kyle Busch's Toyota Camry Nationwide Series car at Charlotte Motor Speedway in North Carolina for a promotional video. By the end of his time on track Rossi was posting lap times that were faster than half the NASCAR field could manage. 'I thought he did pretty good,' said Busch, who, with fifty-five wins to his credit, is one of the most successful NASCAR drivers of all time. 'He started out a little slow, which is fine, but every lap he picked it up a lot. He got to where he was running some competitive laps speeds – times that would have put him in the top fifteen in Nationwide Series practice.'[13]

It seems clear that Rossi's retirement plans will include some form of car racing, given that it's both safer and not as youth-dependent as MotoGP. Most likely he will race on circuits rather than in rallies, as he has stated that reaching the top level in rallying is too hard and that purpose-built racing circuits rather than forests and deserts are more his natural habitat.

Rossi will always be a big draw whatever he races, so, while he may not get the same kicks as he did on a MotoGP bike, he will, in future, at least have an outlet for his competitive nature. 'Nothing will be as fun as the MotoGP and I had already realised that ten years ago,' he told Italian journalist Matteo Aglio in 2019. 'I'd like to race cars but it'll still be something different so I'll continue to ride a bike until I can.'[14]

Those close to Rossi had long been aware of how difficult he would find the transition into retirement. 'His life is a Disneyland,' laughs Carlo Pernat who signed Rossi in 1995. 'For Valentino, Disneyland is to race! He lives in terror of having to stop racing. Racing is his whole life and he doesn't even like to think about when he will have to stop. The engine is Vale's girlfriend and he is very much in love!'

The 2020 season was set to be Rossi's twenty-fifth consecutive year in Grand Prix racing and he had already raced in almost half of all Grands Prix held since the introduction of the world championships in 1949. It's a miraculous achievement and a statistic that has deeply impressed fellow racers as well as fans. Of his astonishing success and longevity, former rival Lucio Cecchinello says, 'It was clear that he had a lot of natural talent from the start, but I don't think anybody expected that he could go on to win so many world championships and do so many races and take so many wins and podiums in his career. That has been simply fantastic. It's fantastic what he has done in his career – nobody could have expected that he could ride for so long. To have signed another two-year contract when he was almost forty years old is simply amazing.

'He is an incredible example of a really fantastic sportsman and he must have an incredible drive and passion for what he's doing because I believe he has enough money to leave the sport and live very well, but he still wants to race and he still wants to fight and that's fantastic. There is only one word to describe what makes him so good – talent! And, of course, I would add that he has a lot of passion for motorcycling and for this sport. He has dedicated his life fully for this sport so, together with his talent, Valentino is simply the best. I truly admire him as a rider because he did a fantastic job.'

While the compliments continued to pour in as Rossi entered the twilight years of his incredible career, there was also some concern about the gaping hole he will leave behind him in MotoGP when he does retire. 'For sure, Valentino Rossi has changed MotoGP,' Pernat says. 'He made so many people fall in love with the sport who otherwise would never have heard of it. Grandmothers, grandfathers, little boys, little girls who know nothing about engines or motorcycles but they love Valentino. Little boys want to be like him, mothers want him as their son… You can go to a circuit in any country in the world and sixty or seventy per cent of the crowd is wearing yellow. What he has done for the sport is simply unprecedented. The problem for MotoGP is that it will probably lose all these people when Valentino retires. I remember one year when he crashed in Holland and 20,000 people left the circuit!'

Pernat doesn't see any obvious replacement for Rossi waiting in the wings either; not even the mercurial Marc Márquez. 'For sure, Márquez is a phenomenon, but he made a stupid mistake in Malaysia in 2015 with Valentino and this meant that Vale's fans would not support him in later years. If Márquez had not behaved this way then he might have inherited many of Vale's fans but that will not happen now.'

Neil Hodgson is another who believes Rossi's contribution to MotoGP cannot be underestimated. 'Valentino's impact on the sport has been massive. Whenever I'm in a taxi and I'm asked what I do for a living and I explain that I cover MotoGP for BT Sport they always say, "Oh, Valentino Rossi!" I mean, he *is* the sport. Even if you're not a motorcycle enthusiast you've heard of Valentino Rossi. You can't say that about Marc Márquez. Or, at least, you can't say that yet.'

Steve Parrish also testifies to the Rossi effect: 'When I was racing people used to ask me what I did for a living and when they didn't understand what motorcycle road racing was I said, "Barry Sheene" and they would know instantly. It was the same when I commentated on MotoGP for the BBC – people would ask what MotoGP was and I'd say, "Valentino Rossi" and they would instantly know.'

Like many others, Hodgson is concerned about how many fans will walk away from MotoGP in the post-Rossi era. 'I do think lots of fans will leave; the question is how many? What percentage? I don't think it will be a silly amount but if you even consider the value of losing twenty per cent of the audience, it's an awful lot. If Márquez continues to dominate then I think a lot of the Rossi fans will simply stop watching MotoGP.'

Parrish sees things slightly differently. 'I'm not sure it will make such a difference. Rossi was brilliant at engaging the casual sports fan so they would watch MotoGP when it was on TV for free. The biggest problem for the sport now, in terms of viewing figures, is that it's almost exclusively on channels that you need to pay for, so there are not so many casual viewers. Those who pay to watch it are clearly dedicated fans and they're not going to walk away from it just because Rossi retires.'

Rossi himself is very aware of the impact he's had on the sport and it's something he's immensely proud of. 'A lot of people started to follow it [MotoGP] because of me and that's a great positive. When I stop, I'm happy that MotoGP will be more famous than it was before me.'

But that was still in the future. For now, there would be one more full season, at least, for the fans, and for Rossi himself, to savour. Or at least, there should have been. But nobody could have foreseen the coming of COVID-19.

CHAPTER 16

THE GREATEST

'He is top of the list, number one,
the greatest of all time.'
KEVIN SCHWANTZ

Jorge Lorenzo was not absent from the MotoGP paddock
for long, but his role upon his return in winter testing
for the 2020 season came as something of a shock. He had
agreed to head up Yamaha's European test team, which meant
his job was to help his once great rival, Valentino Rossi. The
sight of Lorenzo in Rossi's garage advising him on how to get
the best out of the latest version of the Yamaha M1 was one
that no one ever thought they would see. The pair seemed to
have truly buried the once-bitter hatchet that had caused so
much bad blood between them. 'He actually acted as an extra
coach for me,' Rossi said. 'He gave me advice and showed
me certain trajectories. Having Jorge in the garage and on
the track is important. It's strange seeing him in street clothes

while I'm in a race suit, but it's cool and I can see he's really focused on what he's doing.'

With Lorenzo's help, winter testing had gone well and Rossi was confident that Yamaha had finally turned its M1 into a bike he could once more challenge for race wins on. But then, in February of 2020, Yamaha dropped a bombshell by announcing that if Rossi wanted to race on into the 2021 season, he would have to do so in the satellite Petronas Yamaha SRT team. The factory seats had been taken up by Maverick Viñales and Fabio Quartararo as Yamaha had an eye on the future and needed to take the development of the M1 in the direction that the younger riders felt it should be going. Rossi could still have access to a full factory-spec bike and technical support from Yamaha but he would have to run out of a satellite team. As much as he publicly supported Yamaha's decision, it must have been a blow to his ego to finally be pushed aside to make way for a new generation.

There was even speculation that Lorenzo and Rossi would form an old-guard dream team in 2021 as comrades with Petronas Yahama SRT – somewhat ironic, given that the sole reason for the team's existence up to that point had been to nurture new young talent. In any case, Rossi and Lorenzo appeared like long-lost friends as the Spaniard settled into his new Yamaha testing role and was pictured with his arm slung around his erstwhile enemy's shoulder. For race fans it was a pleasure to see and a far cry from the days when Rossi had insisted on a dividing wall in the Yamaha garage to keep Lorenzo out of his sight. It was also a reminder that, in most cases, racing rivalries end when the racing ends, or when one rider is no longer a direct threat to the other. As Rossi said of Lorenzo after the two had worked on developing the

Yamaha M1 together, 'Jorge is in great shape – really nice and laid-back. It looks as if when you stop [racing] your character improves. I hope this happens to me too!'

So Rossi was confident that he had a competitive bike for the 2020 season and, after a successful winter testing programme, was psyched up and ready to begin his twenty-fifth season of Grand Prix racing. Everything was in place. But then came the virus, the coronavirus: COVID-19.

No one could have imagined that the outbreak of a flu-like virus in the Chinese city of Wuhan would have such a devastating global impact and would not only claim hundreds of thousands of lives but would also necessitate 'lockdowns' in many countries, with people being forced to stay in their homes for weeks or even months. The pandemic also caused the almost complete cessation of international travel: borders were closed, airlines were stood down, and those who were able to travel often had to spend fourteen days in quarantine once they reached their destination: Grand Prix racing could clearly not happen under such circumstances.

The first round of the 2020 MotoGP season should have been held in Qatar on 8 March and, in fact, the Moto3 and Moto2 races did go ahead but only because those teams were already in the country for testing before the authorities announced a two-week quarantine period for anyone travelling into Qatar. It meant the MotoGP riders could not travel to the opening round of the season. Plans were quickly made to replace the round later in the year and the intention was to kick off the season in Thailand until the Thai government also announced stringent measures to combat the spread of the virus. The Argentinian and American rounds were also postponed, but Dorna boss Carmelo Ezpeleta continued to assure riders, teams and fans that he and his staff would find a way to stage a MotoGP season, even if that season had to be reduced to thirteen rounds – the minimum number of races required by regulations to count as a full world championship.

When COVID-19 struck Italy, it struck it hard, particularly in Rossi's native Pesaro region. People were forced to stay indoors; travel between villages, towns and cities was forbidden; and, in an alarmingly short period of time, tens of thousands of Italians lost their lives to the pandemic. Rossi was quick to donate money to Marche Nord Hospital to buy ventilators to treat victims and he led calls for further donations, but he too was in lockdown. 'Here in Tavullia the situation is difficult,' he told *Sky Sports Italia*. 'Unfortunately, many people are sick here and also in Pesaro. We must all hold on, waiting for this moment to pass. We cheer for the people of Bergamo and Brescia [two of the hardest hit areas]. I have seen very bad images – it looks like a war zone. I have many friends there and right now I'm the one cheering them on, while usually I'm the one they cheer for.'

With his country amongst the hardest hit anywhere in the world at that point, Rossi suddenly had far more important things than motorcycle racing to worry about, but the timing was particularly unfortunate for his career. The plan had always been to contest a few races of the 2020 season in order to assess how competitive both he and the Yamaha M1 could be before making a decision on his future. But with all the early races postponed or cancelled, Rossi faced the prospect of not racing again until 2021 when he would not only be forty-two years old but would also be on a satellite bike in a satellite team – and with no way of knowing how competitive he might be. 'As for my choice, I was hoping to decide whether to continue after the first part of the season but now everything slips. I would like a few races to understand how competitive I can be, that would be important.'

An unexpected side effect of the enforced break was to give Rossi a chance to sample life without racing, without travelling, without pressure, without the constant threat of injuries. It would be the first year since 1994 that he hadn't travelled the globe to race bikes, but it clearly wasn't to his liking: by late April he announced his intention to race on in 2021. At a special Yamaha Q&A session he said, 'I have enough motivation and I want to continue. It was very important to understand the level of competitiveness because in the second part of last year I suffered and too many times I was too slow and I had to fight outside of the top five. In my mind, I had another year with the factory team and I needed time to decide and understand if I can be strong. The problem is that there's no racing. I will have to decide before racing because in the most optimistic situation we can race in August or September. But I have to make my decision before. It's not the best way to stop [his career]. It's fairer to do another championship, so I hope to continue in 2021.'

And so the greatest career in the history of motorcycle racing was put on hold due to the most bizarre circumstances and Rossi, like countless millions of others, was forced to stay at home and wait for some kind of normality to return. He had faced every kind of challenge over a quarter century of Grand Prix racing and had risen to them all, but this one was insurmountable. There was nothing he could do but wait.

But the downtime gave Rossi, and others, time to reflect on his remarkable career, on his achievements and on the legacy he would leave in MotoGP once he had finally hung up his Dainese leathers. And it became clear, if it wasn't already, that most people consider him to be the greatest motorcycle racer of all time, despite the increasing challenge from Marc Márquez. 'For me, Rossi is still the GOAT but will he still be when Márquez comes to retire?' Neil Hodgson says. 'I mean, just one more title would put him equal with Rossi and yet he's still so young, so unless something bizarre happens then the title of the GOAT will soon be taken by Márquez. But then, a lot of people argue that it depends on how you choose the greatest of all time, because Rossi has done much more for the sport than Márquez. So for Márquez to be considered the GOAT then, in my opinion, he has to beat all Rossi's records by a long way. If their statistics end up being very close then I'd say Rossi still deserves the title because of all the other things he's done for the sport.'

Kevin Schwantz agrees: 'I think you have to put Valentino at the top because of what he's ridden, the era that he's ridden in, the guys that he's raced against, the number of world championships and just the sheer length of time that he's continued to race Grand Prix bikes at world championship level – that makes him top of the list for me. John Surtees, Mike Hailwood, Giacomo Agostini – all those guys are right there near the top as well, but I think Valentino has shown he's a much more diverse rider by being able to win on absolutely anything you put him on. He is top of the list, number one, the greatest of all time.'

Even once bitter rivals now recognise Rossi's astonishing achievements and have paid tribute now that the dust has settled on their rivalries. 'He is great, maybe the greatest ever, and nobody can take away what he has already achieved,' Sete Gibernau said in tribute. 'Despite everything that happened, I still have tremendous respect for him. I'm sorry we had some confrontations but I don't hold a grudge. Quite the opposite, actually: if I was a top rider, it was thanks to him.'

Max Biaggi had also learned to look back on his rivalry with Rossi in a more positive light, saying, 'Recently I was really pleased when he said his greatest battles were with me. We had a great rivalry and I miss it a little. Today he has no equal. His real rival is not Márquez nor Viñales – it's time.'

Dorna boss Carmelo Ezpeleta recognised the genius of his star rider too. 'Valentino has been very important, especially because his legend has been based, from my point of view, not on the celebrations or how funny he is, nor on how well he deals with the press, but on the fact that he is an extraordinary rider.'

But for all his achievements and skill on a racing motorcycle, it is Rossi's character that has most impressed those who know him and have raced against him. Maverick Viñales had this to say after the announcement that Rossi would no longer be his team-mate in 2021: 'What have I learned from Rossi? I have learned many things but what will surely remain for me is his ability to always have a smile, regardless of whether he finished first or seventh.'

Former rival Jeremy McWilliams backs up Viñales' assessment: 'I think that's why he is the fans' favourite – because he never blamed his bike or his team or whatever when he lost races, he just took it on the chin, and that's a lovely trait. If other riders were as good at taking it on the chin as Valentino they might have been liked a lot more. Most riders will find any other excuse but themselves.'

Despite all the fame and the constant attention and all the demands made of him, Rossi has remained the same happy-go-lucky character that he always was and that's what has so deeply impressed Neil Hodgson. 'I interview Rossi most days on a race weekend and I see him behind the camera a lot. I see many other riders behind the camera who are not nice and not friendly and they're arrogant too, but then when the camera is on them they're all smiles and waves, trying to be like Valentino. So what impresses me most about Rossi is that he's the same man you see on TV. Better than all his wins, better than all his last laps, better than all his championships and celebrations, he's just an incredible human being and that's the most impressive thing about him for me.'

By the time COVID-19 had temporarily halted the sport of MotoGP, Valentino Rossi had competed in 402 races, won 115 of them, taken 234 podiums, 65 pole positions, 96 fastest laps, scored 6,247 points and won 9 world championships. He holds the record for the most wins in the premier class with 89 compared to Giacomo Agostini's 68, meaning he is the most successful premier-class Grand Prix race winner of all time. But he remains eight race wins short of Agostini's record of 122 wins across different Grand Prix classes. However, those statistics are subject to change: after all, the story isn't quite over yet. There is still time for the church bells in Tavullia to ring out once more in celebration of the local boy who made good; the local boy who conquered the world but never lost his soul. The legend of Valentino Rossi continues.

NOTES

CHAPTER 1

[1] Mackenzie, Niall, 'The God's Father', www.visordown.com
15 September 2010

[2] Mackenzie, Niall, 'The God's Father', www.visordown.com
15 September 2010

[3] *Faster* (Director: Mark Neale), Dorna Sports S.L.,
Spark Productions 2003

[4] Mackenzie, Niall, 'The God's Father', www.visordown.com
15 September 2010

[5] Oxley, Mat, *Valentino Rossi: MotoGenius* (2nd edition),
Haynes Publishing, 2003

[6] Scott Michael, *Motocourse 1997–98*, Hazleton Publishing,
1997, p45

[7] Lieback, Ron, 'Rossi's Right-Hand Man: Uccio Interview',
www.ultimatemotorcycling.com 28 May 2011

[8] Scott Michael, *Motocourse 1997–98*, Hazleton Publishing, 1997, p45

[9] Guidotti, Maria, 'CW Interview: Graziano Rossi', www.cycleworld.com 9 November 2015

[10] McLaren, Peter: 'Rossi on Graziano', www.crash.net 12 August 2005

[11] 'Valentino Rossi: The Iconic Rider', www.myitalianlink.com 4 September 2017

[12] Guidotti, Maria, 'CW Interview: Graziano Rossi', www.cycleworld.com 9 November 2015

[13] Rossi, Valentino with Borghi, Enrico, *Valentino Rossi: What If I Had Never Tried It*, Century, 2005, p75

CHAPTER 2

[1] McLaren, Peter and Scott, Michael, *Valentino Rossi: Record Breaker*, Icon Publishing Limited, 2009, p7

[2] Prontelli, Michele, 'Valentino Rossi's Cagiva Myth: Interview with Claudio Lusuardi' www.moto.it 9 October 2014

[3] Oxley, Mat, *Valentino Rossi: MotoGenius* (2nd edition), Haynes Publishing, 2003, p47

[4] Prontelli, Michele, 'Valentino Rossi's Cagiva Myth: Interview with Claudio Lusuardi' www.moto.it 9 October 2014

[5] Mackenzie, Niall, 'The God's Father' www.visordown.com 15 September 2010

[6] Rossi, Valentino with Borghi, Enrico, *Valentino Rossi: What If I Had Never Tried It*, Century, 2005, p80

[7] Russo, Antonio, 'Valentino Rossi?: At 15 I Put Him in

Trouble', www.tuttomotoriweb.com 15 March 2018

[8] Rossi, Valentino with Borghi, Enrico, *Valentino Rossi: What If I Had Never Tried It*, Century, 2005, p82

[9] Russo, Antonio, 'Valentino Rossi?: At 15 I Put Him in Trouble', www.tuttomotoriweb.com 15 March 2018

[10] 'Breeding a World Champion: Part One – Mauro Noccioli', www.motogp.com 16 October 2001

[11] Rossi, Valentino with Borghi, Enrico, *Valentino Rossi: What If I Had Never Tried It*, Century, 2005, p89

[12] 'Breeding a World Champion: Part One – Mauro Noccioli', www.motogp.com 16 October 2001

CHAPTER 3

[1] Rossi, Valentino with Borghi, Enrico, *Valentino Rossi: What If I Had Never Tried It*, Century, 2005, p86

[2] Oxley, Mat, *Valentino Rossi: MotoGenius* (2nd edition), Haynes Publishing, 2003, p52

[3] *Rossi: 20 Years of GP Racing*, MCN Special Edition, Bauer Media, 2015, p26

[4] Rossi, Valentino with Borghi, Enrico: *Valentino Rossi: What If I Had Never Tried It*, Century, 2005, p90

[5] *Rossi: 20 Years of GP Racing*, Special MCN Edition, Bauer Media, 2015, p26

[6] *Rossi: 20 Years of GP Racing*, MCN Special Edition, Bauer Media, 2015, p27

[7] Oxley, Mat, *Valentino Rossi: MotoGenius* (2nd edition), Haynes Publishing, 2003, p59

[8] Oxley, Mat, *Valentino Rossi: MotoGenius* (2nd edition), Haynes Publishing, 2003, p57

[9] Rossi, Valentino with Borghi, Enrico: *Valentino Rossi: What If I Had Never Tried It*, Century, 2005, p116

[10] 'Breeding a World Champion: Part One – Mauro Noccioli', motogp.com 16 October 2001

CHAPTER 4

[1] Scott, Michael, *Motocourse: 1997–98*, Hazleton Publishing, 1997, p44

[2] Falsaperla, Filippo, *Valentino Rossi: Legend*, Yellow Jersey Press, 2006, p38

[3] 'Breeding a World Champion Part Two: Rossano Brazzi', www.motogp.com 16 September 2001

[4] 'Breeding a World Champion Part Two: Rossano Brazzi', www.motogp.com 16 September 2001

[5] 'Why Valentinik?', www.thedoctor.ru 23 March 2013

[6] 'Breeding a World Champion Part Two: Rossano Brazzi', www.motogp.com 16 September 2001

[7] Oxley, Mat, *Valentino Rossi: MotoGenius* (2nd edition), Haynes Publishing, 2003, p67

[8] McLaren, Peter and Scott, Michael, *Valentino Rossi: Record Breaker*, Icon Publishing Limited, 2009, p8

[9] Falsaperla, Filippo, *Valentino Rossi: Legend*, Yellow Jersey Press, 2006, p55

CHAPTER 5

[1] Adams, Dean, 'Interview, Master Crew Chief Jeremy Burgess', www.superbikeplanet.com 21 July 2017 (originally published 2010)

[2] Tiburtius, Christian, 'MotoGP Q&A: Mick Doohan', www.crash.net 10 September 2014

[3] Oxley, Mat, *Valentino Rossi: MotoGenius* (2nd edition), Haynes Publishing, 2003, p84

[4] Adams, Dean: 'Interview, Master Crew Chief Jeremy Burgess', www.superbikeplanet.com 21 July 2017 (originally published 2010)

[5] Oxley, Mat, *Valentino Rossi: MotoGenius* (2nd edition), Haynes Publishing, 2003, p27

[6] McLaren, Peter, 'Rossi's Love for London, Anger at Bombings', www.crash.net 21 July 2005

[7] Lupi, Michele, *Racers: Stori di uomini con la velocità cuore*, Feltrinelli, 2003

[8] Downes, Andy, 'Look Back: Colin Edwards', www.motorcyclenews.com 28 July 2016

CHAPTER 6

[1] Scott Michael, *Motocourse 2001-2002*, Hazleton Publishing, 2001, p19

[2] Oxley, Mat, *Valentino Rossi: MotoGenius* (2nd edition), Haynes Publishing, 2003, p95

[3] 'Rossi: When I Stop I'll Miss This Most', www.crash.net 23 March 2020

[4] English, Steve, 'Look Out, The Boss Is Coming', *Rossi: 20 Years of GP Racing, MCN Special Edition*, Bauer Automotive, 2015, p118

[5] 'Rossi and Biaggi Feud Hots Up', www.motogp.com 10 April 2001

[6] Rossi, Valentino with Borghi, Enrico, *Valentino Rossi: What If I Had Never Tried It*, Century, 2005, p101

[7] Downes, Andy, 'Look Back: Colin Edwards', www.motorcyclenews.com 28 July 2016

[8] Scott, Michael,, 'The Midas Touch', *Two Wheels Only*, January 2002, p134

[9] Rossi, Valentino with Borghi, Enrico, *Valentino Rossi: What If I Had Never Tried It*, Century, 2005, pp4-5

[10] Scott Michael, *Motocourse 2001-2002*, Hazleton Publishing, 2001, p5

CHAPTER 7

[1] Falsaperla, Filippo, *Valentino Rossi: Legend,* Yellow Jersey Press, 2006, pp120-121

[2] Oxley, Mat, *Valentino Rossi: MotoGenius* (2nd edition), Haynes Publishing, 2003, p110

[3] Falsaperla, Filippo, *Valentino Rossi: Legend*, Yellow Jersey Press, 2006, pp123-124

[4] MCN, 6 November 2002

[5] MCN, 11 December 2002

[6] MCN, 18 December 2002

[7] MCN, 24 December 2002

[8] MCN, 9 July 2003

[9] Scott Michael, *Motocourse 2003-2004*, Hazleton Publishing, 2003, p143

[10] MCN, 13 August 2003

[11] MCN, 13 August 2003

[12] MCN, 13 August 2003

[13] Rossi, Valentino with Borghi, Enrico, *Valentino Rossi: What If I Had Never Tried It*, Century, 2005, p53

[14] MCN, 24 September 2003

[15] Ryder, Julian, *MotoGP Season Review 2004*, Haynes Publishing, 2004, p7

CHAPTER 8

[1] *MCN Sport* Winter 2003, EMAP, 2003, p50

[2] Van Leeuwen, Andrew, 'What's It Really Like to Work With Valentino Rossi?', www.motorsport.com 19 October 2017

[3] MCN, 21 April 2004

[4] MCN, 21 April 2004

[5] MCN, 27 October 2004

[6] MCN, 20 October 2004

[7] McLaren, Peter and Scott, Michael, *Valentino Rossi: Record Breaker*, Icon Publishing Limited, 2009, p123

CHAPTER 9

[1] Scott, Michael, *Valentino Rossi: Life of a Legend*, Quarto Publishing Group, 2017, p110

[2] 'Words of a Champion: Nicky Hayden On...'
www.motogp.com 22 May 2017

[3] 'Hayden Claims Shock World Title', www.bbc.co.uk
29 October 2006

[4] Broadbent, Rick, *Ring of Fire: The Inside Story of Valentino Rossi and MotoGP*, Bantam Press, 2009, p287

[5] Broadbent, Rick, *Ring of Fire: The Inside Story of Valentino Rossi and MotoGP*, Bantam Press, 2009, p287

[6] 'Rossi Responds to Tax Evasion Claims', www.autosport.com
8 August 2007

[7] 'Taxman Wants 112 Million Euros from Valentino Rossi',
www.italymagazine.com, 10 August 2007

[8] 'Taxman Wants 112 Million Euros from Valentino Rossi',
www.italymagazine.com, 10 August 2007

[9] Lostia, Michele: 'Rossi Reaches Settlement in Tax Probe',
www.autosport.com 7 February 2008

[10] MCN, 2 October 2002

[11] MCN, 17 March 2004

[12] MCN, 28 April 2004

[13] Scott, Michael, *Valentino Rossi: Life of a Legend*, Quarto
Publishing Group, 2017, p113

[14] McLaren, Peter and Scott, Michael, *Valentino Rossi:
Record Breaker*, Icon Publishing Limited, 2009, p10

[15] McLaren, Peter and Scott, Michael, *Valentino Rossi:
Record Breaker*, Icon Publishing Limited, 2009, p11

[16] Stoner, Casey with Roberts, Matthew, *Casey Stoner:
Pushing the Limits*, Orion, 2013, p230

CHAPTER 10

[1] Stoner, Casey with Roberts, Matthew, *Casey Stoner: Pushing the Limits*, Orion, 2013, p196

[2] Stoner, Casey with Roberts, Matthew, *Casey Stoner: Pushing the Limits*, Orion, 2013 p197

[3] Lorenzo, Jorge and Tobia, Ernest Riveras, *Jorge Lorenzo: My Story So Far*, Haynes, 2009, p108

[4] McLaren, Peter and Scott, Michael, *Valentino Rossi: Record Breaker*, Icon Publishing Limited, 2009, p162

[5] Scott, Michael, *Motocourse 2008-2009*, Crash Media Group Ltd, 2008, p146

[6] McLaren, Peter and Scott, Michael, *Valentino Rossi: Record Breaker*, Icon Publishing Limited, 2009

[7] MCN, 30 October 2019

[8] Scott, Michael, *Valentino Rossi: Life of a Legend*, Quarto Publishing Group, 2017, p127

[9] Scott, Michael, *Valentino Rossi: Life of a Legend*, Quarto Publishing Group, 2017, p128

[10] Scott, Michael, *Valentino Rossi: Life of a Legend*, Quarto Publishing Group, 2017, p121

[11] Lorenzo, Jorge, and Tobia, Ernest Riveras, *Jorge Lorenzo: My Story So Far*, Haynes, 2009, p102

[12] Lorenzo, Jorge, and Tobia, Ernest Riveras, *Jorge Lorenzo: My Story So Far*, Haynes, 2009, p102

[13] Lorenzo, Jorge, and Tobia, Ernest Riveras, *Jorge Lorenzo: My Story So Far*, Haynes, 2009, p344

[14] 'Valentino Rossi retains world title after third place in Malaysia', www.theguardian.com 25 October 2009

CHAPTER 11

[1] Scott, Michael, *Valentino Rossi: Life of a Legend*, Quarto Publishing Group, 2017, p137

[2] 'Valentino Rossi fractures leg in practice for Italian Grand Prix', www.theguardian.com 5 June 2010

[3] Stoner, Casey with Roberts, Matthew, *Casey Stoner: Pushing the Limits*, Orion, 2013, p232

[4] Scott, Michael, *Motocourse 2012-2013*, Icon Publishing Limited, 2012, p20

[5] Stoner, Casey and Roberts, Matthew, *Casey Stoner: Pushing the Limits*, Orion, 2013, p229

[6] MCN *Sport Review 2011*, Bauer, 2011, p34

[7] *La Gazetta dello Sport*, 20 February 2018

[8] MCN *Sport 2011 Review*, Bauer, 2011, p34

[9] MCN *Sport 2011 Review*, Bauer, 2011, p37

[10] *Rossi: 20 Years of GP Racing*, MCN Special, Bauer, 2015, p32

[11] 'Rossi on staying competitive and relationship with Lorenzo', www.motogp.com September 2014

[12] Scott, Michael, *Valentino Rossi: Life of a Legend*, Quarto Publishing Group, 2017, p155

CHAPTER 12

[1] Stoner, Casey with Roberts, Matthew, *Casey Stoner: Pushing the Limits*, Orion, 2013, p229

[2] Guidotti, Maria, 'CW Interview: Valentino Rossi', www.cycleworld.com 2 October 2015

CHAPTER 13

[1] Guidotti, Maria, 'CW Interview: Graziano Rossi', www.cycleworld.com 9 November 2015

CHAPTER 14

[1] Pecino, Manual: 'MotoGP: Rossi is a Frankenstein Rider – Cadalora', www.cycleworld.com 13 May 2016

[2] Pecino, Manual: 'MotoGP: Rossi is a Frankenstein Rider – Cadalora', www.cycleworld.com 13 May 2016

[3] MCN, 5 December 2018

[4] *Rossi: 20 Years of GP Racing*, MCN Special Edition, Bauer Automotive, 2015, p131

[5] Turner, Victoria: 'Valentino Rossi: Six Reasons Why Fans Continue Their Devotion to MotoGP Superstar', www.bbc.co.uk 16 March 2019

[6] Woodroffe, James, 'Why Rossi Still Smiles', *MCN Sport* Autumn 2011, Bauer, 2011

[7] Guidotti, Maria, 'Rossi's Moto3 Team', www.cycleworld.com 5 March 2015

[8] *La Gazetta dello Sport*, 15 September 2015

[9] Morrison, Neil, 'MotoGP Exclusive: Luca Marini Interview', www.crash.net 17 October 2018

CHAPTER 15

[1] Oxley, Mat, *Valentino Rossi: MotoGenius* (2nd edition), Haynes Publishing, 2003, p23

[2] Oxley, Mat, *The Valentino Rossi Files: Everything I've Ever Written About VR*, 2014

[3] Hedge, Trevor, 'Rossi – A Little More Insight to The World Champion', www.mcnews.com.au 22 October 2002

[4] 'Fast Talk: Valentino Rossi', www.*amcn.com.au* 9 April 2019

[5] 'MotoGP: Rossi at Radio 1 Rai', www.gpone.com 19 August 2019

[6] Oxley, Mat, *MotoGP Season Review 2018*, Motocom Limited, 2018, p26

[7] MCN, 20 February 2019

[8] *Rossi: 20 Years of GP Racing*, MCN Special Edition, Bauer Automotive, 2015, pp62-64

[9] Guidotti, Maria, 'CW Interview: Valentino Rossi', www.cycleworld.com 2 October 2015

[10] MCN, 30 October 2019

[11] Patterson, Simon: 'Lorenzo on Retirement, Rossi, and Much More', www.the-race.com 10 February 2020

[12] Scott, Michael, *Motocourse 2009-2010*, Icon Publishing Limited, 2009, p32

[13]'Valentino Rossi on the Pace in NASCAR Nationwide Promotional Test', www.autosport.com 23 April 2013

[14] Aglio, Matteo, 'Rossi: Life After Retirement? Nothing Could Be Better than the MotoGP', www.gpone.com 16 November 2019

CAREER RESULTS

1993
125cc Italian Sport
Production Championship
Bike: Cagiva Mito

Final Championship Position:
3rd

1994
125cc Italian Sport
Production Championship:
Bike: Cagiva Mito

Final Championship Position:
1st

125cc GP Italian
Championship
Bike: Santorini RS125R

Final Championship Position:
6th

1995
125cc GP Italian
Championship
Bike: Aprilia RS125R

Final Championship Position:
1st

125cc European
Championship
Bike: Aprilia RS125R

Final Championship Position:
3rd

VALENTINO ROSSI

1996
125cc Grand Prix World
Championship
Bike: Aprilia RS125
Team: Team Polini
Shah Alam, Malaysia: 6th
Sentul, Indonesia: 11th
Suzuka, Japan: 11th
Jerez, Spain: 4th
Mugello, Italy: 4th
Paul Ricard, France: DNF
Assen, Netherlands: DNF
Nürburgring, Germany: 5th
Donington Park, Britain: DNF
Zeltweg, Austria: 3rd
Brno, Czech Republic: 1st
Imola, San Marino: 5th
Catalunya, Barcelona: DNF
Rio de Janeiro, Brazil: DNF
Eastern Creek, Australia: 14th

Final Championship Position:
9th
Wins: 1
Pole Position: 1
Fastest Laps: 2
Points: 111

1997
125cc Grand Prix World
Championship
Bike: Aprilia RS125
Team: Nastro Azzurro Aprilia
Shah Alam, Malaysia: 1st

Suzuka, Japan: DNF
Jerez, Spain: 1st
Mugello, Italy: 1st
A-1 Ring, Austria: 2nd
Paul Ricard, France: 1st
Assen, Netherlands: 1st
Imola, San Marino: 1st
Nürburgring, Germany: 1st
Rio de Janeiro, Brazil: 1st
Donington Park, Britain: 1st
Brno, Czech Republic: 3rd
Barcelona, Catalunya: 1st
Sentul, Indonesia: 1st
Phillip Island, Australia: 6th

Final Championship Position:
1st
Wins: 11
Pole Positions: 4
Fastest Laps: 7
Points: 321

1998
250cc Grand Prix World
Championship
Bike: Aprilia RS250
Team: Team Aprilia Racing
Suzuka, Japan: DNF
Johor, Malaysia: DNF
Jerez, Spain: 2nd
Mugello, Italy: 2nd
Paul Ricard, France: 2nd
Jarama, Spain: DNF
Assen, Netherlands: 1st

Donington Park, Britain: DNF
Sachsenring, Germany: 3rd
Brno, Czech Republic: DNF
Imola, San Marino: 1st
Barcelona, Catalunya: 1st
Phillip Island, Australia: 1st
Buenos Aires, Argentina: 1st

Final Championship Position:
2nd
Wins: 5
Pole Positions: 0
Fastest Laps: 3
Points: 201

1999
250cc Grand Prix World
Championship
Bike: Aprilia RS250
Team: Team Aprilia Racing
Sepang, Malaysia: 5th
Motegi, Japan: 7th
Jerez, Spain: 1st
Paul Ricard, France: DNF
Mugello, Italy: 1st
Barcelona, Catalunya: 1st
Assen, Netherlands: 2nd
Donington Park, Britain: 1st
Sachsenring, Germany: 1st
Brno, Czech Republic: 1st^t
Imola, San Marino: 2nd
Valencia, Spain: 8th
Phillip Island, Australia: 1st
Phakisa, South Africa: 1st

Rio de Janeiro, Brazil: 1st
Buenos Aires, Argentina: 3rd

Final Championship position:
1st
Wins: 9
Pole Positions: 2
Fastest Laps: 10
Points: 309

2000
500cc Grand Prix World
Championship
Bike: Honda NSR500
Team: Team Nastro Azzurro
Honda
Phakisa, South Africa: DNF
Sepang, Malaysia: DNF
Suzuka, Japan: 11th
Jerez, Spain: 3rd
Le Mans, France: 3rd
Mugello, Italy: 12th
Barcelona, Catalunya: 3rd
Assen, Netherlands: 6th
Donington Park, Britain: 1st
Sachsenring, Germany: 2nd
Brno, Czech Republic: 2nd
Estoril, Portugal: 3rd
Valencia, Spain: DNF
Rio de Janeiro, Brazil: 1st
Motegi, Japan: 2nd
Phillip Island, Australia: 3rd

Final Championship Position:

2nd
Wins: 2
Pole Positions: 0
Fastest Laps: 5
Points: 209

2001

500cc Grand Prix World
Championship
Bike: Honda NSR500
Team: Nastro Azzurro Honda
Suzuka, Japan: 1st
Phasika, South Africa: 1st
Jerez, Spain: 1st
Le Mans, France: 3rd
Mugello, Italy: DNF
Barcelona, Catalunya: 1st
Assen, Netherlands: 2nd
Donington Park, Britain: 1st
Sachsenring, Germany: 7th
Brno, Czech Republic: 1st
Estoril, Portugal: 1st
Valencia, Spain: 11th
Motegi, Japan: 1st
Phillip Island, Australia: 1st
Sepang, Malaysia: 1st
Rio de Janeiro, Brazil: 1st

Final Championship Position:
1st
Wins: 11
Pole Positions: 5
Fastest Laps: 11
Points: 325

2002

MotoGP World
Championship
Bike: Honda RC211V
Team: Repsol Honda Team
Suzuka, Japan: 1st
Phakisa, South Africa: 2nd
Jerez, Spain: 1st
Le Mans, France: 1st
Mugello, Italy: 1st
Barcelona, Catalunya: 1st
Assen, Netherlands: 1st
Donington Park, Britain: 1st
Sachsenring, Germany: 1st
Brno, Czech Republic: DNF
Estoril, Portugal: 1st
Rio de Janeiro, Brazil: 1st
Motegi, Japan: 2nd
Sepang, Malaysia: 2nd
Phillip Island, Australia: 1st
Valencia, Spain: 2nd

Final Championship Position:
1st
Wins: 11
Pole Positions: 6
Fastest Laps: 10
Points: 355

2003

MotoGP World
Championship
Bike: Honda RC211V
Team: Repsol Honda Team

Suzuka, Japan: 1st
Phakisa, South Africa: 2nd
Jerez, Spain: 1st
Le Mans, France: 2nd
Mugello, Italy: 1st
Barcelona, Catalunya: 2nd
Assen, Netherlands: 3rd
Donington Park, Britain: 3rd
Sachsenring, Germany: 2nd
Brno, Czech Republic: 1st
Estoril, Portugal: 1st
Rio de Janeiro, Brazil: 1st
Motegi, Japan: 2nd
Sepang, Malaysia: 1st
Phillip Island, Australia: 1st
Valencia, Spain: 1st

Final Championship Position:
1st
Wins: 9
Pole Positions: 9
Fastest Laps: 12
Points: 357

2004
MotoGP World
Championship
Bike: Yamaha M1
Team: Gauloises Fortuna
Yamaha Team
Phakisa, South Africa: 1st
Jerez, Spain: 4th
Le Mans, France: 4th
Mugello, Italy: 1st

Barcelona, Catalunya: 1st
Assen, Netherlands: 1st
Rio de Janeiro, Brazil: DNF
Sachsenring, Germany: 4th
Donington Park, Britain: 1st
Brno, Czech Republic: 2nd
Estoril, Portugal: 1st
Motegi, Japan: 2nd
Losail, Qatar: DNF
Sepang, Malaysia: 1st
Phillip Island, Australia: 1st
Valencia, Spain: 1st

Final Championship Position:
1st
Wins: 9
Pole Positions: 5
Fastest laps: 3
Points: 304

2005
MotoGP World
Championship
Bike: Yamaha M1
Team: Gauloises Yamaha
Team
Jerez, Spain: 1st
Estoril, Portugal: 2nd
Shanghai, China: 1st
Le Mans, France: 1st
Mugello, Italy: 1st
Barcelona, Catalunya: 1st
Assen, Netherlands: 1st
Laguna Seca, USA: 3rd

Donington Park, Britain: 1st
Sachsenring, Germany: 1st
Brno, Czech Republic: 1st
Motegi, Japan: DNF
Sepang, Malaysia: 2nd
Losail, Qatar: 1st
Phillip Island, Australia: 1st
Istanbul Park, Turkey: 2nd
Valencia, Spain: 3rd

Final Championship Position:
1st
Wins: 11
Pole Positions: 5
Fastest laps: 6
Points: 367

2006
MotoGP World
Championship
Bike: Yamaha M1
Team: Camel Yamaha Team
Jerez, Spain: 14th
Losail, Qatar: 1st
Istanbul Circuit, Turkey: 4th
Shanghai, China: DNF
Le Mans, France: DNF
Mugello, Italy: 1st
Barcelona, Catalunya: 1st
Assen, Netherlands: 8th
Donington Park, Britain: 2nd
Sachsenring, Germany: 1st^t
Laguna Seca, USA: DNF
Brno, Czech Republic: 2nd

Sepang, Malaysia: 1st
Phillip Island, Australia: 3rd
Motegi, Japan: 2nd
Estoril, Portugal: 2nd
Valencia, Spain: 13th

Final Championship Position:
2nd
Wins: 5
Pole Positions: 5
Fastest Laps: 4
Points: 220

2007
MotoGP World
Championship
Bike: Yamaha M1
Team: Fiat Yamaha Team
Losail, Qatar: 2nd
Jerez, Spain: 1st
Istanbul Circuit, Turkey: 10th
Shanghai, China: 2nd
Le Mans, France: 6th
Mugello, Italy: 1st
Barcelona, Catalunya: 2nd
Donington Park, Britain: 4th
Assen, Netherlands: 1st
Sachsenring, Germany: DNF
Laguna Seca, USA: 4th
Brno, Czech Republic: 7th
Misano, San Marino: DNF
Estoril, Portugal: 1st
Motegi, Japan: 13th
Phillip Island, Australia: 3rd

Sepang, Malaysia: 5th
Valencia, Spain: DNF

Final Championship Position:
3rd
Wins: 4
Pole Positions: 4
Fastest Laps: 3
Points: 241

2008
MotoGP World
Championship
Bike: Yamaha M1
Team: Fiat Yamaha Team
Losail, Qatar: 5th
Jerez, Spain: 2nd
Estoril, Portugal: 3rd
Shanghai, China: 1st
Le Mans, France: 1st
Mugello, Italy: 1st
Barcelona, Catalunya: 2nd
Donington Park, Britain: 2nd
Assen, Netherlands: 11th
Sachsenring, Germany: 2nd
Laguna Seca, USA: 1st
Brno, Czech Republic: 1st
Misano, San Marino: 1st
Indianapolis, USA: 1st
Motegi, Japan: 1st
Phillip Island, Australia: 2nd
Sepang, Malaysia: 1st
Valencia, Spain: 3rd

Final Championship Position:
1st
Wins: 9
Pole Positions: 1
Fastest Laps: 5
Points: 373

2009
MotoGP World
Championship
Bike: Yamaha M1
Team: Fiat Yamaha Team
Losail, Qatar: 2nd
Motegi, Japan: 2nd
Jerez, Spain: 1st
Le Mans, France: 16th
Mugello, Italy: 3rd
Barcelona, Catalunya: 1st
Assen, Holland: 1st
Laguna Seca, USA: 2nd
Sachsenring, Germany: 1st
Donington Park, Britain: 5th
Brno, Czech Republic: 1st
Indianapolis, USA: DNF
Misano, San Marino: 1st
Estoril, Portugal: 4th
Phillip Island, Australia: 2nd
Sepang, Malaysia: 3rd
Valencia, Spain: 2nd

Final Championship Position:
1st
Wins: 6
Pole Positions: 7

VALENTINO ROSSI

Fastest Laps: 6
Points: 306

2010
MotoGP World
Championship
Bike: Yamaha M1
Team: Fiat Yamaha Team
Losail, Qatar: 1st
Jerez, Spain: 3rd
Le Mans, France: 2nd
Mugello, Italy: DNS
Silverstone, Britain: DNS
Assen, Holland: DNS
Barcelona, Catalunya: DNS
Sachsenring, Germany: 4th
Laguna Seca, USA: 3rd
Brno, Czech Republic: 5th
Indianapolis, USA: 4th
Misano, San Marino: 3rd
Aragon, Spain: 6th
Motegi, Japan: 3rd
Sepang, Malaysia: 1st
Phillip Island, Australia: 3rd
Estoril, Portugal: 2nd
Valencia, Spain: 3rd

Final Championship Position:
3rd
Wins: 2
Pole Positions: 1
Fastest Laps: 2
Points: 233

2011
MotoGP World
Championship
Bike: Ducati Desmosedici
Team: Ducati Marlboro Team
Losail, Qatar: 7th
Jerez, Spain: 5th
Estoril, Portugal: 5th
Le Mans, France: 3rd
Barcelona, Catalunya: 5th
Silverstone, Britain: 6th
Assen, Netherlands: 4th
Mugello, Italy: 6th
Sachsenring, Germany: 9th
Laguna Seca, USA: 6th
Brno, Czech Republic: 6th
Indianapolis, USA: 10th
Misano, San Marino: 7th
Aragon, Spain: 10th
Motegi, Japan: DNF
Phillip Island, Australia: DNF
Sepang, Malaysia: DNF
Valencia, Spain: DNF

Final Championship Position:
7th
Wins: 0
Pole Positions: 0
Fastest Laps: 1
Points: 139

2012
MotoGP World
Championship

Bike: Ducati Desmosedici
Team: Ducati Team
Losail, Qatar: 10th
Jerez, Spain: 9th
Estoril, Portugal: 7th
Le Mans, France: 2nd
Barcelona, Catalunya: 7th
Silverstone, Britain: 9th
Assen, Netherlands: 13th
Sachsenring, Germany: 6th
Mugello, Italy: 5th
Laguna Seca, USA: DNF
Indianapolis, USA: 7th
Brno, Czech Republic: 7th
Misano, San Marino: 2nd
Aragon, Spain: 8th
Motegi, Japan: 7th
Sepang, Malaysia: 5th
Phillip Island, Australia: 7th
Valencia, Spain: 10th

Final Championship Position:
6th
Wins: 0
Pole Positions: 0
Fastest Laps: 1
Points: 163

2013
MotoGP World
Championship
Bike: Yamaha M1
Team: Yamaha Factory
Racing

Losail, Qatar: 2nd
Circuit of the Americas: USA:
6th
Jerez, Spain: 4th
Le Mans, France: 12th
Mugello, Italy: DNF
Barcelona, Catalunya: 4th
Assen, Netherlands: 1st
Sachsenring, Germany: 3rd
Laguna Seca, USA: 3rd
Indianapolis, USA: 4th
Brno, Czech Republic: 4th
Silverstone, Britain: 4th
Misano, San Marino: 4th
Aragon, Spain: 3rd
Sepang, Malaysia: 4th
Phillip Island, Australia: 3rd
Motegi, Japan: 6th
Valencia, Spain: 4th

Final Championship Position:
4th
Wins: 1
Pole Positions: 0
Fastest Laps: 1
Points: 237

2014
MotoGP World
Championship
Bike: Yamaha M1
Team: Movistar Yamaha
MotoGP
Losail, Qatar: 2nd

Circuit of the Americas, USA:
8th
Termas de Rio Hondo,
Argentina: 4th
Jerez, Spain: 2nd
Le Mans, France: 2nd
Mugello, Italy: 3rd
Barcelona, Catalunya: 2nd
Assen, Netherlands: 5th
Sachsenring, Germany: 4th
Indianapolis, USA: 3rd
Brno, Czech Republic: 3rd
Silverstone, Britain: 3rd
Misano, San Marino: 1st
Aragon, Spain: DNF
Motegi, Japan: 3rd
Phillip Island, Australia: 1st
Sepang, Malaysia: 2nd
Valencia, Spain: 2nd

Final Championship
Position: 2nd
Wins: 2
Pole Positions: 1
Fastest Laps: 1
Points: 295

2015
MotoGP World
Championship
Bike: Yamaha M1
Team: Movistar Yamaha
MotoGP
Losail, Qatar: 1st

Circuit of the Americas, USA:
3rd
Termas de Rio Hondo,
Argentina: 1st
Jerez, Spain: 3rd
Le Mans, France: 2nd
Mugello, Italy: 3rd
Barcelona, Catalunya: 2nd
Assen, Netherlands: 1st
Sachsenring, Germany: 3rd
Indianapolis, USA: 3rd
Brno, Czech Republic: 3rd
Silverstone, Britain: 1st
Misano, San Marino: 5th
Aragon, Spain: 3rd
Motegi, Japan: 2nd
Phillip Island, Australia: 4th
Sepang, Malaysia: 3rd
Valencia, Spain: 4th

Final Championship Position:
2nd
Wins: 4
Pole Positions: 1
Fastest Laps: 4
Points: 325

2016
MotoGP World
Championship
Bike: Yamaha M1
Team: Movistar Yamaha
MotoGP
Losail, Qatar: 4th

Termas de Rio Hondo,
Argentina: 2nd
Circuit of the Americas, USA:
DNF
Jerez, Spain: 1st
Le Mans, France: 2nd
Mugello, Italy: DNF
Barcelona, Catalunya: 1st
Assen, Netherlands: DNF
Sachsenring, Germany: 8th
Red Bull Ring, Austria: 4th
Brno, Czech Republic: 2nd
Silverstone, Britain: 3rd
Misano, San Marino: 2nd
Aragon, Spain: 3rd
Motegi, Japan: DNF
Phillip Island, Australia: 2nd
Sepang, Malaysia: 2nd
Valencia, Spain: 4th

Final Championship Position:
2nd
Wins: 2
Pole Positions: 3
Fastest Laps: 2
Points: 249

2017
MotoGP World
Championship
Bike: Yamaha M1
Team: Movistar Yamaha
MotoGP
Losail, Qatar: 3rd

Termas de Rio Honda,
Argentina: 2nd
Circuit of the Americas, USA:
2nd
Jerez, Spain: 10th
Le Mans, France: DNF
Mugello, Italy: 4th
Barcelona, Catalunya: 8th
Assen, Netherlands: 1st
Sachsenring, Germany: 5th
Brno, Czech Republic: 4th
Red Bull Ring, Austria: 7th
Silverstone, Britain: 3rd
Misano, San Marino: DNS
Aragon, Spain: 5th
Motegi, Japan: DNF
Phillip Island, Australia: 2nd
Sepang, Malaysia: 7th
Valencia, Spain: 5th

Final Championship Position:
5th
Wins: 1
Pole Positions: 0
Fastest Laps: 0
Points: 208

2018
MotoGP World
Championship
Bike: Yamaha M1
Team: Movistar Yamaha
MotoGP
Losail, Qatar: 3rd

Termas de Rio Hondo, Argentina: 19th
Circuit of the Americas, USA: 4th
Jerez, Spain: 5th
Le Mans, France: 3rd
Mugello, Italy: 3rd
Barcelona, Catalunya: 3rd
Assen, Netherlands: 5th
Sachsenring, Germany: 2nd
Brno, Czech Republic: 4th
Red Bull Ring, Austria: 6th
Silverstone, Britain: Race cancelled
Misano, San Marino: 7th
Aragon, Spain: 8th
Buriram, Thailand: 4th
Motegi, Japan: 4th
Phillip Island, Australia: 6th
Sepang, Malaysia: 18th
Valencia, Spain: 13th

Final Championship Position: 3rd
Wins: 0
Pole Positions: 1
Fastest Laps: 0
Points: 198

2019
MotoGP World Championship
Bike: Yamaha M1
Team: Monster Energy

Yamaha MotoGP
Losail, Qatar: 5th
Termas de Rio Hondo, Argentina: 2nd
Circuit of the Americas, USA: 2nd
Jerez, Spain: 6th
Le Mans, France: 5th
Mugello, Italy: DNF
Barcelona, Catalunya: DNF
Assen, Netherlands: DNF
Sachsenring, Germany: 8th
Brno, Czech Republic: 6th
Red Bull Ring, Austria: 4th
Silverstone, Britain: 4th
Misano, San Marino: 4th
Aragon, Spain: 8th
Buriram, Thailand: 8th
Motegi, Japan: DNF
Phillip Island, Australia: 8th
Sepang, Malaysia: 4th
Valencia, Spain: 8th

Final Championship Position: 7th
Wins: 0
Pole Positions: 0
Fastest Laps: 1
Points: 174

Key
DNS = Did Not Start
DNF = Did Not Finish

BIBLIOGRAPHY

BOOKS

Broadbent, Rick, *Ring of Fire: The Inside Story of Valentino Rossi and MotoGP*, Bantam Press, 2009

Falsaperla, Filippo, *Valentino Rossi: Legend*, Yellow Jersey Press, 2006

Lorenzo, Jorge, and Tobia, Ernest Riveras, *Jorge Lorenzo: My Story So Far*, Haynes, 2009

Lupi, Michele, *Racers: Stori di uomini con la velocità cuore*, Feltrinelli, 2003

McLaren, Peter and Scott, Michael, *Valentino Rossi: Record Breaker*, Icon Publishing Limited, 2009

Oxley, Mat, *MotoGP Season Review 2018*, Motocom Limited, 2018

Oxley, Mat, *MotoGP 2019: The Official Season Story*, Motocom Limited, 2019

VALENTINO ROSSI

Oxley, Mat, *The Valentino Rossi Files: Everything I've Ever Written About VR*, 2014

Oxley, Mat, *Valentino Rossi: MotoGenius'*(2nd edition), Haynes Publishing, 2003

Perez de Rozas, Emilio, *Marc Márquez: Dreams Come True: My Story*, Ebury Press, 2014

Rossi, Valentino with Borghi, Enrico, *Valentino Rossi: What If I Had Never Tried It*, Century, 2005

Ryder, Julian, *MotoGP Season Review 2004*, Haynes Publishing, 2004

Ryder, Julian, *MotoGP Season Review 2005*, Haynes Publishing, 2005

Ryder, Julian, *MotoGP Season Review 2006*, Haynes Publishing, 2006

Ryder, Julian, *MotoGP Season Review 2007*, Haynes Publishing, 2007

Ryder, Julian, *MotoGP Season Review 2008*, Haynes Publishing, 2008

Ryder, Julian, *MotoGP Season Review 2009*, Haynes Publishing, 2009

Ryder, Julian, *MotoGP Season Review 2010'*, Haynes Publishing, 2010

Ryder, Julian, *MotoGP Season Review 2011*, Haynes Publishing, 2011

Ryder, Julian, *MotoGP Season Review 2012*, Haynes Publishing, 2012

Ryder, Julian, *MotoGP Season Review 2013*,
Haynes Publishing, 2013

Ryder, Julian, *MotoGP Season Review 2014*,
Evro Publishing, 2014

Ryder, Julian, *MotoGP Season Review 2015*,
Evro Publishing, 2015

Ryder, Julian, *MotoGP Season Review 2016*,
Evro Publishing, 2016

Ryder, Julian, *MotoGP Season Review 2017*,
Motocom Limited, 2017

Scott, Michael, *Motocourse 1996–97*,
Hazleton Publishing, 1996

Scott Michael, *Motocourse 1997–98*,
Hazleton Publishing, 1997

Scott, Michael, *Motocourse 1998–99*,
Hazleton Publishing, 1998

Scott, Michael, *Motocourse 1999–2000*,
Hazleton Publishing, 1999

Scott, Michael, *Motocourse 2000–2001*,
Hazleton Publishing, 2000

Scott Michael, *Motocourse 2001–2002*,
Hazleton Publishing, 2001

Scott, Michael, *Motocourse 2002–2003*,
Hazleton Publishing, 2002

Scott Michael, *Motocourse 2003–2004*,
Hazleton Publishing, 2003

VALENTINO ROSSI

Scott, Michael, *Motocourse 2004–2005*,
Hazleton Publishing, 2004

Scott, Michael, *Motocourse 2005–2006*,
Crash Media Group Ltd, 2005

Scott, Michael, *Motocourse 2006–2007*,
Crash Media Group Ltd, 2006

Scott, Michael, *Motocourse 2007–2008*,
Crash Media Group Ltd, 2007

Scott, Michael, *Motocourse 2008–2009*,
Crash Media Group Ltd, 2008

Scott, Michael, *Motocourse 2009–2010*,
Icon Publishing Limited, 2009

Scott, Michael, *Motocourse 2010–2011*,
Icon Publishing Limited, 2010

Scott, Michael, *Motocourse 2011–2012*
Icon Publishing Limited, 2011

Scott, Michael, *Motocourse 2012–2013*,
Icon Publishing Limited, 2012

Scott, Michael, *Motocourse 2013–2014*,
Icon Publishing Limited, 2013

Scott, Michael, *Motocourse 2014–2015*,
Icon Publishing Limited, 2014

Scott, Michael, *Motocourse 2015–2016*,
Icon Publishing Limited, 2015

Scott, Michael, *Motocourse 2016–2017*,
Icon Publishing Limited, 2016

Scott, Michael, *Motocourse 2017–2018*,
Icon Publishing Limited, 2017

Scott, Michael, *Motocourse 2018–2019*,
Icon Publishing Limited, 2018

Scott, Michael, *Motocourse 2019–2020*,
Icon Publishing Limited, 2019

Scott, Michael, *Valentino Rossi: Life of a Legend*,
Quarto Publishing Group, 2017

Stoner, Casey with Roberts, Matthew, *Casey Stoner:
Pushing the Limits*, Orion, 2013

WEBSITES

www.amcn.com.au

www.autosport.com

www.bbc.co.uk

www.crash.net

www.cycleworld.com

www.gpone.com

www.italymagazine.com

www.mcnews.com.au

www.moto.it

www.motogp.com

www.motorcyclenews.com

www.motorsport.com

www.myitalianlink.com

www.superbikeplanet.com

www.thedoctor.ru

www.theguardian.com

www.the-race.com

www.tuttomotoriweb.com

www.visordown.com

BOOKAZINES

Rossi: 20 Years of GP Racing, MCN Special Edition,
Bauer Automotive, 2015

Just Rossi, Mortons Media Ltd, 2008

MAGAZINES AND NEWSPAPERS

*Il Resto del Carlino, Italy Magazine, La Gazetta dello Sport,
MCN Sport, Motor Cycle News, Riders, Two Wheels Only*

FILMS

Faster (2003) Director: Mark Neale, Dorna Sports S.L.

Fastest (2011) Director: Mark Neale, Dorna Sports S.L.

Hitting the Apex (2015) Director: Mark Neale,
Dorna Sports S.L.

Valentino Rossi's MotoGP Trail of Glory (2003),
Dorna Sports S.L.

ACKNOWLEDGEMENTS

Many people refused to be interviewed for this book and many, many more did not even respond to my emails and texts regarding interview requests. So I am doubly grateful to those who did take the time to share their stories and insights with me. I would like to say a huge thanks to the following (in alphabetical order) without whom this book would not have been possible: Lucio Cecchinello, Alison Forth, Ivan Goi, Chris Herring, Neil Hodgson, Niall Mackenzie, Jeremy McWilliams, Don Morley, Steve Parrish, Carlo Pernat, Kevin Schwantz, and Andrew Smith.

I'm also grateful to Giulio La Bua for giving me a tour of Rossi's hometown of Tavullia and for helping with Italian translations and also to Maria Dalla Cola for her translation work. Thanks must also go to Jan McCormick for her assistance at the British Grand Prix in 2019 and to Ben Purvis for his computer wizardry and advice. I am also indebted to Graham Pennington of the Grammar Police ('to correct and to serve') for spotting my mistakes.

I would like to thank my agent, David Luxton, of David Luxton Associates, for getting the project off the ground and to Matt Roberts for introducing us. Thanks also to Rebecca Winfield, head of rights and contracts at David Luxton Associates. I am most grateful for the hard work put in by my senior editor, James Hodgkinson, of Bonnier Books and to senior rights executive, Valentina Paulmichi, senior publicity manager, Nikki Mander, audio manager Laura Makela, copy editor Nicky Gyopari and editorial assistant Sophie Nevrkla.

Thanks also to Lisa Tams for her continued support during the writing of this book and to my mum and dad, Josie and Jim Barker, for speaking my interest in motorcycle racing in the first place.

I am especially indebted to Rossi's own hero, Kevin Schwantz, not only for his invaluable insights but for being kind enough to supply a foreword. Thanks also to Marnie Lincoln for making that happen.

INDEX